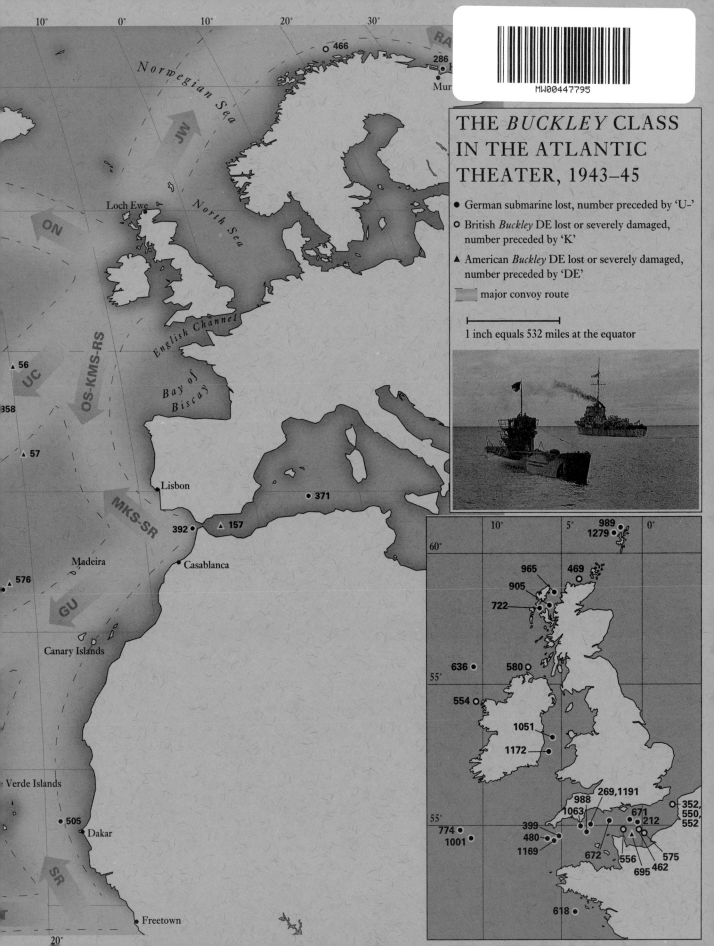

The *Buckley*-Class Destroyer Escorts

The *Buckley*-Class

NAVAL INSTITUTE PRESS • *Annapolis, Maryland*

Destroyer Escorts

Bruce Hampton Franklin

Library of Congress Cataloging-in-Publication Data
Franklin, Bruce Hampton, 1962–
    The Buckley-class destroyer escorts / Bruce Hampton Franklin.
        p.   cm.
    Includes bibliographical references and index.
    ISBN 1-55750-280-3 (alk. paper)
    1. Destroyer escorts—United States. 2. Destroyer escorts—Great
Britain. 3. World War, 1939–1945—Naval operations. I. Title.
V825.F73 1999
623.8′254—dc21   98-46329

Printed in the United States of America on acid-free paper ∞
06 05 04 03 02 01 00 99   9 8 7 6 5 4 3 2
First printing

For my father

RICHARD LAWSON FRANKLIN

Contents

Preface

In the few months that I had commanded her I had become very fond of this mass-produced tin-can of a ship. She could never be the aristocrat that *Hesperus* was, or the faithful old war-horse like *Walker*, but she had shown that she could "take it" and "hand it out" as well as either of them.

—Cdr. Donald Macintyre, D.S.O.**, D.S.C., Commanding Officer, *Bickerton*

The World War II destroyer escort (DE) was developed in response to Great Britain's pressing need for a long-range convoy escort capable of safeguarding Allied shipping from German submarines. Existing emergency escorts were not suited for open ocean warfare, while more-customary antisubmarine types such as fleet destroyers and sloops were in short supply due to the ravages of combat and the prohibitive costs and time required to build them. Therefore, on behalf of Great Britain the United States initiated the DE program, with the key ability to adapt the ship's basic destroyer-like design to economical multiple production processes so that large numbers of nearly identical warships could be produced over a short period of time. The DE was a successful design and the United States ended up acquiring the ship for its own navy.

By June 1943 orders for 1,005 DEs were placed with United States shipyards, although nearly half of these orders ended up being canceled due to competition from other construction programs—notably landing craft production—and the decline of U-boat activity in the wake of the Allied antisubmarine initiative throughout the balance of 1943.

Built specifically for conditions encountered in World War II, the DEs' strategic value dropped following the end of the conflict. But with so many new and robust hulls on hand and the huge investment in their construction, the U.S. government encouraged the Navy to utilize some of these vessels into the ensuing decades, despite their inadequate size and performance for postwar ASW.

The rapid disappearance of the destroyer escort from the operational navy has obscured the role of these ships in World War II, and although DEs were produced in greater numbers than any other kind of Allied fighting ship, served in four Allied navies during wartime, sank more enemy submarines than any other escort vessel, and contributed to combat operations in the Atlantic and Pacific theaters from late 1943 on, the destroyer escort has been one of the least studied American warship types. It is the goal of this book to lay the foundation for a more thorough examination of the DE program and its classes.

The *Buckley* was the largest of the six classes of destroyer escort, and with 154 units completed (six as high-speed transports), it was the second most numerous class of major combatants built by the United States during World War II.[1] Ships of this class also represented the

1. The *Fletcher* class was the largest, with 175 units completed, and *Balao* submarines were third, with 121 completed.

greatest number of warships of a single class to be transferred to the United Kingdom through lend-lease. In service, American *Buckley* DEs sank or assisted in sinking the second-highest number of submarines credited to a class of U.S. Navy ship during the war, while British *Buckley*s teamed with their *Evarts* lend-lease counterparts to claim the most U-boats destroyed by a single class of warship in the Royal Navy.[2]

This book contains the only complete photographic record of all 154 *Buckley*-class destroyer escorts and their variants produced between June 1942 and March 1945. Photographs of a portion of the *Buckley* class are not present in either the American or British national photographic archives, or in the collections of museums and private archives in those countries. A relatively small number of official photographs of the lend-lease vessels exists because these ships entered the Royal Navy in the midst of war and were returned shortly after the cessation of hostilities and scrapped. For those ships without photographs in national archives or museums, the author was fortunately able to locate former crew members who had photographs of their ships and were willing to share them for this project. A few private collectors and photographers also generously donated pictures. Without the direct involvement of these gentlemen, it would have been impossible to assemble this book and gaps would remain in the material history of the class. The timing of this photographic history is critical: The existence or significance of these nonofficial photographs would have been, in some cases, lost to future generations had this inquiry been made at a later date. The value of the photographs is obvious. Pho-

tographs can capture details and subtleties that are absent from paintings, sketches, or written descriptions, and due to the authenticity inherent in the process, a photograph can be our strongest tool for interpreting the recent past.[3]

The text provides details of *Buckley*-class ships in American and British service as well as a description of the class's design, armament, major conversion programs, and weapons upgrades. Throughout the book, excerpts from interviews and letters from former *Buckley*-class officers and crew members have been placed in screened boxes alongside areas in the text where the topic discussed is enhanced by their recollections and experiences. In addition, several passages from a remarkable contemporary diary of a DE sailor have been included. The appendixes contain statistical data for the entire class, including key construction dates. An effort has been made to correct errors about these ships that have appeared in other sources.

In the text, all named DEs are *Buckley* class unless otherwise noted, and ships' hull numbers are listed only following the first occurrence of the ship's name. "U-boat" refers only to German submarines, and all numbered U-boats are Type VIIC except where indicated.

2. The top four totals by class for each navy were: (USN) *Fletcher* DDs—26 (all Japanese); *Buckley* DEs—19 (8 German, 11 Japanese); *Benson-Livermore* DDs—16 (9 German, 1 Italian, 6 Japanese); *Edsall* DEs—15 (all German). (RN) V & W DDs—36 (33 German, 3 Italian); Captains frigates (*Evarts* and *Buckley* DEs)—35 (all German); Flower corvettes—33 (30 German, 3 Italian); *Black Swan* sloops—29 (all German). Totals include assists, captured submarines, and submarines shared between classes. See appendix D for a complete list of U-boats credited to the Captains-class.

3. The coloration in color photographs from this period is an exception and must be regarded with caution.

Abbreviations

AA	antiaircraft		IFF	identification, friend or foe
APD	high-speed transport		LCVP	landing craft, vehicle, personnel
ASW	antisubmarine warfare		MF/DF	medium frequency direction-finder
CIC	combat information center		nm	nautical mile
CO	commanding officer		PPI	plan position indicator
CortDiv	escort division (U.S.)		RAF	Royal Air Force
CTL	constructive total loss		RN	Royal Navy
DD	destroyer		rpm	revolutions per minute
DE	destroyer escort; diesel-electric (RN)		SCB	Ship Characteristics Board
DER	radar picket escort		SO	senior officer (RN)
DF	direction-finding		TBS	"talk between ships" (line of sight T-series U.S. Navy VHF radio)
ECM	electronic countermeasure			
EG	escort group (RN)		TE	turboelectric
GM	distance between ship's metacenter and center of gravity		TEG	power supply ship
			TG	task group
HF/DF	high-frequency direction-finder		UDT	underwater demolition team
HUK	antisubmarine hunter-killer group		USNR	U.S. Naval Reserve

The *Buckley*-Class Destroyer Escorts

Part One

DESIGN AND DEPLOYMENT

1   *Historical Background*

At the outset of World War II, Great Britain discounted the immediate need for large numbers of long-range, destroyer-like escort vessels to protect shipping, since the hazardous and fuel-consuming passage from Germany to the western Atlantic through the North Sea and around the Shetland Islands made it unlikely that many U-boat attacks would occur far at sea (the shorter route through the English Channel was not an option due to the dense minefields and antisubmarine traps). In addition, during the first months of the war, Britain was aware that fewer than fifty U-boats were operational at any given time and a portion of these were coastal types not capable of cruising into the open ocean. Existing sloops and older destroyers appeared numerous enough to meet any deep-sea U-boat threat.

Entering the waters around Great Britain and the continent, however, merchantmen came within striking range of German submarines, but a local convoy system that could be screened by smaller, readily constructed vessels such as corvettes and trawlers was instituted upon the declaration of war and did not require escort from warships with the size or sophistication of destroyers. The fact that the light escort vessels were gradually being equipped with asdic, an echo-ranging device capable of detecting a submerged U-boat, furthermore appeared to give the escort a distinct advantage over the submarine. Aircraft were an important element of the defense against sub-

marines as well, and their patrols provided reconnaissance of U-boat activities, particularly alerting the Royal Navy to enemy submarines in transit across the North Sea.

According to Britain's initial assessment of the current strategic situation, German surface ships—both disguised raiders and capital ships—constituted the greatest threat to British supply lines, and as a result the Admiralty deployed its main naval battle units in several concentrated groups at key bases along the British coast to provide the most efficient and powerful response to any movements of enemy warships.

An integral element of the British plan to protect its trade routes was an agreement with France that the French Navy would assist in the defense of the Mediterranean and help protect regional convoys. With the French support to the south, the Royal Navy was able to station more of its major warships in home waters and along Britain's northern and western approaches. These forces were then capable of countering forays by German surface ships as well as effecting a blockade to check neutral merchant shipping headed for Germany.

The unanticipated success of the German campaign of 1940, however, suddenly forced Great Britain to abandon its early war strategy and focus almost exclusively on the defense of its transoceanic supply lines for survival. The German occupation of Norway and France cut Britain off from the continental military sup-

U-660, a Type VIIC U-boat, forced to the surface by a depth charge attack from the Flower-class corvette *Star-wort* (K 20) on November 12, 1942. The Type VIIC was the most numerous kind of U-boat of World War II and was the largest single major warship construction program of any nation in the conflict. More than six hundred were completed between 1939 and 1945. This submarine was the chief predator of Allied convoys and a prized quarry of Allied escorts. The Type VIIC was 216 feet in overall length and had a surfaced standard displacement of 769 tons and a complement of forty-four (on average). It was capable of traveling approximately 9,500 miles at 10 knots while running on the surface with its two diesel engines. Its maximum surfaced speed was 17.7 knots. Submerged, the U-boat had a range of about eighty miles at 4 knots on electric battery power. The Type VIIC was designed to withstand depths of 600 feet below the surface, although it could on occasion dive much deeper. The submarine's armament consisted of four bow torpedo tubes and one stern tube. It was also capable of laying mines. Up to twelve torpedoes or a combination of torpedoes and mines were carried aboard. A medium-caliber deck gun and a variety of automatic antiaircraft cannon were also fitted, and the configuration of these weapons changed radically over the course of the war. The Type VII series was similar in size and shape to its World War I predecessors, but unlike the submarines of the Great War, the Type VII was employed more often in mid-ocean patrols rather than along the European continental shelf for which it was better suited. Despite its relatively small size, the Type VIIC U-boat proved readily adaptable for carrying out unrestricted warfare from the Gulf of Mexico to the Bay of Bengal. Submarines were quite vulnerable once submerged, so their early detection on the surface by convoy escorts or aircraft in order to force them to dive was an important countermeasure. (IWM AX 70A)

port, manufactured goods, and natural resources it required and allowed German submarines (including smaller types), aircraft, and surface ships closer and less-contested access to the Atlantic shipping lanes by means of bases along the French and Norwegian coasts. Therefore, even though British emergency corvettes and trawlers became available in greater numbers to protect local convoys and air patrols increased around Great Britain, Germany was able to extend the Battle of the Atlantic farther to sea, where coastal escorts were much less effective in the mid-ocean conditions and air cover could not be provided. As a result, the German campaign against British shipping reached its most effective point in the war, despite the small number of U-boats patrolling on any given day.[1] Not only did the loss of merchant ships to German submarines, aircraft, mines, and surface ships rise dramatically—from an average of 194,500 tons per month (sixty-two ships) in the nine months before the fall of France to an average of 413,351 tons per month (one hundred ships) in the nine months following that debacle—but the reduction of carrying capacity due to convoy tactics and the strains on available port facilities jeopardized Britain's ability to prosecute the war.[2]

The North Atlantic trade routes were only part of the overall strategic situation. Cargo ships from Asia and the Near East, steaming around Cape Horn and along the coast of West Africa to Great Britain, needed escort as well, while German capital ships, now able to anchor safely within a few hours' cruising time of British supply lines, and the threat of amphibious invasion from the continent tied up a considerable number of British naval and air forces—at the expense of ships and aircraft that would otherwise have been available for escort duty.

In response to German advances, Britain continued to expand the range and administration of its convoys, even though the desirable type and number of escorts to accompany convoys would have to wait for new construction. The majority of escorts in service were inadequate for deep-sea convoy duties, and a large portion of the British destroyer force had been lost or damaged through the ravages of the first year of the war, leaving Great Britain without enough of these valuable ships to offer protection to both its fleet and merchant convoys. The difficulties for Great Britain were compounded by an ominous increase in the number of operational U-boats, the vanguard of Germany's stepped-up commitment to submarine production.

The most effective countermeasure to U-boat attacks during this period was the ability for Great Britain to reroute convoys around known U-boat positions with information gleaned from special intelligence, although it was apparent that this advantage could end at any given moment, leaving convoys at the mercy of existing conventional antisubmarine strategies.[3] Although Great Britain stood fast through the first year and a half of the war (in the process dealing crushing blows to both the German surface fleet and air force), the menace to its shipping from submarines remained its chief strategic problem, and the acquisition of escort vessels continued to be among its highest priorities.

During this same period, President Franklin D. Roosevelt steered the United States toward outright support of the British cause. In September 1940, he authorized the exchange of fifty flush-decker destroyers from American reserves for ninety-nine-year leases to six British naval and air bases in the Caribbean (to which Great Britain added bases in Bermuda and Argentia, Newfoundland, as "gifts"), and in November, he approved the construction of sixty British-designed emergency cargo ships (the progenitors of the Liberty ships) in U.S. shipyards. The overage flush-decker destroyers were an important stopgap in the British war against the U-boats, but not a permanent solution to the shortage of suitable escort vessels.

By February 1941, after eighteen months of war, the last third of which it fought Germany and Italy essentially alone, Great Britain had exhausted its hard currency used to purchase war materials from abroad. The passage of the Lend-Lease Act on March 11, 1941, however, allowed cash-strapped Great Britain promissory access to American munitions, including warships. Britain's desperate need for escort vessels could now be realistically addressed.

Great Britain therefore requested in June 1941 that the United States design and manufacture an oceangoing convoy escort and antisubmarine vessel for British use. The United States Navy had been debating whether to embark on

---

1. The monthly average of the daily number of U-boats at sea between June 1940 and March 1941 was just over twelve submarines. See V. E. Tarrant, *The U-boat Offensive, 1914–1945* (Annapolis, Md.: Naval Institute Press, 1989), 93–96.

2. These statistics were calculated using figures from Stephen W. Roskill, *The War at Sea, 1939–1945*, vol. 1 (London: HMSO, 1954), appendix R, 615–16.

3. F. H. Hinsley, *British Intelligence in the Second World War*, vol. 2 (London: HMSO, 1981), 170.

The Canadian Flower-class corvette *Barrie* (K 138) at sea in 1945. "Flower"-class corvettes made up the bulk of emergency escort construction deployed along the transatlantic shipping routes during the critical second and third years of the war, even though they were designed for coastal rather than mid-ocean service. The Flower-class corvette had a tight turning radius and could safely ride out heavy weather, but due to its short hull length and deep draft, the corvette pitched and heaved excessively in the waves of the North Atlantic, to the discomfort of the crew and detriment of the ship as a fighting unit. The Flowers were wet, underpowered, and overcrowded (due to the necessity of increasing the crew to alleviate the exhaustion incurred on longer convoy routes). Nevertheless, Great Britain's survival was an accomplishment shared by the British, Canadian, and Commonwealth crews of these valuable small ships. The Flower corvette underwent several revisions to its superstructure and armament, but its inability to perform as an efficient fighting platform in ocean conditions would only be alleviated by the introduction of completely new designs with greater overall length and more powerful machinery, such as the River-class frigate and the destroyer escort. (PA 115357, National Archives of Canada)

an escort destroyer program since late 1939, and the British interest decided the issue. Characteristics for a suitable escort vessel had already been prepared by Capt. E. L. Cochrane of the Bureau of Ships (BuShips) and as a consequence the design was completed quickly.

For American planners, the chief obstacle to embarking on an austere escort vessel program had been the difficulty of justifying the manufacture of ships that were similar in size and cost to the 1,630-ton (*Benson*-class) fleet destroyers already on the ways, but that were designed purposely to be less capable (e.g., slower, with fewer guns) in order to facilitate multiple production. The SC—a small and inexpensive escort vessel that was clearly not a destroyer—had been selected as the mobilization prototype for coastal escort purposes, but the war dictated that escorts would have to navigate and fight in the open ocean, something the SC, and the later PC, simply could not do.

Cochrane's draft of the original design for an escort vessel was influenced by his observations of Royal Navy antisubmarine operations and escort ships—particularly the "Hunt"-class escort destroyer and the "Flower"-class corvette—during a mission to Great Britain in the autumn of 1940. From this experience, Cochrane sketched a ship that was larger than the British corvette and equipped with a heavy combination of antiaircraft (AA) and antisubmarine warfare (ASW) armament. Cochrane had envisioned the vessel as being adapted for fast, economical multiple production (since he had witnessed the importance of employing sufficient numbers of oceangoing escorts to successfully combat German submarines) and therefore attempted to simplify the hull and superstructure construction requirements and, in the process, lower the unit cost. Although his proposals had been shelved by the General Board prior to the British request, he pursued the idea until he was able to further reduce the unit cost from three-quarters to about half of the cost of a 1,630-ton destroyer.[4]

In August 1941, President Roosevelt authorized the construction of the new escort vessels on the recommendation of the chief of naval operations, Adm. Harold Stark (who had finally acquiesced to the British requests and BuShips assurances that the Cochrane design was the best solution to the escort problem), and orders for the first fifty units were placed with four Navy shipyards—Boston, Mare Island, Philadelphia, and Puget Sound—in November 1941. When the time came to put the new ship into production, the working plans for the initial design were prepared by the firm of Gibbs and Cox, the same marine architects that prepared the drawings for the Liberty emergency cargo ship. All of these escort vessels were earmarked for transfer to Great Britain under the provisions of the Lend-Lease Act. This new ship, slightly smaller and less complex than a fleet destroyer but equipped with a more formidable antisubmarine battery (which included the British Hedgehog ahead-throwing spigot mortar), was initially designated the British destroyer escort (BDE). This designation was soon simplified to destroyer escort (DE) when the United States officially entered the war and ended up taking over most of the British orders.[5] The first DE design was designated the *Evarts* class in U.S. service.

The design incorporated the latest techniques for multiple production, such as welding and prefabrication, so that these ships could be launched and fitted out as quickly as possible. (Prefabrication was originally called the "American method" by the British Admiralty and was adopted for the production of similar, subsequent British wartime escort designs, such as the "Castle"-class corvette and the "Loch"-class frigate.) By war's end, 504 DEs had been built—the most of any major Allied combatant ship—and were distributed among six classes, distinguished primarily by their power plants, bridge structures, and armament: the *Evarts, Buckley, Cannon, Edsall, Rudderow,* and *John C. Butler* (fifty-six more DEs were completed as APDs and three others were commissioned following the war for a grand total of 563 ships; see appendix A).[6] Great Britain eventually received seventy-eight destroyer escorts, rated as frigates in the Royal Navy (thirty-two *Evarts* and forty-six *Buckley*-class), while France was loaned eight (all *Cannon*-class) and Brazil was given twelve (all *Cannon*-class). The remaining DEs served exclusively in the U.S. Navy.

When construction began on DEs, they were intended to be built without delay. The keels of the first two destroyer escorts were laid down at the Philadelphia Navy Yard on February 12,

4. One source states that a destroyer escort cost $5.3 to $6.1 million in 1943, compared to $10.4 million for a repeater *Benson*-class destroyer. (Norman Friedman, *U.S. Destroyers: An Illustrated Design History,* Annapolis, Md.: Naval Institute Press, 1982, 141.) The Navy Department, however, reported in late 1943 that a DE cost $3.5 million, but it is possible that this figure is a wartime estimate rather than the actual cost. Ashley Halsey, Jr., "Those Not-So-Little Ships—The DEs," *Proceedings* 69, no. 9 (September 1943): 1203.

5. The only destroyer escorts that retained the BDE designation were the first six transferred to Great Britain (BDEs 1, 2, 3, 4, 12, and 46); these were also the only ships Great Britain received from their initial fifty ship lend-lease order, as the remaining forty-four ships were reclassified to DE on January 25, 1943, and taken over by the United States.

6. The classes were also known by abbreviations based on their propulsion systems: GMT (*Evarts*), General Motors diesel-electric tandem drive; TE (*Buckley*), turboelectric drive; DET (*Cannon*), diesel-electric tandem drive; FMR (*Edsall*), Fairbanks-Morse diesel reduction gear drive; TEV (*Rudderow*), turboelectric drive with 5-inch guns; WGT (*John C. Butler*), Westinghouse geared turbine drive.

1942,[7] but the program was slowed immediately—at times to a standstill—by an executive order giving higher priority to the manufacture of landing craft needed for a possible Allied assault on Western Europe in September 1942 (Operation Sledgehammer).[8] Most of the shipyards building the lead DEs were also assigned contracts for landing craft, and since landing craft, particularly the LST and the LCI(L), shared key mechanical components with DEs, the builders could not support both programs simultaneously and still retain the completion rates requested by the Navy. (Ironically, the lack of escort vessels during early 1942 forced the United States to accept emergency British assistance, beginning in February 1942 with the transfer of twenty-two minor ASW craft with Royal Navy crews to American service and the reverse lend-lease loan of ten Flower-class corvettes to the U.S. Navy.)

Construction of DEs finally received the Navy's highest priority rating in November 1942, and the team of dedicated scheduling and procurement specialists that helped accelerate landing craft production was assigned to the DE program, but the projected number of completed ships that had been anticipated for the beginning of 1943 was not achieved until the final months of that year, due to bottlenecks in power plant and component production.[9] As a result, DEs did not participate in the critical convoy battles of the spring of 1943 and ended up carrying out their duties in the afterglow of the Allied Atlantic offensive. The return of Allied control to the major Atlantic shipping lanes by late 1943 led to the cancellation of hundreds of planned DEs, and in their stead, a second round of landing craft production was authorized to support Operation Overlord.

More than 300 DEs did serve, however, in the Atlantic theater—a formidable number despite cancellations—and these ships ensured the safe delivery of supplies to Allied armies in the Mediterranean, Russia (via Arctic routes), and Western Europe. DEs proved adept at the grueling task of tracking and destroying U-boats in shallow waters, particularly the shoals around Great Britain and the European continent

Although the production situation was, of course, far better than it had been at the first meeting in Washington a year before, there was one item of insufficiency on the gigantic list which seriously affected all the strategic calculations of the time—and that item was escort vessels. There were not enough destroyers and destroyer escorts to defend the convoys to Russia and to all the other far-flung theaters of war. After the war, I asked a group of men who had been engaged in grappling with the production problems whether they could name any outstanding failures, the avoidance of which might have shortened the war; their answer was unanimous: the escort vessel program.

Robert E. Sherwood, *Roosevelt and Hopkins: An Intimate History* (New York: Harper Brothers, 1948)

where, by the last year of the war, the majority of German submarines had strategically retreated. The difficulty of this effort, conducted mostly by DEs in British service, was compounded by the advent of the *schnorkel*-equipped submarine.

DEs also helped thwart any renewed U-boat offensive in the Atlantic: in addition to close convoy escort, their long endurance and heavy ASW batteries made DEs ideal vessels for hunter-killer (HUK) groups, the dedicated U.S. Navy antisubmarine forces usually built around escort aircraft carriers. Aided with special intelligence, HUK groups waged a search-and-destroy battle against U-boats in the final two years of the war. American DEs were credited with the outright destruction of twenty U-boats while operating in this capacity between March 1944 and May 1945 and had their most notable success during Operation Teardrop, the counterattack to the last-ditch effort by U-boats to infiltrate the U.S. Eastern Seaboard shipping routes in the waning months of the war. Both of these characteristics

---

7. *Andres* (DE 45, ex–BDE 45) and *Drury* (BDE 46, K 316).

8. These landing craft were ultimately used during Operation Torch, the invasion of French North Africa in November 1942.

9. G. E. Mowry, "Landing Craft and the War Production Board," War Production Board Special Study No. 11 (Washington: GPO, 1946), 22, 74.

of the final stage of the Battle of the Atlantic—shallow-water warfare and the deployment of HUK groups—underscored the need for sufficient numbers of surface ships in cooperation with aircraft to prosecute submarines.

In the Pacific, DEs were an unexpected boon to U.S. operations, since the high design quality and large numbers of these ships allowed the Navy to deploy capable forces simultaneously in several areas of this vast theater. One of the most important functions of DEs in the Pacific was screening fleet oilers—a generally unheralded task, yet one that was critical to the operations of the highly mobile, but fuel-thirsty, fast carrier task forces. This duty underscores one of the great benefits of the DE program: Had DEs been unavailable to screen service groups, fleet destroyers would have to have been deployed to escort these valuable units, thereby bleeding the strength of the task force screens and, indeed, hindering the fighting capabilities and influencing the strategic decisions of the Navy. Escorting fuel-oil tankers was not light duty; as Donald Tillotson writes in his diary, "No one wants a tanker close to them in an air raid."

DEs did not always operate as convoy escorts in the Pacific, however, but were often deployed as sophisticated patrol ships and were the most immediate American naval presence in some engagements. Destroyer escorts, for example, provided support for minor, but necessary, landings along the coasts of New Guinea, the Philippine Islands, Indonesia, and China. DEs also surveyed and charted the region, conducting soundings to find navigable passages, and helped broadcast the end of the war throughout the archipelagoes and atolls dotting the western Pacific Ocean. DEs accepted the surrender of Japanese troops on several islands, including the first enemy garrison to lay down their arms to American forces following Japan's capitulation announcement on August 14, 1945, when *Levy* (DE 162, *Cannon* class) accepted the surrender of the Japanese garrison on Mili Atoll, Marshall Islands, on August 22, 1945.

The *Buckley* class was the second type of DE designed, and with 154 members it was the

August 4. O div. called together and told to have all weapons in top shape, so something is developing. We were informed we were going to shell a beach still in Japanese hands. We intend to go in within 800 yards and fire for 12 minutes doing 5 knots, make a turn and do it over again. We will take on a full Capt and a doctor. This mission was carried off with no return fire. Our guns worked real well and we expended many, many rounds. After we were done, five A29 Hudsons finished it off by dive bombing and strafing the beach. For this we got to paint our first island on the bridge. This will be in our service jackets.

Diary of Donald Tillotson, Seaman, *Bowers*

largest class of escort vessel produced by one nation during the war.[10] The first ship of the class was laid down on June 29, 1942 (DE 52, the future HMS *Bentinck*), and the first to commission was *Reuben James* (DE 153) on April 1, 1943. The final ship of the class to enter the fleet as a DE, *Vammen* (DE 644), was commissioned on July 27, 1944, while the last ship of the class to be built, *Jack C. Robinson* (APD 74, ex–DE 673) was completed as a high-speed transport and commissioned on March 15, 1945. Forty-six *Buckley*s were transferred to Great Britain in 1943 and 1944 through lend-lease—the most of any American-built warship—and they made an immediate and critical contribution to Royal Navy operations. *Buckley*-class ships in American and British service sank or captured at least forty-six enemy submarines, including U-841, destroyed by HMS *Byard* (K 315, ex–DE 55) on October 17, 1943, the first submarine credited to a DE in World War II.[11]

Forty-three *Buckley*-class ships were converted into high-speed transports (redesignated

10. The largest class of escort vessel produced during the war was the "Flower" corvette, with 215 completed—135 by Great Britain and 80 by Canada. The two countries also combined resources to build an additional 52 Modified Flower–class corvettes.

11. *Buckley*-class ships serving in the Royal Navy sank or assisted in sinking twenty-seven U-boats, while American *Buckley* DEs sank or assisted in sinking seven U-boats and eleven Japanese submarines and helped capture one U-boat for a combined total of forty-six. See appendix D.

Charles Lawrence–class APDs) beginning in mid-1944 and were used to land reconnaissance parties ahead of amphibious operations in the Pacific, notably for the invasions of Iwo Jima and Okinawa. Four American and three British *Buckley*-class DEs were converted into power supply ships (TEGs) between 1945 and 1949 and were capable of providing emergency electricity for civilian or military use. (These power supply ships were listed as one of the thirteen major American military innovations of World War II, which included self-propelled projectiles, individual rations, and the atomic bomb.[12]) Seven other ships of the class were modified into radar pickets (DERs) immediately after the war, although these vessels were not as successful as the power supply ships and all but one were placed in the inactive reserve before the end of the decade. A second round of DER conversions in the 1950s using thirty-four *Edsall*- and two *John C. Butler*–class DEs, however, did make an important contribution to the U.S. Cold War effort as mid-ocean monitors of Soviet long-range aircraft movements, among their many tasks.

Several *Buckley* ships distinguished themselves during World War II. *England* (DE 635) sank six Japanese submarines in the space of twelve days (May 19–31, 1944), considered the greatest American antisubmarine performance of the war; *Bassett* (APD 73) rescued the largest number of survivors of the sunken cruiser *Indianapolis* (CA 35) on August 2, 1945; and HMS *Duckworth* (K 351, ex–DE 61) was involved in the destruction of five U-boats, the most of any DE in the Atlantic theater.[13]

The *Buckley* class was well regarded immediately following the war, and by the end of 1948, twelve *Buckley*s were the only DEs of any class that remained in full, active commission. Six of these ships served in the Korean War, including all four power supply ships. The combat usefulness of DEs declined rapidly, however, due to their inadequate speed compared to postwar submarine designs, their light armament, and their inability to achieve a suitable machinery and ordnance upgrade.[14] They also suffered

from a high ratio of crew members to firepower. The most important postwar function of *Buckley*-class DEs became their use as training vessels and platforms for weapons tests.

All ships of the class, save one APD and a DE that was used for research purposes, were deactivated by 1963. A few vessels remained in service in reserve into the early 1970s, but all were gradually disposed of—either scrapped, sunk as targets, or sold to foreign countries—before the end of 1975.[15] One *Charles Lawrence*-class APD converted from a *Buckley*-class DE is still listed on the register of the Mexican navy (1998)—the last *Buckley*-class vessel in existence—but it is probably slated for disposal in the near future.[16]

---

12. Marcel Baudot, et al., eds. *The Historical Encyclopedia of World War II* (New York: Facts On File, 1980), 474.

13. *Duckworth* is credited in the destruction of five submarines, although the identity of one of them has not been conclusively established. The *Evarts*-type Captains-class frigate *Bayntun* (K 310, ex–BDE 1) positively destroyed or assisted in the destruction of four U-boats, while *Affleck* (K 462, ex–DE 71), another *Buckley*-type ship, is also credited with four kills, although the success of one of these attacks has been questioned (see appendix D). *Bronstein* (DE 189, *Cannon* class) had the highest total for a U.S. Navy destroyer escort in the Atlantic theater, with credit for sinking one German submarine single-handedly and assisting in the destruction of two others in March 1944.

14. Surface escorts were expected to have a 10-knot advantage over a submarine, and the fact that the German Type XXI and Type XXIII U-boats introduced at the end of World War II were capable of trial submerged speeds of just under 16 and 12 knots, respectively, for just over one hour meant that even the 24-knot DEs would have difficulty tracking these submarines. It was assumed (correctly) by the West that the postwar Soviet Union would eventually prepare a submarine force based on captured German technology, effectively rendering the DEs obsolete as first-line ASW vessels.

15. Eighteen former *Buckley*-class DEs converted into *Charles Lawrence*-class APDs were sold to foreign navies between 1961 and 1971. All of the other ships of the class were disposed of by the U.S. Navy. The *Buckley* class ended up being the only type of destroyer escort that was not sold to a foreign navy.

16. *Vincento Guerrero* (E-21), the former USS *Barber* (DE 161, APD 57) is the last of the *Buckley*s. Originally called *Coahuila* (B-07), *Vincento Guerrero* was renamed around 1994. Two *Crosley*-class APDs and one *Edsall* DE are still listed on the naval register of Mexico as well, but these ships, too, are probably nearing the end of their active careers.

2 *Design and Armament*

The *Buckley*-class DE was a specialized antisubmarine and convoy escort vessel capable of protecting merchant and auxiliary ships from submarine and aircraft attacks while accompanying these ships across thousands of miles of ocean and in heavy seas. It had enough bunkerage, beam, and hull length to navigate the open ocean successfully (although the DE received some criticism early on for excessive pitching and rolling), while its twin rudders and maximum speed of 24 knots gave the ship a tight turning radius, excellent maneuverability, and a decisive performance margin over contemporary submarines.

The original destroyer escort built for Great Britain (the *Evarts* class in U.S. service) was powered by a bank of four General Motors V12 diesel engines in tandem with electric drive. Electric drive was chosen in order to sidestep a bottleneck in gear production, so that instead of reduction gears, an electrical generator powered by the diesel engines was coupled to a motor to regulate propeller shaft revolution. Although this design was intended to be powered by eight diesel engines, the Navy anticipated a shortage of diesel engines and therefore halved the number of engines, reducing the shaft horsepower from 12,000 shp to 6,000 shp and thus lowering the design speed of the class from 24 to about 19 knots.[1]

Despite these measures, the Navy realized that it still would not have enough diesel engines to supply the DE program and therefore began work immediately on an alternative DE design that utilized a steam turboelectric power plant. The Navy had been contemplating using turboelectric power plants for smaller warships since mid-1941 as a means of alleviating propulsion bottlenecks, and faced with the ambitious DE program, which called for hundreds of these vessels to be completed on fast schedules, the Navy now had the circumstances to sanction its introduction.[2] In January 1942, General Electric was contracted to produce turboelectric power plants of its own design, while Bethlehem Shipbuilding prepared the vessel's working drawings and broke ground for a shipyard at Hingham, Massachusetts, to build the new DEs. The design was named after the first numbered ship of the class, the *Buckley* (DE 51).[3]

The *Buckley* class was not part of the British

---

1. All three diesel-powered DE classes—*Evarts*, *Cannon*, and *Edsall*—ended up having only four diesel engines; as a consequence, all of these classes had top speeds well under the original DE design speed of 24 knots.

2. Charles H. Coleman, "Shipbuilding Activities of the National Defense Advisory Commission and the Office of Production Management, July 1940 to December 1941," War Production Board Special Study No. 18 (Washington: GPO, 1946), 121–22.

3. American destroyer escorts, like fleet destroyers, were named in honor of deceased persons who served in or were of service to the U.S. Navy. In several cases the name of a destroyer lost early in the war, e.g., *Reuben James*, was reassigned to a DE.

Sixteen *Buckley*-class DEs including *Bates* (DE 68) and *Joseph E. Campbell* (DE 70) along the outfitting docks at the Bethlehem-Hingham shipyard in August 1943. Two of the ships have SL surface-search radars and armament fitted; one of them (the sixth ship from the foreground flying a U.S. flag) has started its boilers and is beginning to back away from the dock. Most of the ships in this photograph were transferred to Great Britain. (Courtesy, Mr. D. Glaser, from the collection of Mr. W. B. Ackroyd)

fifty-ship lend-lease order that led to the *Evarts*-class design but was instead authorized by Public Law 440 (passed February 6, 1942), which called for the construction of 1,799 small combatant and auxiliary vessels for Great Britain, including 250 additional DEs that had been ordered by Great Britain in January 1942. A provision was added to the bill, as with the Lend-Lease Act, that gave the United States the authority to repossess any vessel prior to delivery.[4]

The propulsion system of a *Buckley*-class DE consisted of two nearly identical units, each com-posed of a high-pressure, superheater boiler in a fire room and a main GE 4,600-kW steam turbine-generator, synchronous propulsion motor, and motor-generator set in an adjacent engine room. At full power, each shaft was driven by an entire unit; the forward unit operated the starboard propeller and the after unit operated the port propeller. For reduced (cruising) speed, or in the event one engine or boiler were lost, either

4. Samuel E. Morison, *History of United States Naval Operations in World War II* (Boston: Little, Brown & Co., 1956), vol. 10: *The Atlantic Battle Won*, 34.

The Bethlehem-Hingham shipyard in February 1944. The outfitting docks are to the left-center and the ways are on the right. The long buildings below the ways are assembly shops, and further down are the steel plate storage and shop areas. The buildings below the docks are outfitting warehouses. Large cranes line the ways, where at least eighteen ships are in various stages of construction. At this time, the shipyard was finishing its last *Buckley*-class DEs, including the final two TEs transferred to Great Britain (these two ships may be at the extreme left, moored to the outfitting docks). Bethlehem-Hingham was also in the midst of converting *Rudderow*-class DEs into *Crosley*-class APDs. The outfitting docks appear to be servicing at least sixteen DEs. (80-G-218183)

Each of the fire rooms had a water tube boiler that burned, I believe, No. 6 crude oil. The boilers generated 430-psi, 980-degree superheated steam. Each engine room had a turbine that was driven by the steam from the fire room. These two turbines drove a generator that generated electricity to propel the drive motors hooked up to the two propellers (or screws) that moved the ship through the water. The speed of the ship was controlled by the voltage applied to the motors. The maximum speed of the ship was 24 knots. Care had to be taken not to drop the steam pressure below 235 psi or you could pull water from the boiler into the turbine, destroying it. . . . When I first went aboard the *Fechteler* I was the evaporator man. I made the fresh water for use in the boilers. If the water wasn't pure it would coat the boiler tubes decreasing the efficiency of the boilers.

Curtis Toombs, Fireman, *Fechteler*

unit could provide parallel power to both shafts through a cross-connection.[5] Propeller speed was regulated with a lever on a control panel located in each engine room. Levers to apply a DC excitation field to the generator and propulsion motor and to reverse the electrical connection for propeller reversal were also located on these panels (during a cross-connection, one control panel would operate both propeller shafts).

The main turbine-generators turned at 5,600 rpm at full speed and together produced the equivalent shaft horsepower of the originally specified eight linked diesels (12,000 shp). As designed, the speed ratio between each turbine-generator and propulsion motor was to be a constant 14:1 (achieved through a governor motor control). The actual performance of the *Buckley*-class power plant was closer to 13:1, however, with the motor turning 153 rpm at 10 knots, 237 rpm at 15 knots (standard speed), 327 rpm at 20 knots (full speed), and 430 rpm at 24 knots (flank speed).[6] Compared to geared drive, electric drive gave a ship excellent response: acceleration and maneuvering—particularly switching to reverse—were almost immediate. Electric drive was, however, more expensive to produce, operate, and maintain than the geared steam turbine power plant installed in the *John C. Butler* class, the final wartime DE design.

In order to accommodate the new GE machinery, which required greater longitudinal space than the arrangement of the diesel-electric drive in the *Evarts* class, Bethlehem Shipbuilding had to lengthen the existing DE hull from 283.5 feet to 300 feet at the waterline and increase the extreme beam by almost two feet. These changes had the added benefit of improving the ship's seakeeping qualities. The *Buckley*-class long hull design ended up being adopted for all four subsequent classes of World War II DE: *Cannon, Edsall, Rudderow,* and *John C. Butler.* The uptakes from the *Buckley*'s two fire rooms angled toward each other and joined to form a single, flat-sided stack. This arrangement gave the *Buckley*-class exhaust system its distinctive, upside-down Y appearance. Bethlehem also modified the ship's superstructure so that it extended unbroken from the base of the bridge, back to the number three gun position on the quarterdeck, in contrast with the original *Evarts* DE design, which had a large gap between the bridge superstructure and a

5. Although the *Buckley*'s steam turbine power plant provided great propulsion power, its endurance was low compared to the diesel plants installed in the *Cannon* and *Edsall* classes due to the high volume of fuel burned to retain efficient steam pressure. Endurances for the steam classes of DEs were calculated on a cross-connection, since that provided the most efficient cruising power. Even so, the wartime cruising endurance of the *Buckley* class was roughly half that of the long-hulled diesel classes (*Cannon* and *Edsall*), which is what led to the latter's general adoption for HUK groups. Steam turbines had several advantages over diesels that helped mitigate their lack of endurance, however, including efficiency at low speeds and quieter operation, both of which provided better opportunities for successful sonar use and ASW maneuvering. Interestingly, a relatively small number of long-hulled diesel ships served in the Pacific theater (in fact, no *Edsall*-class ships operated in this ocean until the war was virtually over) despite the great distances required for some convoy routes; clearly, the advantage that the added endurance of these ships brought to the Atlantic HUK groups was not simply great range but the critical ability to prosecute possible submarine contacts for long periods without having to top off their fuel supply, something that was of less importance along the convoy routes of the Pacific, which were virtually uncontested by submarines.

6. William Johnson, course notes, GE turboelectric power plant training course, Hadley Tech, St. Louis, Missouri, May–September 1943. The maximum rpm for each main turbine generator was 5,780, producing roughly 12,200 shp, which can account for some of the difference between the two performance ratios.

The main propulsion control panel in the forward engine room aboard *Torrington* (K 577, ex–DE 568). The rating's left hand is on the reverse lever and his right hand is on the speed lever. The ship's speed dial is at eye level, along with gauges for steam pressure and turbine rpm. (Courtesy, Mr. A. E. D'Auriol)

We hit a lot of storms in the Atlantic. At times the ship pitched so violently the bow would come up out of the water; you could drive a semi under it without touching, at times the lines to the stack would be pulled tight enough to sound the horns on the stack; this is a lot of flexing! The flying bridge is forty-two feet from the water, and water would come over it, at times the next DE could not be seen for a couple seconds, it would be in a trough, all you could see was the radar antenna. One time three or four nights out we hit heavy storms; one of our sister ships lost a man over the side about midnight. The commodore took a risk that night, he ordered the two closest DEs to turn their searchlights on for a few minutes to try and locate the man; no luck. It was in November, I recall, and cold. At night in heavy weather, and going to your watch, you always had one hand on something solid. I recall one night in a heavy storm, going up the ladder to the bridge from the boat deck, I had both hands wrapped around a rung, and the ship pitched and rolled and I was almost perpendicular to the ladder. The DEs were good ships, it was tough duty, you were hammered day and night in heavy weather, sometimes for ten to twelve days.

George Farral, Gunner's Mate, *Weber*

deckhouse toward the stern. As a result of the continuous superstructure and ability to ride heavy waves, *Buckley* DEs remained remarkably dry belowdecks even in the worst sea weather.

The building plans for the *Buckley* class, like all classes of DE, were prepared for multiple production. Each ship was entirely welded, and prefabricated sections were used throughout to accelerate assembly. The DE was a flush-decked, thin-skinned vessel built from steel plate ranging in thickness from $\frac{1}{2}$ inch along the outboard strake above the keel to $\frac{3}{16}$ inch for the superstructure bulkheads. Most of the hull and deck plating was $\frac{1}{4}$-inch-thick steel plate, although areas of greater stress were built with heavier plate, up to $\frac{7}{16}$ of an inch. The *Buckley*-class hull was made up of thirteen prefabricated sections and contained 171 transverse frames (eleven of which were watertight bulkheads) and fifteen longitudinal frames on either side of the keel which ran the length of the ship.[7] The watertight compartmentation of the DE proved to be a major factor in the survivability of these ships with severe bow or stern damage, and wartime experience proved that even a fleet destroyer could not have been expected to perform much better with a similar torpedo hit in the screws or bow. The DE's relatively large engine room and fire room spaces were vulnerable to rapid flood-

7. Al Ross provides further details of the hull construction and machinery functions in his book, *Anatomy of the Ship: The Destroyer Escort* England (London: Conway Maritime Press, 1985).

Top: *Barber* (DE 161) under construction at the Norfolk Navy Yard on May 20, 1943, being prepared for launch later that day. The prefabricated director station for the X position is on the stern waiting to be lifted into place. Bottom: *Pavlic* (DE 669) on December 18, 1943, being launched sideways into the Ohio River from the Dravo Corporation's east yard on Neville Island, Pittsburgh, Pennsylvania. Most of the DEs launched at this yard ended up being floated down the Ohio and Mississippi Rivers to the Gulf of Mexico, where they were completed. *Pavlic* was converted into an APD at Consolidated Steel in Orange, Texas, prior to commissioning. DEs were usually launched light and fitted with their power plants once the ship was in the water, but some DEs, like *Pavlic*, were launched with their main machinery already installed. (Top: NH S-112-C; bottom: LCM-19-55540)

Buckley (DE 51) undergoing evaluation trials on July 3, 1943, off Rockland, Maine. The twin-ruddered *Buckley* has completed a circle with a diameter of about 1,000 feet while steaming at 20 knots. Two rudders gave DEs excellent maneuverability—and therefore a tactical advantage when attacking submarines—compared to ships of similar size with a single rudder, such as the "River"- and *Tacoma*-class frigates manufactured in Great Britain and the United States. These frigates had a turning diameter of about 1,440 feet at 12 knots. A *Fletcher*-class destroyer with its single rudder would make a circle approximately 2,850 feet in diameter while steaming at a brisk 30 knots. (80-G-269442)

ing if opened to the sea, and therefore, like all smaller warships, a DE stood little chance of survival if hit square amidships by a torpedo.

The *Buckley*-class DE had an overall hull length of 306 feet; an extreme beam of 36 feet, 11.5 inches; a standard displacement of 1,400 tons (1,740 full load, 1,800 wartime); a mean draft of 9 feet, 5 inches, at standard displacement (11 feet, 3 inches, full load); and a maximum speed of 24 knots.[8] It had a bunkerage of 358 tons of fuel oil and a wartime cruising radius of roughly 3,700 nm, depending on sea conditions and duties.[9] The ship had two 8.5-foot solid manganese-bronze screws and twin rudders. The resulting turning radius for the class was about 500 feet at 20 knots, a significant improvement over ships of similar size with single rudders.

The crew consisted of eight to fifteen officers and 180 to 210 petty officers and enlisted men. During World War II, many of the officers, including the commanding officer, and the major-ity of enlisted men aboard both American and British DEs were naval reservists. Destroyer escorts were the largest warships that USNR officers were routinely assigned to command. British sailors were mostly "hostilities only" volunteers or draftees, and in addition to the RN, the officers' ranks drew from RNR, RNVR, and Commonwealth naval reserve pools. The chief petty officers (artificers in the RN) were often regular

8. Some published *Buckley*-class data tables indicate an extreme beam of 37 feet for ships built at Bethlehem Steel shipyards and 36 feet, 10 inches, for those built at all other yards. The former measurement is not documented on the Bethlehem design plans and may simply be an approximation, while the latter measurement is actually the extreme molded breadth of the class. *Buckley* (DE 51) was rated at 23.7 knots during its initial trials, but there is no doubt that these ships could achieve 24 knots without difficulty. *Calder* (K 349) claimed burst speeds of 26.8 knots.

9. The *Buckley*-class trial endurance was 4,920 nautical miles at 15 knots and 1,673 tons displacement. *Eichenberger* (DE 202) recorded its average wartime endurance as 3,708 nautical miles, while *Conn* (K 509) recorded 3,722 miles.

A sign proclaiming the incredible speed in which a DE could be built. This is *Halsted* (K 566, ex-*Reynolds*, DE 91), one of forty-six *Buckley*-class DEs transferred to Great Britain during World War II. All of the *Buckley*-class lend-lease ships were built at the Bethlehem–Hingham shipyard. *Halsted* ended up being the second-fastest-built DE: *Fieberling* (DE 640) was completed in just under twenty-four days in April 1944, at Hingham's fellow shipyard, Bethlehem–San Francisco. (Courtesy, Cdr. R. Fowler, RN, Ret.)

navy, however, so that each DE had persons with technical experience in key positions aboard the ship as an aid to train reservists.

Three navy yards and six commercial shipyards were eventually contracted to build *Buckley*-class DEs (see appendix B). In order to expedite construction, shipyards made bulk purchases of identical components such as hull frames, funnels, boilers, propellers, and rudders from subcontractors scattered throughout the country. These assemblies and components were then brought to the shipyard by rail. The speed with which a *Buckley*-class DE could be built and delivered to the Navy was impressive. *Fieberling* (DE 640) was laid down at the Bethlehem–San Francisco shipyard on March 19, 1944, and commissioned a mere twenty-four days later, on April 11.[10] This was the fastest building time of any escort vessel during the war.

The *Buckley* class ended up being the most evenly distributed type of DE between the Atlantic and Pacific theaters owing to its large numbers, the construction of ships on both coasts, and the fact that the class was produced over the longest period of time. Delivery of the first units began in April 1943 and continued until March 1945, although the majority of the ships of the class (119) were commissioned between August 1943 and March 1944. The greatest monthly total of *Buckley*-class deliveries occurred in November 1943, when twenty-one ships were commissioned (see appendix C).

The most significant British influence on the

10. *Fieberling* was also the last *Buckley*-class ship laid down. All other ships of the class, including the six vessels destined to be completed as APDs, had been laid down before the end of 1943. The Bethlehem–San Francisco shipyard had last laid down a DE five months earlier, in October 1943.

In 1943, as a young sub-lieutenant, I suppose age nineteen, I and others took the *Queen Elizabeth* to the states, at New York, where we were destined to make the first crew for the American built frigates, which were of the Captains class. From New York, where we stayed at the Barbizon Plaza Hotel for about a week I think, we were sent by train to Boston—about three or four officers and fifty odd ratings. At Boston, we lived at Dry Dock Barracks (it doesn't exist now), where we had a tidy little office and one desk on which stood the out tray and in tray, both empty; we all arrived and sat down and wondered what are we to do now, nobody seemed to know. This went on for a little bit and gradually things picked up, and we were sent in due course to Hingham, Massachusetts, where the Bethlehem-Hingham corporation had a shipyard which certainly a year before had been just virgin meadow land. The building process [of the DEs] was quite interesting. The ships were made in sections, which I think were probably one-seventh of the total length of a completed ship, fabricated in the shed, then wheeled onto the slipway and welded up by teams of women welders, the skin, the frames, and the keel welded together, and the system was that every ship was one week ahead of the ship on the next slipway; every week, maybe it was Monday, one ship was launched without fail. If there was any hold up— there just couldn't be a hold up!—that ship had to be launched, as the next user of that slipway had to come up. So it was a magnificent process: everyday the railway came into Bethlehem-Hingham shipyard; you might see a train load of funnels coming in, a train load of engines, a train load of rudders, train load of propellers, all coming from all over the states—what ever they need; it was a magnificent system.

Lt. Christopher Eason, Navigation Officer, *Calder*

initial DE design was the high, open bridge, which was the prominent feature of the first four classes of DE. The open bridge provided an ideal position for conning, particularly for keeping an eye on ships in close formation or in heavy seas, or during an aircraft attack when an all-around view of the sky was preferable to assist gun control, notably against kamikazes. Visual spotting, too, remained an important means of submarine detection throughout the war, and the ability to scan the horizon from an unobstructed position proved invaluable; in fact, toward the end of the war, scanning the sea with binoculars for a telltale sign, such as a puff of diesel exhaust or a small wake, became more productive than radar for locating *schnorkel*-equipped U-boats.[11] Although the British Admiralty required an open bridge for its escorts, the chief architect of the DE, Capt. E. L. Cochrane, was sufficiently impressed with the efficacy of the British-style open bridge that he planned to include it in the DE design anyway.[12]

The sound room, as requested by the Admiralty, was located above the pilothouse, forward of the open bridge. The original *Buckley*-class design placed portholes on either side of the sound room, but these were eliminated by August 1943 in favor of two additional portholes in front of the pilothouse. Rounded conning positions were also added at this time to each forward corner of the open bridge to eliminate some of the blind spots that resulted from the placement of the high bridge relatively close to the bow. The boxy, balconylike lookout stations on either side of the flying bridge of the *Evarts* design were simplified into single, curved plates to eliminate additional steel plate cutting, fitting, and welding.

The British Admiralty had also requested a dual-purpose weapon for the main battery, which resulted in the adoption of the 3-inch/50 Mk22 gun, in three single mounts, two forward of the bridge and one on the quarterdeck. (The superior 5-inch/38 would have been preferred, but this gun was not yet available in sufficient quantities to supply the DE program. The final two classes of DE and the high-speed transport conversions, however, were armed with this

11. Charles M. Sternhell and Alan M. Thorndike, *Anti-submarine Warfare in World War II* (Washington: Office of the Chief of Naval Operations, 1946), 74.

12. Philip K. Lundeberg, *American Anti-Submarine Operations in the Atlantic, May 1943–May 1945*, Ph.D. diss., Harvard University, 1953 (Ann Arbor: University Microfilms, 1997), 11.

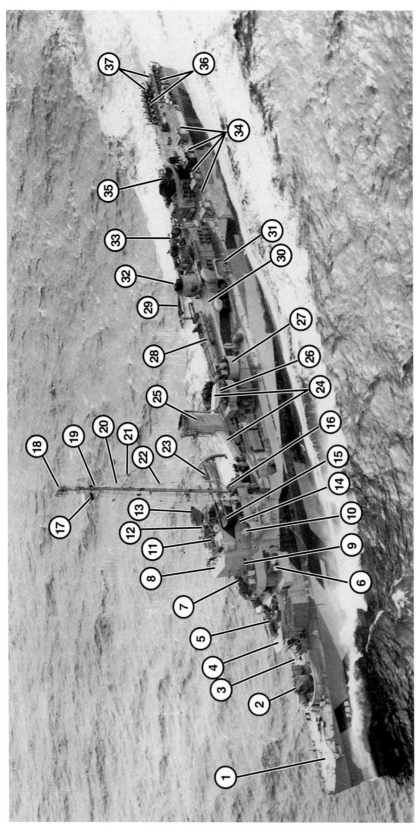

The topside architecture of a *Buckley*-class DE consisted of four decks, beginning with the main deck, or 00 level. Above the main deck was the superstructure deck, which ran almost the entire length of the ship; this was also called the upper deck, or 01 level. The next highest deck was the navigating bridge, or 02 level, and on top of that was the open flying bridge—the uppermost deck—at the 03 level (which was also called the steering station and sky lookout level). An observer on the flying bridge was about 42 feet above the water, roughly the same height as the pilothouse in a *Fletcher*-class destroyer. Most British lend-lease DEs added a crow's nest above the yard; this vantage point was about 68 feet above the water.

Legend: *1,* main deck (00 level); *2,* number one gun; *3,* Hedgehog; *4,* Hedgehog blast shield; *5,* number two gun; *6,* 01 level 20mm guns (numbers three and four); *7,* 02 level 20mm guns (numbers one and two); *8,* sound room; *9,* pilothouse; *10,* 24-inch carbon arc searchlight; *11,* flying bridge (03 level); *12,* 12-inch signal light; *13,* 2.5-meter range finder; *14,* navigating bridge (02 level); *15,* lookout station; *16,* signal flag locker; *17,* surface-search radome (SL); *18,* air-search radar array (SA); *19,* mast; *20,* yard; *21,* TBS antenna; *22,* signal flag halyards; *23,* whaleboat and davits; *24,* fire room uptakes; *25,* stack; *26,* 01.5 level 20mm guns (numbers five and six); *27,* 01 level 20mm guns (numbers seven and eight); *28,* torpedo tubes; *29,* torpedo handling hoist; *30,* superstructure deck (01 level); *31,* life raft; *32,* X position fire-control director station; *33,* X position; *34,* depth charge throwers, K-guns; *35,* number three gun; *36,* depth charge tracks; *37,* smoke screen generators (80–G–419678)

weapon.) The DE would also be equipped with the Hedgehog, a British antisubmarine weapon that was a significant improvement over the conventional depth charge.

The Admiralty had originally specified each DE be furnished with a bank of torpedo tubes, but this requirement was dropped before the first ships were laid down in favor of including additional antiaircraft guns. As a result, the *Evarts* class was not designed to carry torpedo tubes, even though the antiaircraft guns requested were never fitted since the supply of these weapons and their mounts was quite scarce at the time. The *Buckley* class retained the general deck layout and superstructure adopted for the *Evarts* class in order to avoid a complete, time-consuming redesign, but the class did receive a bank of three torpedo tubes amidships just aft of the stack. All U.S. *Buckley*-class ships completed as DEs had a torpedo mount, but it was left off those ships transferred to Great Britain.[13]

Britain ultimately received thirty-two *Evarts*-class and forty-six *Buckley*-class DEs.[14] These seventy-eight ships were pooled together into a single group called the "Captains"-class frigates.[15] Captains-class ships were named in honor of Royal Navy officers from the eighteenth and nineteenth centuries, many of whom served under Lord Nelson. These ships were officially rated as frigates rather than escort destroyers because, although they were slightly larger than the British "Hunt"-class escort destroyers, ships classified as destroyers in the Royal Navy not only had to satisfy certain size and speed requirements but also had to be fitted with guns or torpedo tubes capable of countering other destroyers or large torpedo boats. This requirement excluded the Captains-class ships since they were fitted with a modest 3-inch dual-purpose battery and, as specified by the Admiralty, had no torpedo tubes.

The major design criticism of the DE in British service was the ship's high metacentric height (GM) and excessive stiffness that caused the ship to roll rapidly, almost violently, in heavy

seas.[16] The *Buckley*s performed better than the shorter-hulled *Evarts* class, but both types benefited from subsequent lengthening and deepening of the bilge keels. The bilge keels were modified following transfer to Great Britain and took from three to eight weeks to complete, depending upon congestion at the shipyard. Increasing topweight was also a means of decreasing GM, and this strategy was employed by British DEs with additional depth charge stowage along the main deck to compensate for their lack of four K-guns, ready racks, and (on *Buckley* vessels) a torpedo mount. The U.S. Navy suggested that the lack of a torpedo mount accounted for most of the instability of the Captains-class ships, but the British calculated that the weight of the mount alone would have had a negligible effect on decreasing GM. Cochrane believed that the substitution of the 3-inch main battery for the preferred 5-inch guns was the main cause of the large GM of these ships.[17] Following modifications, complaints about excessive rolling in the Captains class disappeared.

---

13. Four *Buckley*-class ships, hull numbers 575–578, are sometimes reported as not ever having had torpedo tubes, but this is not the case. All were commissioned with a triple torpedo bank, but three of these ships, like many others, had the torpedo mount removed early in their careers in favor of additional antiaircraft guns; the fourth, DE 576, was torpedoed during its first escort mission, towed back to the United States, and converted into APD 39.

14. Six *Evarts* ships were transferred under the original lend-lease order authorized on August 15, 1941; fifteen *Evarts* and thirty-four *Buckley*-class were transferred from the "1799" act of February 6, 1942, while the final eleven *Evarts* and twelve *Buckley*s were transferred under the Naval Construction Act of July 9, 1942.

15. When distinguishing the two types of Captains-class vessels, the Royal Navy referred to the *Evarts* ships as DEs (diesel-electric frigates) and the *Buckley*s as TEs (turboelectric frigates). Since the British did not use the term "destroyer escort," there was no ambiguity with their *Evarts* abbreviation. Note that the name of this class is often shortened to Captain, but the class name was officially pluralized.

16. David K. Brown, "Atlantic Escorts, 1939–1945," in *The Battle of the Atlantic, 1939–1945*, edited by Stephen Howarth and Derek Law (Annapolis, Md.: Naval Institute Press, 1994), 467.

17. Friedman, *U.S. Destroyers*, 161.

The outboard profile of the *Buckley*-class DE. This and the following plans were prepared by Bethlehem Shipbuilding and approved on November 17, 1943. The plans incorporate all of the superstructure modifications added to the production line by this time, including lookout sponsons at the forward end of the open bridge and additional 20mm gun tubs along the superstructure. It is fortunate that a copy of the original plans for the *Buckley* class still exists, although the drawings were not clearly duplicated before the master was destroyed, leaving some of the writing difficult, if not impossible, to make out and scratches occasionally breaking up the lines. The bilge keels extend from frame 59 to 113 on either side of the main keel, a length of 94.5 feet. Following trials of early units, the Admiralty found that the Captains-class ships rolled too excessively for service and ordered the bilge keels lengthened to frame 120 (an additional 14 feet). This modification increased the ship's roll period to a satisfactory level. It has been noted that American officers and crews did not express any official dissatisfaction with the seakeeping quality of their DEs, and American DEs did not have their bilge keels lengthened. Reasons for this contrast have been offered, including the lack of American experience with other vessels of similar size that could afford comparison; the much heavier weather conditions regularly encountered by British ships in the North Sea; and the added weight of American DEs, which carried larger crews, more stores, four more K-guns, and a torpedo mount.

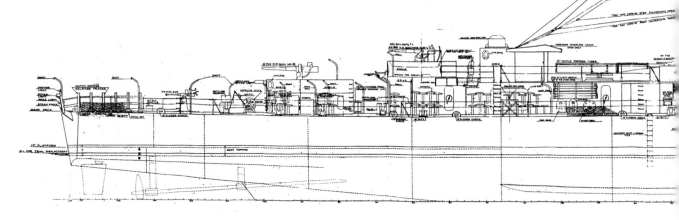

Inboard profile showing the general arrangement of the ship's interior compartments. The large engine room and fire room spaces amidships reveal an unavoidable weakness in smaller warship design: An opening across one or more compartments caused by a torpedo or mine could result in rapid and potentially fatal flooding if the breach was too large for damage control parties to secure. Note the access hatches to belowdeck platforms—the aft crew quarters from a hatch on the main deck aft of the number three gun and two hatches beneath the X position, the engineering spaces from hatches within the machine shop areas in the superstructure, and the forward crew and CPO quarters from a hatch aft of the Hedgehog.

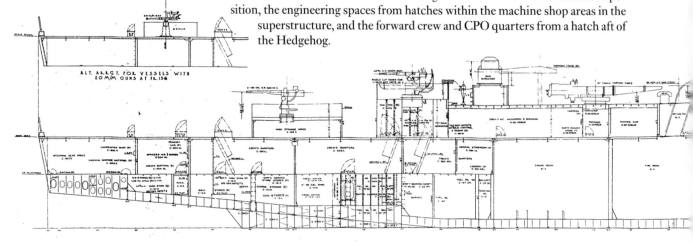

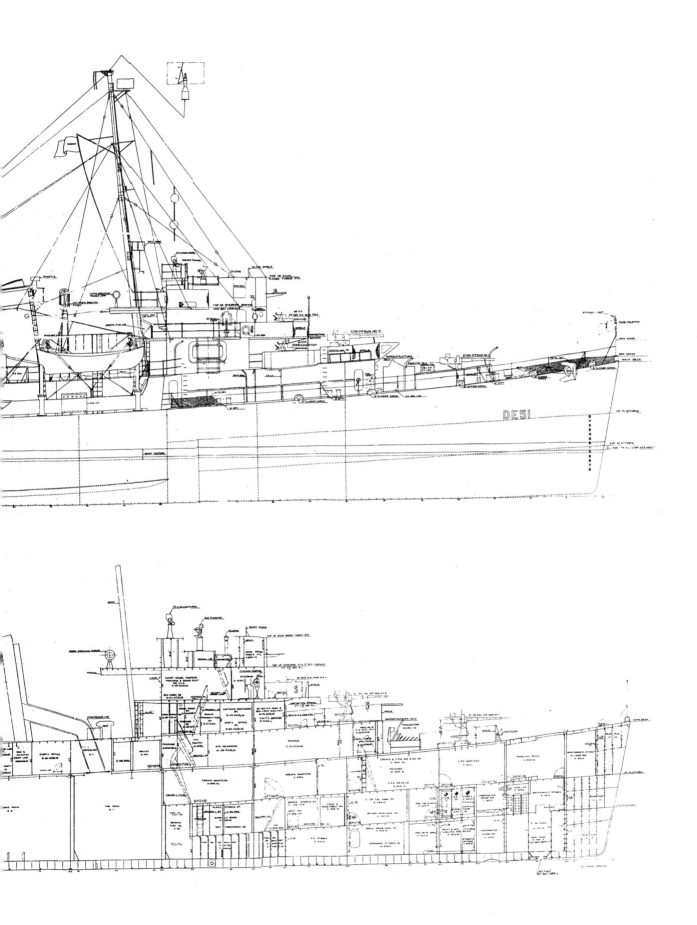

General arrangement of the flying bridge and sky look-out. The sonar room (asdic cabinet in the Royal Navy) is forward, containing the sonar amplifier, sound range recorder, and attack plotter. The sonar room is flanked by two observation posts with portable seats and footrests. Immediately aft along the center-line is the pelorus, followed by the Mk51 gun director station and the 2.5-meter optical range finder. On the port side of the flying bridge is the log desk and radar plot viewer, while an accessway to the steering station is on the starboard side. The two sky lookout positions are port and starboard, each containing two stations: one for air lookout (aft) and one for sea lookout (forward). Each lookout had binoculars and an alidade at his service.

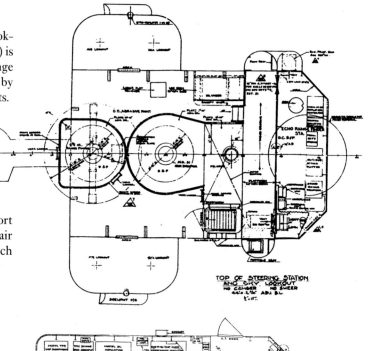

General arrangement of the navigating bridge. The steering station, or wheel house, is forward with port-holes indicated and the sextant locker on the starboard side; the CIC (combat information center) was aft of the wheel house and contained the chart house port-side along with the SL and SA radar control units, radar plot, and the HF/DF station. The officers' sea cabin was in the aft starboard corner. All of these stations were illuminated with red light at night in order to conceal the ship and preserve night vision.

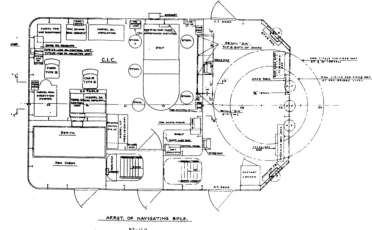

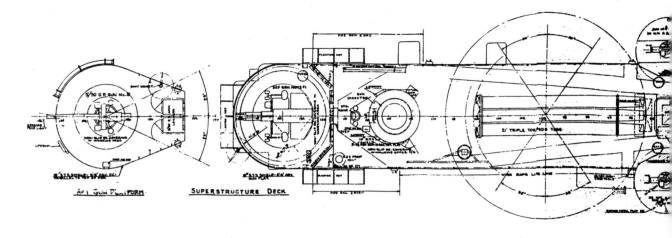

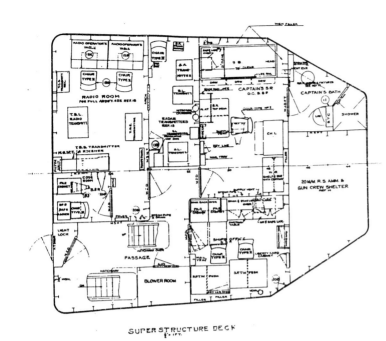

General arrangement of the bridge superstructure deck. Aft of the 20mm ready service locker and gun crew shelter on the starboard side is the ship's office containing the liberty card cabinet and other files, followed by hatchways to belowdecks and the code room. From the port side, the captain's bath is forward, followed by the captain's stateroom, the SA and SL radar room, and the radio room containing TBL, TBE, and TBS equipment.

General plan of the superstructure deck. The superstructure deck begins with the Hedgehog blast shield and is followed by the number two gun, the numbers three (starboard) and four 20mm guns, and the bridge portion of the superstructure (the only fully enclosed portion on the deck; see plan above), containing the captain's stateroom, ship's office, and radio room. Aft of the bridgehouse is the ship's boat with gravity davits, the exhaust uptakes and stack, the numbers five through eight 20mm guns, and the triple torpedo mount. The Mk51 director station and X position heavy antiaircraft gun mount complete the superstructure deck.

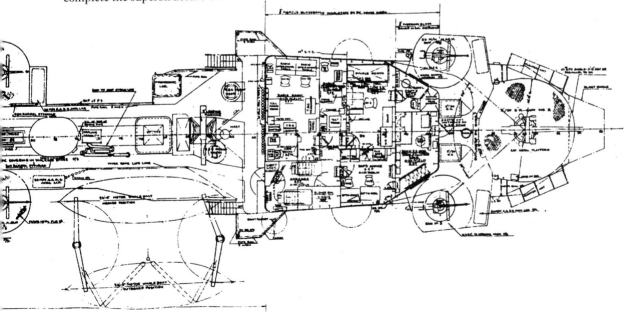

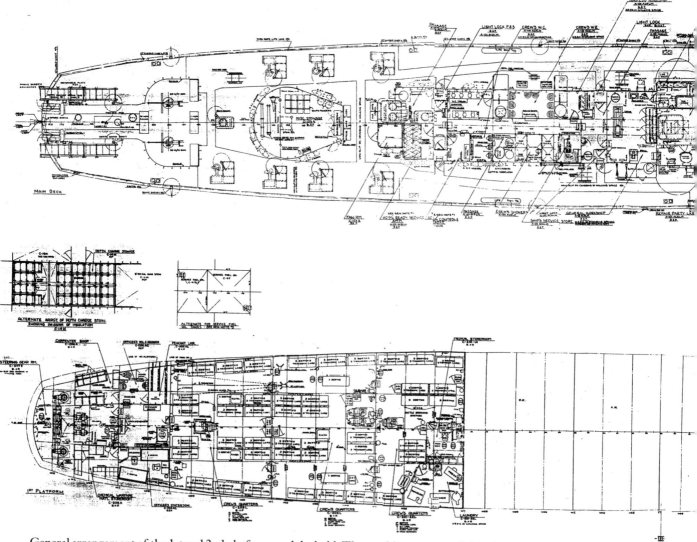

General arrangement of the 1st and 2nd platforms and the hold. The machinery spaces divide the 1st platform and hold into forward and aft sections, while the 2nd platform extends only from the bow to the forward bulkhead of the first fire room (frame 59). The area belowdecks not taken up with machinery, service fuel, water, ammunition, or ballast was reserved mostly for ship's stores and crew quarters, including berthing and messing. The underwater sound room containing the retractable sonar apparatus was located between frames 14 and 18 of the hold, roughly 25 feet aft of the bow along the keel, and was followed by a narrow room on the port side where a pitot tube could be lowered manually into the water to obtain the ship's speed. The forward portion of the 1st platform contained CPO and crew quarters. Aft of the engine and fire room spaces, the 1st platform contained additional crew quarters, the ship's laundry, pharmacy, officers' quarters, the carpenter shop, and the steering gear room. The latter was an important damage control station because if control were lost from the bridge, the rudder could be operated from this room. Most casualties incurred from acoustic torpedo hits were members of the steering gear party. The hold aft of frame 113 stored ammunition and depth charges.

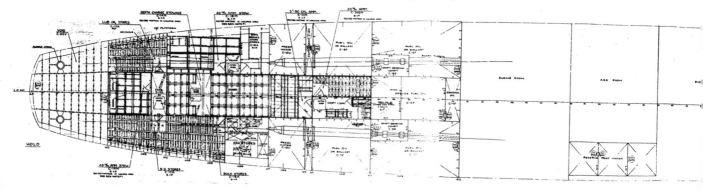

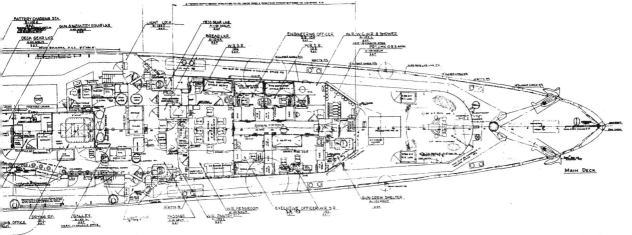

General plan of the main deck. The enclosed deckhouse begins aft of the Mk10 Hedgehog projector; at its forward end is ready storage for Hedgehog bombs (port) and the gun crew shelter with access hatch to belowdecks. Berths and washrooms for officers follow and surround the officers' mess. Various lockers, passageways, offices, and workshops continue down the deckhouse, which ends with the crew's washrooms and ready service ammunition lockers for the 1.1-inch or 40mm gun. The K-gun stations, number three gun with depth charge arbor stowage, a 20mm gun gallery, and depth charge tracks complete the main deck layout.

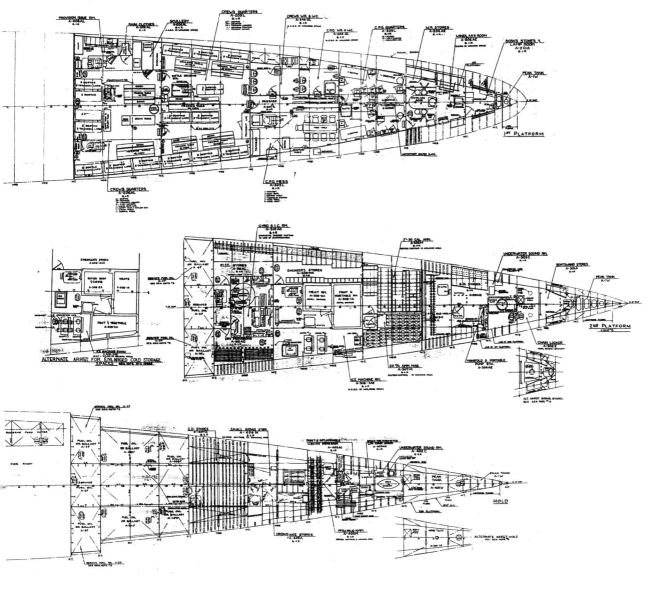

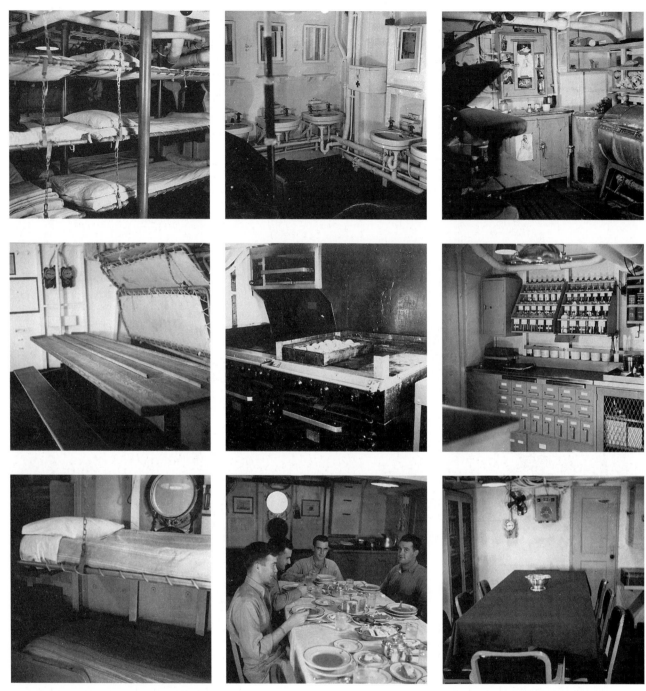

Interior compartments of a *Buckley*-class DE photographed aboard the *Durik* (DE 666) in 1945. *Left to right, top to bottom:* crew's quarters, crew's head, ship's laundry, crew's mess table, ship's galley with electric range, pharmacy, officers' cabin, officers' mess in the wardroom, wardroom. Wartime photographs of DE living spaces are uncommon. (Courtesy, Mr. F. Niepp)

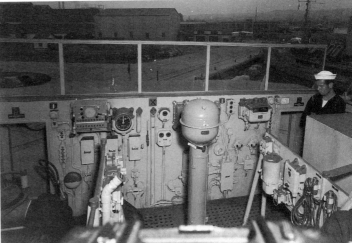

A view from the open bridge (*top right*) of *Sims* (DE 154) in May 1943. The windscreen is raised. The door on the port side leads to the sound room. The pelorus is on the stand in the center of the photograph and the ship's speed indicator is the larger black dial to the left. The sailor is standing where round observation posts would eventually be installed. The bottom photograph shows the outside view of the bridge layout of *William T. Powell* (DE 213). The enclosed sound room is forward with the windscreen on its top, flanked by rounded observation posts; seats for the conning officer were located at these posts as seen in the photograph (*left*) taken from the mast of *Neuendorf* (DE 200). The photograph of *William T. Powell* also shows the arrangement of the two-man lookout stations on either side of the open bridge. The T-shaped range finder is under a protective tarpaulin at the aft end of the bridge. The 02 level begins with the 20mm tub forward, followed by the pilothouse, which has five portholes on its face and two more on the corner bevels. The starboard door to the pilothouse is open and leads to one of the 24-inch searchlight positions. The signal flag locker can just be made out at the aft end of the 02 level, above the forward boiler room uptake. In the photograph of *Neuendorf*, the pelorus is at the bottom center with a 12-inch signal light to its right. Bins for floater nets are attached to the number two gun tub. The large dials of the match-pointer system are visible on the number two 3-inch/50. (Top, 80-G-100105; bottom, 80-G-239228; left, courtesy, Mr. R. L. Franklin)

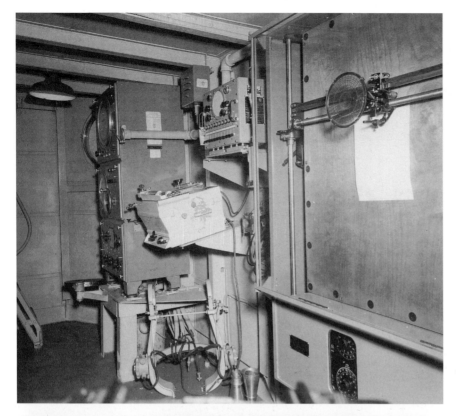

Looking to the port side of the sound room, or "asdic cabinet" in Royal Navy parlance, aboard *Sims* (DE 154). The sound room was located forward of the open bridge and above the steering station. The sonar station is to the left, with the plotting board to record data from the echo range finder to the right. (80-G-100108)

The steering station aboard *Weber* (DE 675). The quartermaster has both hands on the ship's wheel and is facing the ship's speed indicator and a gyrocompass. The voice tube from the flying bridge is at head level. Part of the massive amount of a destroyer escort's wiring is visible above the door leading to the searchlight station. Although the rapid assembly of the ship's hull and superstructure was an impressive characteristic of the entire DE program, the miles of intricate wiring needed to complete a ship were also installed at an equally brisk pace. Because the wiring demanded such high precision and workmanship in order to function, this task was, perhaps, a more outstanding achievement. (Courtesy, *Popular Science*)

Reuben James (DE 153), the first *Buckley*-class DE to be completed, on April 17, 1943, off Hampton Roads, Virginia. The original *Buckley*-class bridge had two portholes on the side of the sound room and three portholes in front of the pilothouse; the original design also lacked conning stations at the forward corners of the open bridge. *Reuben James* carries only four 20mm guns (two forward of the pilothouse and two abreast the aft uptake amidships). In the X position, it has a 40mm Mk1 twin mount, which was the originally specified weapon; the unavailability of these guns, however, led to the installation of the inferior 1.1-inch Mk2 quad for all but two of the U.S. Navy ships of the class. (80-G-62414)

The armament of the first *Buckley*-class units delivered to the U.S. Navy consisted of three 3-inch/50 Mk22 single, open mounts (two on the forecastle and one aft), four single 20mm guns in Mk4 mounts (two forward of the pilothouse and two in tubs amidships), a director-controlled 40mm Mk1 twin mount in the X position superfiring the number three gun, a Mk10 Hedgehog ahead-throwing spigot mortar, eight Mk6 Mod1 depth charge projectors (K-guns), two Mk9 depth charge tracks, and a triple 21-inch torpedo tube bank with three Mk8 or Mk15 torpedoes (no reloads).[18] The original *Evarts* design had only a single 20mm gun forward of the pilothouse along the centerline, but the *Buckley*-class bridge was modified to accommodate two 20mm guns in this position to be able to engage targets port and starboard simultaneously from this vantage.

The 3-inch/50 main battery could not be automatically directed since each mount was manually operated, but an optical 2.5-meter range finder and a Mk51 director located on the open bridge provided distance and bearing information to the guns. (Both of these instruments were left off of most ships transferred through lend-lease.) A second Mk51 director was located aft to automatically direct the 40mm twin mount (or 1.1-inch quad) through electrical links to the gun's motorized mount. All *Buckley*-class ships that had a heavy antiaircraft gun, including lend-lease vessels, were equipped with a corresponding Mk51 director. Toward the end of the war some DEs were fitted with a Mk52 director which incorporated a Mk26 S-band range-only

18. The term X position will be used throughout to identify the main automatic antiaircraft gun position at the after end of the DE's superstructure.

radar on the face of the director on the bridge and a below-deck Mk6 computer to track the target acquired by the director. Following World War II, select *Buckley*-class DEs were equipped with the Mk63 director that could be used with both the 40mm and late-model 3-inch mounts. The director incorporated a Mk34 X-band range-only radar that attached to the gun mount and a Mk28 computer belowdecks.

It was apparent that the original AA armament was much too light for wartime conditions, and by July 1943 four more 20mm gun positions were added, two in tubs abreast the stack and two at the 01 level on either side of the bridge, for a total of eight of these guns. During availability, many ships also began adding two more 20mm guns in a gallery forward of the depth charge tracks at frame 156. This modification was incorporated into the *Buckley*-class design in early 1944. On March 13, 1944, *Willmarth* (DE 638) became the first *Buckley*-class ship to commission with ten 20mm guns.

The heavy antiaircraft weapon in the X position was the only fully powered and automatically directed gun on the ship. The original *Buckley*-class design specified a 40mm Mk1 twin mount, but the scarcity of these assemblies due

A view aft from the mast of *Neuendorf* (DE 200) showing the standard destroyer escort layout amidships and toward the stern. The triple 21-inch torpedo mount is on the centerline atop the superstructure and is surrounded by collapsible life lines. Aft of the torpedo mount are the Mk51 director station and the 1.1-inch quad machine gun in the X position. The number three 3-inch/50 gun is on the quarterdeck, trained portside, while crews are busy installing two 20mm single mounts just forward of the depth charge tracks at the stern. Most DEs that had additional 20mm guns installed at the stern received a gun tub designed to house both guns, but in some cases the mounts were simply bolted to the deck. A movie screen has been raised above the fantail in anticipation of the evening's entertainment. Life rafts and the eight K-guns are outboard port and starboard. Note that the camouflage pattern divides the Mk51 director station and extends to the K-gun ready service racks. (Courtesy, Mr. R. L. Franklin)

The number three 3-inch/50 Mk22 single mount aboard *Durik* (DE 666). The trainer (*left*) and pointer are in position. The hand wheel on the left trained the mount 2°52′48″ for each revolution. The hand wheel in front of the pointer elevated or depressed the gun 3° for every full turn. The gun was capable of being elevated to 85° above the horizontal or depressed to 13° below the horizontal. Since the Mk22 mount was operated manually, pipe guards prevented the gun from being inadvertently trained into the ship. The trainer and pointer both have telescopic sights in front of them at eye level. The round objects connected by a rod below the hand wheels on either side of the mount are part of the automatic match-pointer system, gun elevation indicator Mk21, and gun train indicator Mk23. Each indicator contained a zero reader and a dial consisting of an inner and outer wheel with markers indicating either gun bearing or elevation; the inner wheel was fed target bearing and elevation information electronically from the Mk51 director on the bridge, while the outer wheel was controlled by the gunners. By keeping the markers aligned, the gunners would remain on target. The boxlike structure above the chase is a counterweight. Ammunition stowage is to the left of the trainer. The 3-inch/50 was breech-loaded and fired a 13-pound fixed shot (antiaircraft, armor piercing, or starshell) at a muzzle velocity of 2,700 feet per second. It had a range of 14,600 yards at 45° and an effective antiaircraft ceiling of about 28,000 feet. A well-drilled crew—gun captain, pointer, trainer, two loaders, and two hot shell casing men—could get off five rounds of AA in under 14 seconds. The gun was mechanically reliable with regular maintenance and operation was straightforward, two qualities that lent themselves to speedy command by novice gun crews. (Courtesy, Mr. F. Niepp)

to their redirection to other building programs, such as the *Fletcher*-class DDs, forced the Navy to install the outdated 1.1-inch Mk2 quad machine gun instead, the antiaircraft weapon formerly used aboard DDs, cruisers, and battleships. Only two U.S. *Buckley*-class DEs (the first two delivered, DEs 51 and 153) received a 40mm gun; in addition, eight lend-lease *Buckley*s (ex–DEs 52, 55, 58, 61, 64, 67, 77, and 84) were so equipped. All other ships of the class had a 1.1-inch quad, except for the remaining thirty-eight lend-lease vessels, which were transferred without any weapon installed (most of these ships added a 20mm gun in the X position and

The after 5-inch/38 Mk30/69 single enclosed mounts fitted to four *Buckley*-class DEs, including *Harmon* (DE 678), the inboard ship with modifications circled. The Mk38 blast shield designed for this mount was beveled at its upper back edge to allow clearance for Hedgehog bombs. The mount was standardized for all DE and APD installations; therefore, the blast shield's characteristic bevel remained no matter in which position the gun was placed, as in this case on the quarterdeck, or whether or not the ship was equipped with a Hedgehog projector. The 5-inch/38 Mk30/69 assembly weighed approximately 45,000 pounds, compared to the 3-inch/50 Mk22 single mount, which weighed about 7,510 pounds. An important design feature of the long-hulled 3-inch DE classes was their built-in ability to handle the increased weight of the much heavier 5-inch mount without major structural reinforcement or compromising the ship's reserve buoyancy. The 5-inch/38 is acknowledged as the premier medium-caliber dual-purpose gun of World War II. Its high rate of fire for its size (12 to 15 rounds per minute), reliability, accuracy, relatively light weight, and ability to fire various types of semi-fixed ammunition—including shells with proximity (VT) fuses—made it the preferred fleet antiaircraft gun and main battery for American destroyers. The gun propelled a standard 55.2-pound AA shell 2,600 feet per second to an effective altitude of about 36,000 feet. This photograph also shows the substantial weapons upgrades amidships, with a 40mm Mk2 quad and two 40mm Mk1 twin mounts (all director-controlled), and a 20mm gun aft of each of the 40mm twin mounts. (19-N-91497)

another in its empty director station). A very few ships did have the 1.1-inch quad replaced with a 40mm twin mount during wartime.

The most potent wartime antiaircraft refit for *Buckley*-class DEs was the replacement of the torpedo tubes with four single, Army-type 40mm Mk3 guns. These guns were installed in individual tubs, two to a side, in place of the torpedo mount. Since the guns were manually operated, pipe guards surrounded each tub to prevent the crews from training the guns into the ship while following a target. (Ideally, the torpedo tubes would have been replaced by two director-controlled 40mm Mk1 twin mounts, but this was not

Troops surrounding a 20mm Mk10 single mount aboard the high-speed transport *Newman* (APD 59) during the landings at Palawan, Philippine Islands, in February 1945. The magazine is above the chase and a bag for collecting spent cartridges is below. The Mk14 sight is above the breech block, just forward of the shoulder rests. The cocking lever is below the barrel; trunnion height was adjusted with the hand wheel on the pedestal. The gun does not have a shield. The gun captain (talker) is leaning against the tub, wearing sound-powered phones. Evidently, there is no danger of air attack at this moment.

The 20mm gun was an independent, manually controlled, light antiaircraft weapon designed by the Swiss company Oerlikon. It was ubiquitous in both the British and American navies and was popular, especially early in the war, because of its simple installation, ease of use, high rate of fire, and explosive shell. It differed from most automatic guns in that its breech block was never locked, its barrel did not move in recoil, and it fired only in automatic—although with good touch an operator could squeeze off single rounds. The gun fired by inertia; instead of a firing pin, a striker contacted the shell, and the force of the recoil enabled the gun to fire automatically. The 20mm Oerlikon had a firing rate of 430 to 480 rounds per minute, depending on the type of barrel springs used (rounded springs cycled at a higher rate than the alternative square-finished barrel springs); it had a muzzle velocity of 2,725 feet per second and an effective range of about 1,000 yards. The Mk10 was a single mount that had a fabricated steel tripod to reduce the installation's overall weight; Mk10 mounts were commonly fitted to APDs and late production DEs.

The Mk14 relative-rate sight was the most significant small-caliber fire-control device of the war and proved ideal for the 20mm gun. This sight was first installed on 20mm guns aboard DEs in late 1943. The sight used two gyroscopes to track the relative position of the gun to a moving target. While looking through the sight, the operator kept a small red light on the target. The light was reflected onto the eyepiece from mirrors connected to springs that moved in response to the gyroscopes. The force necessary to keep the gun on target became the measure of the target's angular motion as calculated by the gyroscopes; therefore, the greater the force to keep the red light on target (that is, the faster the speed of the target being tracked), the greater the actual lead angle of the gun to the target due to the movement of the spring and mirror mechanism in relation to the force applied to the gyroscopes. The Mk14 predicted target position but could not estimate range. Range, however, was not an important consideration for a fully automatic close-in weapon like the 20mm Oerlikon. (80-G-305561)

The quadruple 1.1-inch Mk2 automatic machine cannon aboard *Francis M. Robinson* (DE 220). Each gun was fed from multi-round clips passed up and loaded into the gun from behind. Cooling hoses are looped underneath and around the barrels to the top of the breech block. The guns are Mk1 Mod1s, which had flash-hiders threaded to the end of their barrels. The 1.1-inch/75 cannon was a water-cooled, automatic antiaircraft gun developed by the United States Navy beginning in late 1929. Work on the gun continued into the early 1930s, when an individual gun was developed to sustain 140 rounds per minute. The 1.1-inch had a muzzle velocity of 2,700 feet per second, a maximum altitude of 19,000 feet, and a maximum range of 7,500 yards.

In order to achieve a rate of fire equivalent to a .50-caliber machine gun (the other automatic antiaircraft gun adopted by the Navy in the interwar period), an elaborate quadruple mount, the Mk2, was designed. This mount, nicknamed the "Chicago Piano," placed the guns in a horizontal row. The entire assembly weighed about 12,000 pounds and ended up being the only mass-production mount for the 1.1-inch gun. Since dive bombers were considered the greatest aerial threat to surface ships, the Mk2 was designed to elevate to 110°; most models also included a geared mechanism that enabled the guns to be trained 30° from center to either side when the guns were vertical, a point where traverse lost significance.

The gun fired a contact-sensitive, fixed explosive shell with a short delay. Raindrops were said to offer enough resistance to set off the charge, but the round was designed to penetrate an aircraft's fabric and then explode. Problems plagued the 1.1-inch quad from the outset: As a result of a poor recoil and ejection system, the guns jammed and overheated, the delicate ammunition went off in the breech and barrel, and the complex mount tended to seize up; in addition, the installation was difficult to service. Even after the bugs were worked out, it could not shake its reputation for unreliability. Its greatest weakness, however, was not mechanical, but rather the small size of its shell and short range; these qualities made it difficult for the gun to effectively counter mid-1940s aircraft. (80-G-303517)

accomplished until late-war and postwar refits.) Torpedo tube replacement was common on Atlantic-based DEs but was rarely done (if at all) to DEs operating in the Pacific. Most *Buckley*-class DEs on station off Okinawa during the spring of 1945 were forced to engage suicide aircraft with the weak 1.1-inch quad and without the benefit of additional heavy antiaircraft guns.[19]

The ASW armament of the DE indicated that these vessels were primarily antisubmarine escorts. The destroyer escort carried the heaviest

19. Some ships did manage to acquire air-cooled .50-caliber machine guns and mounted them on the bridge and superstructure, although their effectiveness against aircraft was minimal. A few ships may have also acquired additional 20mm guns and mounted them in a similar fashion.

A view of *Joseph E. Campbell* (DE 70) looking forward at the torpedo mount and amidships 20mm gun positions. The torpedo operators sat on the bench just forward of the firing mechanism in the foreground; the mount trainer with sight was to port and the gyro setter was to starboard. The DE, unlike the fleet destroyer, was not an offensive platform for launching torpedoes due to its relatively slow speed: A DE would use its torpedoes only against surfaced or shallow submarines and slower, lightly armed craft, or as a defensive weapon against superior surface ships. (The latter circumstances were encountered by *John C. Butler*–class DEs embroiled in the Battle of Leyte Gulf.) The lack of surface ship threats to convoys, particularly following the capitulation of Italy in September 1943, led to the replacement of the torpedo tube mount with additional heavy AA guns on many DEs. The aft portside 20mm gun is uncovered, giving a clear view of the Mk14 gun sight. The trunnion–height hand wheel of the Mk4 single mount is also visible. The gun tubs have non-slip corrugated floors. (19-LCM-64202)

battery of K-guns of any American warship, as well as the British-designed Hedgehog spigot mortar (an arrangement later duplicated in the *Tacoma*-class frigates). The Hedgehog helped compensate for a significant ASW deficiency of earlier ships. Due to the narrow cone beam and limited downward tilt of most World War II sonars, contact on a potential target would be lost as a ship closed in on it, usually at 100 to 150 yards or at a distance of about three times the depth of the target. By that time, it was hoped, the ship would be near enough and would have

It is felt that ships of this type with their present armament are extremely inadequate to combat aircraft. The ship possesses no means of destroying aircraft at a range that would prevent suicide aircraft from crashing into the ship. The 1.1-inch gun is an old and obsolete piece of ordnance that is of little value to the ship. This gun proved itself to be useless in action. It is also felt that the removal of the torpedo mount and the substitution of 40mm guns should be accomplished without delay.

From an Action Report filed at Okinawa by Lt. Victor Martin, Commanding Officer, *Gendreau*

An unidentified *Buckley*-type Captains-class frigate laying a depth charge pattern during a training exercise. The explosions of the charges fired from K-guns on either side of the ship's wake are easily discerned from the turbulence further astern caused by the charges rolled from tracks off the fantail. (The K-gun could project a depth charge a minimum of 50 yards to a maximum of 150 yards from the ship, depending on the type of pattern desired, amount of black powder charge used, and style of depth charge. U.S. DEs fired Mk6, Mk8 ["ashcan"], or Mk9 ["teardrop"] depth charges, while their British counterparts used MkVII and MkVII-heavy depth charges.) This photo clearly shows the significant horizontal distance between the bow of the ship, which held the sonar transducer, and the placement of the depth charges in the water. Given that sonar contact was temporarily lost when the ship closed within 100 yards of a target (due to physical limitations of the sonar mechanism and angle of the beam) and that a charge took upwards of 20 seconds to reach its preset explosion depth, a submarine had a good opportunity to evade this kind of attack. Techniques such as creeping, where one ship would receive sonar information from another ship via TBS and maneuver quietly into an advantageous position against the unsuspecting submarine, were developed during the war to reduce the blind-time of conventional depth charge barrages and proved more successful. (IWM A25647)

gathered sufficient data to make a successful conventional depth charge attack. However, since depth charges were launched from the stern to avoid an explosion under the ship, there was a significant period of time between the loss of sonar contact at the approach to the target and the descent of the charges to their preset depths, giving the submarine a good chance to maneuver beyond the lethal range of the exploding charges. An added disadvantage for the attacking ship was that sonar contact was difficult to regain once the depth charges began exploding and causing underwater turbulence.

In contrast, the Hedgehog hurled twenty-four contact bombs ahead of the ship, which reduced the blind-time between the acquisition of a target and the delivery of the warhead to the target to about two-thirds that of a conventional depth charge barrage. In addition, if there was no hit, the contact-fuzed bombs would not detonate and sonar operation could be maintained because of the absence of turbulence. Although the near-miss explosion of a depth charge was considered to have a strong negative psychological effect on the crew of a submarine under attack, the lack of non-lethal underwater bursts

A Hedgehog crew *(top)* preparing to fire aboard an unidentified DE. The crew consists of a gunner (*seated,* wearing a helmet that covers his sound-powered phones) and a trainer (*standing*). The trainer used the crank to move the Hedgehog spigots to port or starboard, depending upon the information sent from the bridge to the gun train indicator directly in front of him. Each of the twenty-four bombs carried 31 pounds of TNT (subsequently increased to 35 pounds of torpex), which was enough to breach a submarine hull on contact. Each bomb had a total weight of 65 pounds, and DEs typically carried enough bombs for ten patterns. The bombs were launched sequentially in pairs by setting off the solid propellant in each spigot stalk with an electrical charge. They were armed in flight by a spinner on the bomb nose, and a cylindrical fin on the tail piece provided stability for the flight trajectory. The Hedgehog was able to hurl its bombs (*bottom*) about 250 yards forward of the ship in an elliptical pattern (Mk10, 195 feet in deflection, 168 feet in range, with the bombs discharged at a rate of 2.5 seconds each) or a circular pattern (Mk 11, 267 feet in diameter, with the bombs discharged every 1.8 seconds). (U.S. Navy)

with the Hedgehog was a fair exchange for greater ASW performance.[20] The Royal Navy opted to forgo the Hedgehog and instead develop the Squid weapon, which fired three depth charges forward of the ship with depth settings determined by sonar information. However, no Captains-class DE had its Hedgehog replaced with Squid.

Destroyer escorts were equipped with excellent electronic capabilities. SL, an S-band microwave radar, was specifically designed for the DE program and was the primary surface-search

---

20. The performance of World War II ASW weapons is still debated, but there is no doubt that ahead-throwing weapons were superior to stern-launched depth charge barrages. The initial Royal Navy experience with Hedgehog in the second half of 1943 was a disappointing success rate of 7.5 percent, compared to 4.0 percent for a conventional depth charge attack, but the success rate climbed rapidly to 28.1 percent for the second half of 1944 (Sternhell and Thorndike, *Antisubmarine Warfare in World War II*, 125). There are many factors that contribute to the performance of an ASW weapon (the type of submarine being attacked, the

experience of the submarine's CO, the sea state, and underwater sound conditions, to name a few); in the case of the Hedgehog, evidence pointed to inadequate crew and officer training as the primary culprit for the weapon's poor success rate early in its deployment. Despite the increased success with the Hedgehog, the Royal Navy decided to concentrate on developing the Squid weapon. In American service, the Hedgehog was viewed quite favorably, with the performance of *England* in May 1944 used as a model of Hedgehog operation. The U.S. Navy continued to develop improved versions of Hedgehog following the war.

radar aboard DEs throughout the war. It was located in a radome immediately below the masthead. The air-search set was SA, and its mattress antenna was placed at the masthead, about 88 feet above the waterline. The American SA and SL antennas were capable of being mounted farther from their receivers and therefore higher on the mast than contemporary British radars, which experienced greater signal loss between components. The higher antenna positions afforded greater horizon detection ranges, a fact that contributed to the selection of *Buckley*-type

The SA air-search radar antenna atop the mast of *Loeser* (DE 680). The SL surface-search radar radome is immediately below. A Jacob's ladder runs the length of the mast to give the crew access to the radar service platform. The yard supports IFF antennas port and starboard and a T-shaped TBS antenna on the port side. Three sets of rectangular fighting lights are spaced at regular intervals along the mast. Just above and forward of the lowest set is a loudspeaker. A canopy shades the open bridge from the hot Pacific sun. The floater net bins attached to the face of the sound room and the 20mm gun tub forward of the pilothouse are atypical. (Courtesy, The Mariners' Museum, Newport News, Virginia, Ted Stone Collection)

To me, viewing it from my lookout position on the bridge, the mortar bombs would always spread out in the shape of a pear, the broadest part of the fruit (or base of the fruit) going first. It was immediately followed by moments of excitement and tension. The excitement was hoping for success; the tension was waiting for the actual explosion, almost holding one's breath because the explosion always seemed to occur as the ship sailed over the very spot and the whole ship would shake from the vibrations. Sometimes the Asdic picked up a possible contact and after the first attack it transpired that the suspected contact was nothing but a shoal of cod. "Jack" being a resourceful type of chap, and on command from the ship's captain, would haul the floating cod inboard, thus providing the ravenous crew with fresh fish to supplement our diminishing food supply. And, of course, what could be a better dish to the British matelot than fried fish and chips!

Norman Howgego, Signalman, *Conn*

Captains-class vessels as Coastal Forces control ships. A high-frequency direction-finding (HF/DF) antenna replaced the SA on most British DEs engaged in convoy duty as well as a portion of U.S. DEs, usually those ships operating in the Atlantic.[21] By intercepting German radio transmissions, HF/DF could detect a U-boat at a greater range than radar, allowing Allied ships to calculate the location of a submarine over the horizon. Eventually, as countermeasures began diminishing the effectiveness of HF/DF, a stub mainmast was added on American DEs just forward of the X position to support the HF/DF, and the SA was returned to the top of the foremast. All British DEs earmarked for transfer to the Pacific replaced the HF/DF with SA. In a few instances, SC air-search radar was substituted for the SA aboard a DE.

The next series of surface-search radar, the high-resolution SU X-band set, was fitted to DEs and APDs beginning in mid-1944, but

21. All DEs equipped with a HF/DF were supposed to be assigned to the Atlantic Fleet, but a few ships with HF/DF installed at their mastheads were ordered to the Pacific, where their HF/DF was not useful for acquiring submarines. In all of these cases, the HF/DF was eventually replaced with an air-search radar set (see the caption for *Lovelace*, DE 198, in chapter 5).

A view of *Donnell* (DE 56) in October 1943, from the bow looking aft. Bins for floater nets are fixed on either side of the number two gun position. Three portholes for the pilothouse are visible on the face of the bridge and are flanked by two 20mm single guns. The sound room immediately above the pilothouse has two large portholes on each side; these portholes were part of the original *Buckley*-class design but were eliminated in late 1943. A voice tube to belowdecks is just forward of the number one gun. The mast supports an SL radome and its servicing platform (*4*) and a DAQ HF/DF antenna with mast extension (*2*). The yard has two BK ski pole IFF transponders and a TBS radiating dipole antenna on the port side. Insulators (*3*) have been added to the stays, shrouds, and yard lifts to prevent them from conducting lightning and static electricity. Chain pipe covers (*1*) were added to prevent water from entering the locker below. A British Type FH4 HF/DF antenna is on the top of the mast of the unidentified ship to the left. (19–LCM–53680)

most of the ships that received this radar were assigned to the Pacific. A large number of Captains-class ships had the SL surface-search radar replaced with an SG set. No American DE appears to have carried this radar during wartime. SG was the standard U.S. fleet destroyer surface-search radar and incorporated both an A-scan display and a plan position indicator, or PPI (SL had a PPI only).

As a defense against kamikaze raids during the Okinawa campaign, some DEs had TDY radar jamming devices installed above the flying bridge in an effort to disrupt the frequencies of Japanese airborne and land-based search radars as they attempted to locate targets.

DEs in both American and British service were equipped with secondary radar systems for identifying "friend or foe" (IFF). American BK sets used two "ski-pole" transponders outboard on the yard, while the British Type 244 IFF was composed of four "egg timer" dipoles attached to the mast above the yard. Navigational radio equipment included a medium-frequency direction-finding (MF/DF) receiver with a loop (USN) or rectangular (RN) antenna mounted outside the bridge; LORAN (long-range navigation), first installed in late 1943 and eventually replacing MF/DF; and GEE, a hyperbolic navigational system used by Allied aircraft that was

fitted to some Captains-class vessels operating in the Channel. The primary ship-to-ship communications radio was TBS, a VHF set that, because of the short range of its signal, allowed secure communication between ships without having to code and decode messages.

Most *Buckley*-class DEs were equipped with a QC-series searchlight sonar, usually QCS or QGB, the console version of QC. The sonar's magnetostrictive transducer was enclosed in a British-invented streamlined dome that was lowered into the water from a point along the keel about 25 feet aft of the bow, and when not in operation it could be retracted into the hull. QCS had bearing deviation indicator (BDI) capability, which meant that its signal could be split so that two echoes could be compared simultaneously in order to gain a bearing on a submarine. The sound room (echo range finder station) aboard a U.S. DE contained the sonar transmitter and echo amplification unit, chemical range recorder (another British innovation), and attack plotter.

British DEs were usually fitted with Type 128D or Type 144 asdic, both of which had a retractable sonar dome containing a quartz transducer. Type 128D incorporated a chemical range recorder and was wired for ready conversion into Type 144. Type 144 was developed specifically for ahead-throwing weapons such as the Hedgehog and incorporated both a range recorder and a bearing recorder; it was additionally capable of being trained automatically. Both Type 128D and Type 144 could be equipped with the Q attachment, an additional narrow-beam transducer that was capable of tilting downward to determine a target's depth, information that allowed for greater ASW weapon control; many Captains-class ships received this modification to their sonars. Some Captains-class frigates were fitted with Type 147B asdic, which was essentially an improved Type 144, being equipped with a single narrow-beam quartz transducer capable of tilting to determine a target's depth and feeding this information to range and bearing recorders. Forty Type 147Bs were sent to the United States

The SL radar was subject to sea clutter caused by reflection of the radar signal from waves close to the ship which would result in a loss of any target within the sea clutter range. The rougher the sea, the greater would be the sea clutter range. During one of our early convoys in the Atlantic with rough seas and at night, one of the ships behind the *Blessman* entered the sea clutter area. Fortunately one of the men on lookout duty on the fantail saw the ship close behind our fantail and alerted the bridge. Normally the SL radar did a good job in screening ships in the convoy and helping to keep them in their proper stations. The air search SA radar was not subject to as much sea clutter as the SL but did not have the PPI to produce a map-like image of targets.

Robert G. Wagoner, Radio Technician, *Blessman*

An excellent photograph of *Aylmer* (K 463, ex–DE 72), a *Buckley*-type Captains-class frigate, off the coast of Ireland in mid-1944. *Aylmer* exhibits several modifications made to British lend-lease DEs: A spray shield and illumination rocket rails have been added to the number two gun; a navigational MF direction-finding antenna has been attached to the face of the bridge; a crow's nest has been added to the mast above the yard; a British whaler has been stowed on the port side of the stack, complementing the U.S.-issue ship's boat on the starboard side; life rafts have been added amidships on metal frames; and extra depth charge racks have been added outboard along the quarterdeck (the racks are empty). *Aylmer*'s mast supports an HF/DF aerial at the top, above a Type 244 IFF array and an SG surface-search parabolic radar antenna that replaced the SL radome. The Captains-class frigates that were equipped with the 10cm SG were the only DEs to carry this radar. The X position and its director station are empty, but a 20mm gun eventually was installed in the gun tub. *Aylmer* had several paint schemes during its career. In this photograph the hull is painted dark blue-gray and the upper surfaces are light gray except for a portion of the mast, which is also the darker color. (Courtesy, Mr. L. Gomersall)

under reverse lend-lease in mid-1944, and forty-five more were purchased from Canada.[22] Fifty ended up being allocated to Atlantic fleet DEs, including a few *Buckley*s, and were the most sophisticated sonars fitted to U.S. destroyer escorts during World War II.

Buckley-class ships transferred to Great Britain underwent several interesting modifications, and these changes reflected the conditions encountered as well as tactical preferences. The most significant modification was the arrangement and stowage of depth charges and their projectors. The British DEs only had four K-guns, compared to eight on U.S. ships. Reload racks holding four charges were adjacent to each K-gun on both American and British ships, but the British ships added two sets of two-tiered ready racks capable of holding thirty charges per tier outboard along both sides of the quarterdeck and retained a davit beside each K-gun and behind both depth charge tracks at the stern. These ships were able to carry more than two hundred depth charges, mostly topside, compared to a little over one hundred stowed aboard a U.S. de-

22. Willem Hackmann, *Seek and Strike* (London: HMSO, 1984), 283.

There were several innovations aboard the DEs which appealed to the crews, which we didn't have in our own smaller ships at that time. There were showers, for example, and a ship's laundry! And a water cooling system that supplied cold drinking water and filtered it! Also a cinema with (by the courtesy of USN) the latest films. I remember seeing some films in the *Torrington* before they received their premier in the UK. The DEs also had bunks which saved us slinging our hammocks, although no bunk can equal the comfort of a hammock. Also they had cafeteria messing which was entirely alien to our ratings. Another thing we had to get used to was the complete absence of scuttles in the ship's hull. All later British ships were also built without them and this is now, of course, standard practice. Another good point of the DEs was that although they rolled a lot in heavy weather they were flush decked and the water they shipped simply drained off them, and so they were dry below decks which was a source of deep satisfaction among the crew, unlike many of our older destroyers and corvettes which used to get very flooded through the mess decks when the weather was really foul. If they had a fault it was that they were rather "thin skinned"; in other words, they were built of thinner steel and more liable to be damaged by hard knocks. At anchor off Ryde in the Isle of Wight in a gale we were rammed by an unmanned LCI which had broken its moorings. Despite the fact it was only drifting it hit *Torrington* on the starboard quarter and tore a large hole in the hull which necessitated four days in dock. In our own ships it would have probably buckled a couple of plates. This is my sole criticism, nobody was injured in this incident however.

Christopher Wickenden, Officer's Steward, *Torrington*

stroyer escort.[23] (British DEs had approximately 164 charges on deck: twelve in each stern track, five with each of the four K-guns, and 120 on the outboard ready racks; American DEs shipped sixty-four charges topside: twelve in each stern track and five with each of the eight K-guns.)

Buckley-type Captains-class frigates (along with a few British "River"-class frigates) carried the largest number of depth charges of any Allied escort vessel during the war. Once the charges had been exhausted from the reload racks next to each K-gun, the davits were used to continue to hoist depth charges onto the projectors, rolled over from the outboard ready racks. (American DEs relied on the charges in the reload racks; replenishment was possible by hoisting charges from the locker belowships onto a cart that was then wheeled to the K-guns, but this process was difficult while in action.) British ships were capable, therefore, of engaging a suspected target for a great length of time, sometimes days, saturating an area with depth charges without having to resupply, which might involve a lengthy trip to a base such as Belfast specially equipped to handle Captains-class frigates.[24] The increased depth charge capacity was necessary because Captains-class frigates were often assigned to support groups whose duty was to harry suspected targets, rather than to the straight convoy duty in which most U.S. DEs were engaged. Some Captains-class ships added an observation shelter to the aft portion of the open bridge so that the CO could be on call close to the sound room during long depth charge attacks.

In December 1944, the British authorized the addition of two 3,000-pound MkX* depth charges to some of their DEs. The MkX* was designed to combat the latest German deep-diving submarines with a devastating 2,000-pound charge set to explode at a depth of more than 600 feet. The charges posed no stability problems for the *Buckley*-type ships and were launched from special rails welded to the stern.

Many Captains-class ships added spray shields to their 3-inch/50 guns. If only one shield were added, it was fitted to the number two gun because that was the ready gun during cruising stations and was always manned. When possible, all three positions received shields.

23. As previously noted, Additional topweight was recommended to decrease the GM of these vessels, and it is a happy coincidence that part of the solution—extra depth charges—benefited the fighting capabilities of the ships as well.

24. Captains-class ships of EG 1 were, in fact, credited with the longest continuous hunt for a U-boat; see chapter 5.

A view of the quarterdeck and stern from the open bridge of *Rupert* (K 561, ex–DE 96), a *Buckley*-type Captains-class frigate. Life lines surround the "torpedo" deck in the foreground, where several crew members are working. The large number of depth charges carried topside are evident: depth charge racks are outboard along both sides of the ship and four K-guns and their ready racks are along the stern. Davits to hoist depth charges are located beside each K-gun. Eight life rafts are secured on racks that were designed to allow the rafts to slide directly into the water. Floater nets are stowed in bins on either side of the X position. Twenty-millimeter single guns have been installed in the X position gun tub and its director station; pipe guards surround each gun to prevent them from being trained into the ship. *Rupert* has U.S.-issue Mk4 smoke screen generators between the depth charge tracks at the fantail, as well as British smoke generators that appear as black "dust bins" at the end of each depth charge track. The anti–acoustic torpedo device, foxer, is aft of the Mk4 smoke generator canisters. (Courtesy, Mr. J. Whithouse)

> While in Boston having the final touches done before trials I became friendly with one of the dockyard workers who welded a dime to the base of my gun, the No 1 Oerlikon, to bring me luck and to keep me safe during the war. I have always looked at it as my good luck charm.
>
> David Regan, Seaman, *Aylmer*

The shields helped protect the crews from the wind and spray of the very heavy seas of the North Atlantic, as well as from splinters or fragments from exploding shells. Rails for 2-inch rocket flares were usually attached to the shield, three to a side. These illumination flares were necessary to provide light while in action, particularly since U-boats often attacked at night and daylight was limited during half of the year in the northern latitudes.

A crow's nest was usually added to the mast, above the yard. It was equipped with a buzzer to communicate with the bridge. The crow's nest provided additional security when keeping station in a convoy or searching for a suspected target, because high waves often cluttered the radar plot.

Most Captains-class ships added a British whaler with davits to the starboard side to complement the U.S. Navy–issue (or sometimes RN) whaler on the port side. Additional life rafts were also fitted amidships to provide protection for the crew from the deadly cold water if the ship had to be abandoned.

The American Mk4 single mounts for the 20mm guns were replaced, when possible, with British MkVIIA fixed column mounts.[25] The primary reason for this modification was the fact that the Mk4 mount required at least three persons (gunner, loader, and trunnion operator) to operate, whereas the British single mount only required a gunner and loader because the weapon height was adjusted by a series of steps within the gun emplacement instead of a handwheel. This was an important consideration, because Britain had to cope with manpower shortages, particularly late in the war. If a Mk14 gunsight was added to the Mk4 mount, a fourth gun crew member, the range setter, was required; however, British DEs were not supplied with Mk14 sights. Both American and British gun crews included ammunition loaders when possible.[26]

Of the twenty-eight *Buckley*-type Captains-class ships not equipped with a 40mm twin mount in the X position, few subsequently received a 40mm twin mount, and most ended up installing a 20mm gun in the X position and another in the director station. Some ships added two more 20mm guns amidships on the "torpedo" deck, for a total of twelve of these guns.

Captains-class frigates that engaged German coastal forces, like many Hunt-class vessels assigned to this duty, usually had a 2-pounder MkVIII single mount installed at the bow between the hawse pipes. This automatic gun had a flat trajectory and fired tracer and high-explosive shells at a rate of 115 rounds per minute. It was manually operated with open sights and was a particularly reliable and deadly weapon against enemy craft close aboard during night actions. A splinter shield was fitted around the gun on some ships to protect the crew from return fire.

25. C.A.F.O. 2684. It does not appear that Captains-class ships were fitted with the British-designed, American-manufactured MkV cast iron, fixed column mount.

26. The United States eventually introduced the Mk6 single mount, which adjusted trunnion height hydraulically with a series of foot pedals, eliminating the need for a trunnion operator, but these mounts were equipped with sights that required a range setter, thus keeping the minimum crew at three members.

3　Conversion Programs

Buckley-class ships were involved in several major conversion programs and equipment upgrades during and immediately after World War II. Beginning in mid-1944, *Buckley*-class ships were selected to undergo conversion into specialized vessels because they were faster than the existing diesel DEs and capable of operating efficiently at very low speeds without the danger of the fouling experienced with diesel engines, while their turboelectric power plants gave them the ability to use their generators to produce ship-to-shore electricity. In addition, as 5-inch-armed, geared-turbine DEs entered the fleet in greater numbers, *Buckley*-class ships were no longer needed as urgently for escort duty.

Although the *Buckley*-class conversions provided important military benefits, the choice of DEs for conversion was strongly influenced by the large number of existing building contracts for DEs issued by the Navy. In June 1943, the number of DEs requested under contract had reached 1,005, but it became apparent over the next few months that this number was almost twice what was necessary, given that the majority of the ships under contract would not enter the fleet for another year, long after the demand for ASW vessels had given way to vessels necessary for the invasion of the European continent. Had the U.S. government simply canceled the bulk of the DE contracts outright, however, there was a possibility that shipyards and component manufacturers with millions of dollars

invested in the program would have gone bankrupt or suffered financial hardship, and workers' morale would have plunged given the recent, intense effort to have these ships built as quickly as possible.[1] The Navy chose instead to taper off DE construction as gradually as was feasible, using conversion and overhaul programs until the shipyards were able to shift to other Navy programs such as landing craft production.

The first cancellations of DE contracts occurred in September 1943 at the very moment DEs were beginning to enter the fleet in numbers; so many DEs were under construction (240 ships) and still under contract at the time, however, that these cancellations did not have an immediate impact on the shipyards currently building DEs and actually temporarily increased the number of contracts at some yards due to the curtailment of the shipyard expansion program, which resulted in the transfer of contracts slated for these planned shipyards to existing facilities. Another major round of cancellations occurred in October 1943, but by then shipyards were be-

---

1. In an effort to standardize DE production, the Combined Production and Resources Board (CPRB) had recommended in January 1943 that the DE design be a single geared-turbine type, with the use of turboelectric drives until the program could be fully geared by the end of 1943. But the CPRB directive was disregarded because of the large number of outstanding diesel engine contracts. William Chaikin, "Shipbuilding Policies of the War Production Board, January 1942 to November 1945," War Production Board Special Study No. 26 (Washington: GPO, 1946), 130–34.

ginning to concentrate on landing craft production. The *Buckley* class did not end up suffering any contract cancellations, but the final two DE classes, *Rudderow* and *John C. Butler*, were substantially reduced in numbers built.[2]

The types of conversions suitable for a *Buckley*-class DE were limited by the ship's speed, the bulkiness of its turboelectric power plant (leaving little internal reserve volume), and the design's sensitivity to additional topweight beyond that which was demonstrated aboard late-war 5-inch DE classes. For example, DEs were considered for conversion into light mine layers capable of carrying the same number of Mk6 mines (80) as the earlier flush-decker conversions. But due to the average DE's top speed of just over 20 knots and its inability to carry an equivalent number of Mk16 mines, twelve *Allen M. Sumner* fleet destroyers, with speeds in excess of 30 knots, were ultimately chosen for this role.[3] The shallow draft of the DE did lend itself to important conversions, such as the APD, that could accomplish close-to-shore tasks that would have been difficult for contemporary fleet destroyers, but in the end, there were too many DEs on order for too little strategic demand.

The surfeit of DE orders appears to be a reflection of the Navy's inability to correctly estimate its needs, and the DE program has been criticized as a lesson against the decision to mass produce purposely low-end or austere ships during wartime,[4] but the fact that many proposed DEs were canceled is not as important as it may seem: Given the exigencies of war and the necessity to have industry mobilized, the effort and material geared up for DE production was put into beneficial use in other areas, which meant that these industries were ready for construction—whether to build DEs as originally intended or another kind of military craft or munitions.[5] Of course, had the war against German submarines not shifted decisively into the Allies' favor by mid-1943, U.S. industry would have been capable of supplying enormous numbers of DEs to the Allied navies in record time, and historians may have looked back at the great fortune of the destroyer escort program.

Power Supply Ships

The first destroyer escort reconfigured specifically to supply power was *Donnell* (DE 56). A German acoustic torpedo destroyed *Donnell's* stern and propellers on May 3, 1944, but the DE's power plant and the rest of the ship remained intact. The ship was towed to safety and laid up in Northern Ireland until July 1944, when the Allies captured Cherbourg, France, and needed a source of electrical power. Cherbourg with its great natural harbor had become a critical Allied objective following a severe storm in late June that destroyed the temporary breakwaters along the Normandy landing area, resulting in a lack of places where cargo ships could unload their desperately needed supplies. When the Germans finally evacuated Cherbourg, they demolished the local power station and electrical

2. Two hundred and five DEs were canceled in September 1943, 134 in October 1943, 68 in March 1944, 26 in June 1944, and 9 in September 1944, for a total of 442. See appendix A for a breakdown of cancellations by class.

3. There was no urgency for acquiring light mine layers toward the end of the war, and the selection of *Allen M. Sumner*–class DDs for these conversions was simply a means, as with the DE program, of using excess hulls, since the Navy realized that it was overbuilding fleet destroyers. The minecraft office, in fact, first declined the offer of having 2,200-ton destroyers converted into light mine layers, but it finally acquiesced. It is not the case that the unsuitability of DEs for this conversion forced the Navy to use destroyer hulls that would have otherwise been more profitably employed: They would have been scrapped. Morison, *History of Naval Operations*, vol. 14: *Victory in the Pacific* (1960), 114.

4. Friedman, *U.S. Destroyers*, 163. The operational contributions of DEs are chiefly ignored with this argument, as are the physical and industrial limitations of selecting an option to the DE by the time the U.S. entered the war. Indeed, prior to war, a slightly modified version of an existing destroyer design would have been preferable as the mobilization prototype, but that became impractical. What is clear is that a DE-like ship was necessary during World War II—ultimately in great numbers—and these vessels had to be acquired despite the compromises or shortcomings inherent in a design prepared for multiple production. Their utility after the war—like that of piston-engine aircraft and the Sherman tank—was not as great a concern during the war as defeating the enemy at hand.

5. Between October 1943 and May 1944, 267 LSTs and 353 LCI(L)s were delivered to the Navy, many from shipyards with DE contract cancellations. Mowry, "Landing Craft and the War Production Board," 73.

Donnell (IX 182, ex–DE 56) tied up alongside the dock at Cherbourg, France, on August 15, 1944. The damaged destroyer escort was modified to provide electricity from its turboelectric engines for the port's facilities. *Donnell*'s stern has been plated over and a makeshift rudder has been added. Note the rudder post and tiller operated by a wheel and pulleys on the port side. An unidentified American salvage vessel is outboard of *Donnell*. Following the great gale of June 19–22, 1944, which ravaged the artificial harbors designed to supply the invasion forces, the capture of Cherbourg and its fine natural harbor became the highest priority. Without continual supply, Allied operations were vulnerable to counterattack: The temporary shortage of ammunition, in fact, became so severe in the American sector that offensive operations were briefly suspended. Cherbourg was captured on June 26, and by July 16 the first deep–draft ships were able to enter the harbor. *Donnell*'s electricity was critical to the success of the port and enabled ships to be unloaded around the clock. (80–G–256081)

lines running from Caen that supplied the port city with electricity. *Donnell* was quickly requisitioned and modified into an electrical power hulk, and reclassified IX 182 on July 15, 1944.[6] In August, *Donnell* was towed to Cherbourg and successfully put on line with the city using a transformer that had fortunately been abandoned undamaged by the Germans. The hulk provided all the power to the port from August to December 1944. While *Donnell* was being modified, the

U.S. and Royal navies acknowledged the strategic value of a mobile electricity-generating ship and selected several *Buckley*-class DEs to undergo conversion into permanent power supply vessels.

6. Credit for the idea of using *Donnell* as a power hulk is given to Adm. John Wilkes, who recalled that the carrier *Lexington* (CV 2) used its turbogenerators to supply electricity to Tacoma, Washington, during a drought emergency in 1929. *Marine Engineering and Shipping Review* 50, no. 10 (October 1945), 160.

A detail of the electrical power supply apparatus added amidships to *Wiseman* (DE 667) at the Charleston Navy Yard in January 1945. Three other U.S. *Buckley* DEs underwent a similar conversion. The transformer is to the right, just aft of the main exhaust uptake and forward of two electrical cable reels. Each reel was capable of automatically unwinding an insulated, buoyant cable that would remain on the water's surface once deployed. Note the K-gun arbor stowage along the superstructure bulkhead forward of the access ladder to the far left. (BS 110556)

Six active *Buckley*-class DEs—four from the United States (DEs 59, 634, 667, and 669) and two in British service (ex–DEs 563 and 574)—were ultimately converted into permanent power supply ships. *Wiseman* (DE 667) was the only such ship placed in operation before the end of the war, and it supplied electricity (and fresh water from its evaporators) for Manila in the Philippines beginning in April 1945. Four ships were completed in the months following the surrender of Japan, including *Spragge* (K 572, ex–DE 563), the first British conversion, completed in October 1945, and one (DE 59) was converted in 1949. The U.S. power supply ship

conversion was designated TEG, for "turbo-electric generator."

The TEG had two large cable reels and an enclosed substation consisting of a transformer, switch gear, and water-cooling equipment added amidships in the former torpedo tube position. Since operating voltages varied around the world, the ship was designed to provide six different voltages ranging from 2,400 to 37,500.[7] The British conversion was similar except the

7. John A. Miller, *Men and Volts at War: The Story of General Electric in World War II* (New York: McGraw-Hill, 1947), 123.

> The thing that gave all of us the most anxiety [during the Korean War] was that the enemy army would break through our lines and catch us up a river tied to the dock. At one time we kept fireaxes by all lines so we could cut the lines. We also kept a Thompson submachine gun on the quarter-deck so we could shoot the electrical cable in half in order to get under way faster.
>
> Harold Clemens, Gunner's Mate, *Wiseman*

large cable reels were omitted and electrical power connection points were added at several places amidships and forward of the pilothouse.

The American power supply ships were designed to supply electricity and fresh water for beachheads or war-damaged coastal communities where the power supply hookup point was distant or where the ship, for security reasons, had to be kept away from the coast. The ship's cables were laid on floats from the vessel to the land. American power ships retained all of their weapons except the torpedo tubes. British ships were designed for dockside power supply in noncombat zones, such as British dominions in Asia, where a cable would be provided from the mainland. The British ships were disarmed except for the depth charge tracks on the stern.

The two British ships were eventually returned to the United States and disposed of, but the four U.S. Navy conversions remained in service and were deployed during the Korean War, where their ability to generate electricity proved to be a great asset to United Nations operations.

High-Speed Transports

The high-speed transport, or APD, was used to ferry an advance scouting party or underwater demolition team (UDT) to a landing site before the main amphibious assault in order to reconnoiter beaches and remove obstacles. The first thirty-six APDs were converted from flush-decker destroyers between 1939 and 1943. Beginning in September 1943, when the first cancellation of DEs was announced, DEs were considered for conversion into APDs as an alternative to

greater cutbacks. By March 1944, plans were drawn up for converting long-hulled DEs into high-speed transports, and in May, authorization to convert fifty *Buckley*-class DEs into APDs 37 through 86 was granted. These ships were redesignated the *Charles Lawrence* class, after the first ship earmarked for conversion. Forty-four of the selected ships were active destroyer escorts, and six (hulls 668–673) were units still under construction at the builder's yard. Ultimately, only forty-three *Buckley*-class ships were converted into APDs, as seven proposed APDs (41, 58, 64, 67, 68, 82, and 83) were canceled.[8] *Lloyd* (APD 63, ex–DE 209) was the first conversion to be completed, rejoining the fleet on September 15, 1944. A second round of fifty destroyer escort APDs was authorized in July 1944 as APDs 87 through 136; these ships were converted from *Rudderow*-class DE hulls under construction and redesignated the *Crosley* class.

Destroyer escort APDs were designed to carry up to 162 fully geared troops, or a combination of troops and matériel, including vehicles, artillery, and fuel. The conversion from a *Buckley*-class DE into an APD took about sixty-nine days and involved relocating the sides of the main superstructure out to the extreme beam of the ship in order to provide more internal volume for the troops and equipment. Davits were added amidships to hold four small landing craft, usually LCP(L)s or LCVPs, two port and two starboard. The number three gun was replaced by a lattice cargo derrick with twin booms that had a combined lift capacity of ten tons. The number one gun was removed in favor of a 5-inch/38 Mk30/69 single enclosed base-ring mount. This mount was originally designed for installation aboard DEs, and therefore the mount's Mk38 blast shield was beveled along its upper back edge to permit normal Hedgehog projectile trajectory. For standardization, it was the only 5-inch mount installed aboard DEs and APDs, regardless of gun position or absence of a Hedgehog.

8. The ships selected for these conversions in order of APD numbers were *England* (DE 635), *Witter* (DE 636), *Scott* (DE 214), *Jenks* (DE 665), *Durik* (DE 666), *Borum* (DE 790), and *Maloy* (DE 791).

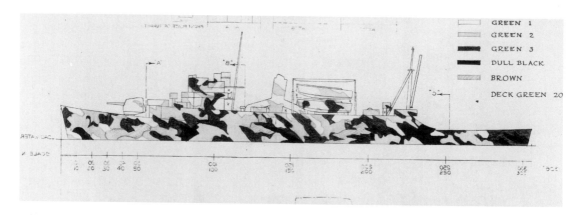

GREEN 1
GREEN 2
GREEN 3
DULL BLACK
BROWN
DECK GREEN 20

The *Buckley*-class ship *Lloyd* (APD 63, ex–DE 209) on September 15, 1944, following its conversion into a *Charles Lawrence*–class high-speed transport. *Lloyd* was the first *Buckley*-class DE to be converted into an APD. Above the photograph is the design sketch for Measure 31/20L as approved on August 15, 1944, composed of green, brown, and black splotches. (Note how closely *Lloyd*'s camouflage matches the sketch.) *Lloyd* retains the original *Buckley*-class high bridge, while a lattice cargo derrick has been added to the quarterdeck. These two features are the distinguishing characteristics of the class. The *Charles Lawrence* APD differs from the *Buckley*-class DE in a number of ways: a 5-inch/38 Mk30/69 enclosed mount and 40mm Mk1 twin mount have replaced the two 3-inch/50s and Hedgehog forward of the bridge; davits holding four LCVPs have replaced the torpedo mount; the four 20mm guns around the stack have been relocated to either side of the landing craft davits; and two 40mm twin mounts have been added to the port and starboard sides of the cargo derrick, replacing the 1.1-inch quad and its director. All K-guns have been removed and the superstructure sides have been extended outboard to the edge of the hull in order to increase the internal volume of the ship for troop accommodations and additional stowage. *Lloyd* has the same SA and SL radar sets that it carried while it served as a DE. (*Top:* 19-LCM-APD 37-2; *bottom:* BS 72334)

A view of *Hollis* (APD 86, ex–DE 794) looking forward at the main and superstructure decks aft. This photograph was taken on August 6, 1945, at Pearl Harbor following *Hollis*'s conversion into a flagship for Pacific UDT forces. A 40mm Mk2 quadruple mount with Mk51 director has been added to the quarterdeck, while a radio mainmast has replaced the heavy cargo derrick. Note the open access hatch to the crew quarters aft of the 40mm quad gun tub. (19-LCM-APD86-1)

The 5-inch mount was automatically controlled by a Mk51, or later Mk52, director located on the open bridge. A 40mm Mk1 twin mount with director replaced the entire Hedgehog, number two gun, and 20mm gun positions forward of the pilothouse. Two more 40mm twin mounts with directors were added in tubs on either side of the cargo derrick's kingpost, while the four 20mm single guns amidships were relocated to positions forward and aft of the extended superstructure sides. All K-guns were removed, but the depth charge tracks were left intact. (The *Crosley*-class APD was almost identical to the *Charles Lawrence* APD except for the low bridge inherited from the *Rudderow* class design and a tripod cargo derrick instead of lattice one.)

Toward the end of World War II, *Blessman* (APD 48), *Laning* (APD 60), and *Hollis* (APD 86) were modified into UDT flagships. The cargo derrick was replaced with a communications mainmast and SCR series radio equipment was installed. In addition, *Laning* had a 40mm twin mount added to the stern, while *Blessman* and *Hollis* had a 40mm quad added in the same position.

Replacement of the Three-Inch Battery

The 3-inch/50 Mk22 was a reliable and easy weapon to use, but because its shell could not penetrate a submarine's pressure hull and its mount was not power operated or automatically director controlled, it frequently proved to be less than adequate.[9] The Navy planned to upgrade the main battery of many of the existing 3-inch-armed de-

9. Cdr. Donald Macintyre, CO of *Bickerton* (K 466), writes, "The principal weakness of these ships was the main gunnery armament. I cannot imagine where the Americans found the short-barreled 3-inch blunderbusses with which they were furnished—elephant guns, I remember, we nicknamed them. They fired a minute shell of, I suspect, solid steel with no explosive charge, for on the only occasion we fired them in anger they were seen to bounce off the target without exploding. I had no confidence whatever in these weapons. But gunnery was a secondary requirement in the Atlantic and the good points of these little ships far outweighed the bad." *U-Boat Killer* (New York: W. W. Norton and Co., 1956), 134–35.

A series of photographs of *Coolbaugh* (DE 217) and an unidentified *Buckley*-class DE taken at Mare Island toward the end of their armament overhaul in November 1945. Circles indicate some of the major alterations. The new armament layout is similar to that of a late-war *John C. Butler*-class DE. The photo at right shows the 5-inch/38 Mk30/69 single, enclosed base-ring mount that replaced the number one 3-inch gun, and the Hedgehog relocated to the former number two 3-inch gun position. The sponsons on the 01 level have been enlarged so that each can accommodate a single 40mm gun. The sound room has been expanded forward, and the 20mm guns in front of the pilothouse have been removed. Bins for floater nets are forward of the 24-inch searchlights on either side of the bridge. Both ships have a Mk57 director on a small platform built into the aft end of the open bridge. The mast still supports SA radar at the top and SL radar in a radome below. The yard has a T-shaped TBS antenna on the port side, inboard from the BK ski pole IFF antenna. A second BK IFF antenna is in the same position on the starboard side. The photograph on the facing page at top shows the area amidships. The four 20mm guns around the stack are in the same positions as when the ship was armed with 3-inch guns. The photograph on the bottom shows the two 40mm Mk1 twin mounts with directors that replaced the torpedo bank, and the 40mm Mk2 quadruple mount in the X position. Two 20mm guns flank the X position director station. A second 5-inch/38 Mk30/69 mount is on the quarterdeck, and a tub for two 20mm guns is on the stern. The K-guns have been moved forward from their previous position, and two depth charge tracks remain at the fantail. (BS 91311; BS 91312; BS 91313)

stroyer escorts to 5-inch/38 guns, but with the end of the war and the ambiguous postwar status of destroyer escorts, very few conversions ultimately took place.

Originally all *Buckley*-class ships not earmarked for a specific conversion program (forty-six ships) were to be rearmed with 5-inch guns, but by mid-1945 that number had been reduced to thirty-one following the DER allocations. The weight difference between the 5-inch single mount and the 3-inch single mount was considerable (45,000 pounds vs. 7,510 pounds), but all 3-inch DEs had been designed to be able to support the weight of the much heavier 5-inch gun in anticipation of receiving this weapon at a future date. *Fogg* (DE 57) was the first *Buckley*-class DE rearmed with 5-inch guns, when it acquired them in May 1945 along with a new fantail while undergoing repairs for torpedo damage. Only eleven more ships ended up being converted (DEs 217, 218, 219, 678, 679, 680, 696, 697, 698, 700, and 701), beginning in August 1945. *Fogg* was further modified into a radar picket escort in late 1945 (see below).

The rearmament conversion resulted in a weapon layout similar to that of the 5-inch DE classes. The number one and number three 3-inch guns were each replaced with a 5-inch/38 Mk30/69 single enclosed base-ring mount. The 5-inch mounts were automatically controlled by a Mk51, Mk52, or (postwar) Mk57 director located on the open bridge. A 40mm Mk1 twin mount with director replaced the number two 3-inch gun, and the 20mm guns at the 01 level on either side of the bridge were replaced with single 40mm guns in extended sponsons. The sound room was expanded forward, and the 20mm guns in front of the pilothouse were removed. The 1.1-inch gun (or 40mm twin mount) in the X position was replaced with a 40mm Mk2 quadruple mount, and two 40mm twin mounts with directors were added in the former torpedo tube position. Two 20mm single guns were placed on either side of the X position director station. The 20mm positions in front of the pilothouse, around the stack, and forward of the depth charge tracks, as well as the Hedgehog and K-guns, remained unchanged.

The upgrade from 3-inch to 5-inch main batteries was successful, but the postwar military capabilities of the newly rearmed *Buckley*s, like DEs in general, were limited; therefore, the Navy did not proceed with the wholesale refitting of the large numbers of reserve 3-inch DEs. All but two of the 5-inch *Buckley*s (DEs 678 and 701) served in the active postwar fleet, with one, *Currier* (DE 700), fighting in the Korean War. Four of these ships, including *Currier*, had their ASW capabilities enhanced in 1947 as a means of further reworking the existing DE design, while another was briefly converted into an amphibious forces control ship (see below). The 5-inch *Buckley*s were ideal for training reservists due to their relatively simple machinery and ease of handling (a built-in benefit of the DE design), and most of them served with distinction in this capacity throughout the 1950s and into the 1960s. The change in antiaircraft technology and their gradual shift from active to reserve training status led to the removal of the single 40mm guns and the portside 40mm twin mount amidships from those ships still in service in the early 1950s, and by the end of the decade all remaining 20mm guns had been landed, along with one of the depth charge tracks and two to four of the K-guns.

Radar Picket Escorts

In response to the mass kamikaze raids of 1945, the U.S. Navy decided to convert a number of destroyers and destroyer escorts into radar picket ships. The DE conversions were reclassified radar picket escorts (DERs). The DER, like its destroyer counterpart, was designed to provide advance warning of air attack, help vector friendly aircraft into favorable counter positions, and jam enemy radar signals to conceal potential targets from the enemy.

Twenty *Buckley*-class ships (DEs 51, 57, 153, 204, 210, 213, 214, 220, 221, 222, 223, 577, 578, 665, 666, 790, 791, 798, 799, and 800) were selected in May 1945 to become radar pickets—the only DEs chosen at the time. Five of those selected (DEs 214, 665, 666, 790, and 791) were already slated for conversion into APDs, and it is not known whether they were scheduled to undergo a combination of the two conversions because all thirteen of the radar picket conversions, including all five APD selections, were canceled a few months later at war's end. Seven conversions proceeded (DEs 51, 57, 153, 213, 223, 577, and 578), even though their tactical necessity had diminished with the end of the war. All seven conversions were completed by January 1946.

Compared to the World War II APD conversions and the *Edsall*-class radar picket conversions of the mid-1950s, the original *Buckley*-class DER required far fewer changes to the superstructure, but the ship was completely rearmed. Two 5-inch/38 Mk30/69 single enclosed mounts replaced the numbers one and three 3-inch guns, a 40mm Mk1 twin mount with director replaced the number two 3-inch gun, two 40mm Mk1 twin mounts were installed on the former torpedo deck, and a 40mm Mk2 quad was fitted in the X position. All single 20mm guns were removed, and four 20mm Mk24 twin mounts, two on each side of the bridge forward

Buckley (DE 51) at the New York Navy Yard in late summer 1945, toward the end of its conversion into a radar picket ship. Very few photographs of *Buckley* in this configuration exist. Two 5-inch/38 single enclosed mounts have replaced the numbers one and three 3-inch/50s, and a 40mm twin mount has replaced the number two gun. All single 20mm guns have been replaced with four 20mm Mk24 twin mounts, two amidships and two at the 01 level on either side of the forward 40mm gun director. Two 40mm twin mounts have been added on either side of the mainmast and a 40mm quad has been installed in the X position. All of *Buckley*'s antisubmarine weapons have been landed except for the depth charge tracks on the stern. The foremast supports an SC-2 air-search radar with IFF panel array on top; beneath that is the SL surface-search radar radome, and below the yard on the foremast is a DBM radar direction-finder in a small radome. The tripod mainmast supports the SP air- and surface-search radar dish, an upright YE aircraft homing beacon, and, on the platform below, a TDY radar jammer with another DBM radome immediately forward. A Mk52 director with Mk26 range-only radar for the 5-inch battery is visible atop the bridge. (Courtesy, Mr. F. Foltz)

and aft on the 01 level, were added. The Hedgehog and all eight K-guns were landed, in part, to offset the additional gun and equipment weight; this modification further emphasized the antiaircraft role of these ships. The stern depth charge tracks were retained, however, as in the APD.

The ship's picket capabilities were provided by a tripod mainmast added aft of the funnel to support an SP surface- and air-search radar dish with IFF dipole in the center, a DBM radar direction-finder, a TDY radar jammer, and a YE aircraft homing beacon. The foremast carried a late-model SC air-search antenna, an SU or SL surface-search set, and an additional DBM radome.

None of the seven *Buckley*-class DERs had the opportunity to fully utilize its new capabilities: *Buckley* (DE 51) was mothballed in July

1946, nine months after its conversion, and all but the *William T. Powell* (DE 213) were placed out of commission and into the inactive reserve by November 1947. *William T. Powell* served as a reserve training ship until 1958.

British Conversion Programs

Thirteen *Buckley*-type Captains-class vessels operated as control ships for Coastal Forces during a portion of their wartime careers (see appendix F). These ships accompanied flotillas of MTBs and MGBs in mostly nighttime attacks on German naval craft and shipping in the Channel. An experienced Coastal Forces officer usually rode aboard each DE as a tactical adviser. The DEs used their radars to locate enemy for-

Calder (K 349, ex–DE 58) and *Essington* (K 353, ex–DE 67) at the Brooklyn Navy Yard on October 20, 1945, upon their return to the United States. Both ships have undergone similar, but not identical, modifications into Coastal Forces control ships and were intended for service with the East Indies Fleet had the war not ended. Most of the standard Captains-class modifications remain, including additional depth charge stowage outboard along the stern, life raft racks amidships, and a crow's nest above the yard. Both ships have SA air-search radar at their mastheads; *Essington* was equipped with SA throughout the war, but *Calder* had its original HF/DF replaced with SA during its conversion. Three 40mm single mounts have been added amidships in boxlike tubs and all the 20mm guns have been landed. Four 40mm single mounts have also replaced the four 20mm guns around the bridge, but these guns are not visible in this photograph. Both of these ships commissioned with a 40mm twin mount in the X position. Each ship is now equipped with seven 40mm single mounts and one 40mm twin mount. All three 3-inch/50 guns aboard *Essington* have spray shields, while *Calder* only received a shield for its number two gun.

mations and then relayed this information with TBS radio to the other ships in the group. There were no major structural or weapons modifications to these control ships, aside from the installation of some specialized radio frequency monitoring devices such as Headache and the addition of a few light automatic weapons.

Toward the end of the European war, the anti-

aircraft armament of at least one Captains-class vessel, *Curzon* (K 513), was improved by the replacement of its two 20mm single mounts forward of the pilothouse with two 40mm single guns and the addition of three 20mm single mounts amidships. *Curzon* was now equipped with four 40mm guns (a twin mount was already present in the X position) and nine 20mm single mounts.

Many Captains-class frigates had added 20mm single mounts along the superstructure amidships to bolster their antiaircraft firepower, but it was not until the end of hostilities in Europe that several *Buckley*-type Captains-class frigates were selected to become specialized vessels for British operations against Japan, conversions which required the addition of heavy automatic antiaircraft weapons. (Ideally, the Admiralty would have preferred to rearm its *Buckley*-type vessels with American 5-inch/38s or British 4-inch guns in either single or twin mounts, but this was simply not practical due to the yard time it would take to make the changes and the paucity of these weapons; 40mm guns were becoming available in larger numbers by war's end, and they ended up equipping the Captains-class conversions.) *Bentinck* (K 314), *Byard* (K 315), *Calder* (K 349), *Duckworth* (K 351), and *Essington* (K 353) were earmarked for conversion into control ships for the East Indies Fleet, while *Bentley* (K 465), *Braithwaite* (K 468), *Cotton* (K 510), *Fitzroy* (K 533), and *Rutherford* (K 558) were to be converted into fighter director ships for the British Pacific Fleet.

The control ship conversions were selected from those ships already equipped with a 40mm twin mount in the X position; each ship replaced the four 20mm single mounts around the bridge with 40mm single guns on a one-for-one basis and landed all four 20mm guns and tubs around the stack in favor of three 40mm single mounts on platforms amidships. Each ship now carried nine 40mm guns. All three 3-inch guns were equipped with spray shields. The electronic capabilities of these ships were modified as well, to include SA air-search radar in place of the HF/DF (if one had been carried) and additional communications equipment.

The fighter director ships received an automatic weapon upgrade similar to the control ship conversions, with 40mm single guns replacing the entire 20mm battery in the same fashion (and a 40mm twin mount installed in the X position if one were not present), but were further modified to include a 40mm twin mount and director in place of the number two 3-inch/50. Spray

shields were fitted to the remaining two 3-inch/50 guns. The fighter director ships carried eleven 40mm guns in two twin mounts and seven single mounts. These ships were to receive communications equipment, an aircraft homing beacon, and late-model air-search radar.

In both conversions, the number of depth charges carried aboard was reduced and ballast was increased to compensate for the added topweight. All of these conversions were in different stages of completion by August 1945, but because the war ended, none steamed to the Pacific and any further conversion work was canceled.

ASW Improvements

With the exception of better sonars, the ASW capability of destroyer escorts was not significantly improved upon during World War II. It is possible that rail- or tube-launched homing torpedoes might have been added to DEs had the war continued, but this was not done until the next decade.[10]

Some attempts were made to increase the ASW performance of a few of the DEs that remained in commission following the war. Four 5-inch-armed *Buckley*-class ships—*Coolbaugh* (DE 217), *Darby* (DE 218), *George* (DE 697), and *Currier* (DE 700)—underwent limited refits in 1947 to upgrade their ASW capabilities. Each ship had its fixed Hedgehog replaced with a Mk14 trainable version and QHB sonar was installed. In addition to being trainable, the Mk14 Hedgehog was linked to a remote fire-control system, which began to address one of the main deficiencies of World War II ASW, the lack of adequate fire control. (The Mk14 was soon replaced with the Mk15 Hedgehog, which was additionally roll-stabilized, giving the attacking ship much greater control over the performance of the weapon.) These ships also had their bridges cut down and enclosed. A new conning platform was added at the 02 level forward of the

10. *Francis M. Robinson* (DE 220) was used as a platform for ASW weapons during the 1950s and tested, for example, the Mk43 homing torpedo from a Mk32 launcher fitted amidships.

pilothouse and was covered with a canvas canopy. During the 1950s other 5-inch-armed *Buckley*s, such as *Spangler* (DE 696), received a Mk15 Hedgehog but did not undergo any bridge reconstruction. By 1960 a few 3-inch DEs, including all three active TEGs (DEs 637, 667, and 669), were reconfigured to have two fixed Hedgehogs installed on platforms on either side of the number two gun.

The most extensive reworking of DE ASW capabilities, SCB 63, was approved in 1950 as a mobilization prototype for reserve DEs. With the large numbers of mothballed DEs on hand (44 *Buckley*s, 48 *Cannon*s, 81 *Edsall*s, 17 *Rudderow*s, and 73 *John C. Butler*–class ships in reserve on January 1, 1949), it was prudent, the Navy supposed, to have an approved plan for converting these ships into an ASW force if necessary, particularly as a buffer against a Soviet attack. Given the comparatively slow speed of these ships, they would have to rely on sheer numbers and defensive deployment to provide effective submarine control. Four ships were ultimately converted into mobilization ASW ships—one *Buckley*-class, one *Edsall*-class, and two *John C. Butler*–class vessels—representing the most promising classes of the remaining DEs.

The *Buckley*-class vessel, *Vammen* (DE 644), ended up receiving a scaled-back version of the plan (SCB 63A) that was completed in March 1952. Instead of the SCB 63's bank of four Hedgehogs in front of a heavily modified bridge, the SCB 63A consisted of two Mk15 trainable and roll-stabilized Hedgehogs installed forward of a less severely reconstructed bridge, replacing the number two 3-inch/50 and the original fixed Hedgehog. The K-gun battery was increased from eight individual projectors to six paired and two single projectors, and SQS 10 (later, SQS 4) sonar was fitted; the ship's radar remained unchanged. *Vammen* did not carry ASW torpedoes at this time, although the one full SCB 63 conversion completed (*Tweedy*, DE 532, *John C. Butler* class) was equipped with a torpedo mount. Following its conversion, *Vammen* conducted two tours of duty during the Korean War, pa-

trolling and providing gunfire support at Wonsan between August and November 1952, and then returned to the Far East nearly ten years later, in early 1962, to help train the nascent South Vietnamese navy. The ship was placed in service in reserve as an ASW training ship in August 1962 and continued this duty until 1969. The general conversion of reserve DEs into enhanced ASW vessels did not prove to be necessary, and most DEs remained mothballed until their disposal.

Amphibious Control Ships

DEs were used extensively during World War II as control ships for amphibious operations in both the European and Pacific theaters. Because of their relatively shallow draft, DEs were capable of approaching beachheads with advancing landing craft and acting as assembly point markers for coordinating multiple waves of vessels during an operation.

Following the war, the U.S. Navy decided to convert three *Buckley*-class DEs into permanent amphibious control ships. Two 3-inch ships, *Cronin* (DE 704) and *Frybarger* (DE 705), and one 5-inch ship, *Raby* (DE 698), were chosen. *Raby* was converted and reclassified to DEC 698 on November 2, 1949, followed by *Cronin* and *Frybarger*, which were reclassified to DECs on September 13, 1950, with the conversions being completed in January 1951.

The conversion to amphibious control ship was not a major undertaking and consisted primarily of expanding the communications room and installing additional radio equipment. *Cronin* and *Frybarger* did have their automatic weapon batteries upgraded at this time, however, to include a 40mm Mk2 quad in the X position and two 40mm Mk1 twin mounts amidships. The DEC program was not pursued when it became apparent that existing APD flagships, such as *Blessman*, *Laning*, and *Hollis*, were better suited to operate with amphibious forces. All three DEC conversions were decommissioned and placed in the reserve fleet by 1954 and were officially returned to DE status on December 17, 1957.

4 *Service History*

Buckley-class ships served in World War II, the Korean War, the Berlin Crisis, and at the beginning of United States involvement in Vietnam. This chapter narrates the kinds of tasks these ships performed while in American and British service, as well as the operational demands placed upon them in wartime. This history is intended to complement the photographs and explanatory captions of the individual *Buckley*-class ships that follow. The conduct of the entire DE program—particularly during World War II—has yet to be studied in sufficient detail and is the subject of a future volume by this author.

World War II

INTRODUCTION OF THE DE: 1943

The first two DEs, both *Evarts* class, were delivered to the U.S. and Royal navies on January 20, 1943. By March only seven more DEs were completed, all *Evarts* class, four for the U.S. and three for Britain.

Delivery of *Buckley*-class DEs began in April 1943, at the same time the Battle of the Atlantic was shifting decisively to the Allies' favor. The earliest units were used for design evaluation and training, but by July the first British escort group to include *Buckley*-class vessels (EG 4) became operational.[1] (The Royal Navy typically combined their diesel-powered and turboelectric DEs in the same escort group; see appendix F.) The U.S. Navy deployed its first *Buckley*-class escort division (CortDiv 6) on August 15, 1943. This was also the first American escort division composed entirely of DEs to cross the Atlantic, arriving at Casablanca, Morocco, with a supply convoy on September 2, 1943.[2]

Italy capitulated in September 1943 and subsequently declared war on its former ally, leaving Germany alone to contest the Allied advance up the Italian Peninsula. DEs did not, therefore, have an opportunity to engage any Italian submarines or surface ships.

The first success for a DE against a submarine occurred on the night of October 17, 1943, when *Byard* (K 315) sank U-841 (Type IXC/40) with gunfire and depth charges south of Iceland while escorting convoy ONS 20 from Belfast to St. John's, Newfoundland. *Byard*'s kill occurred toward the end of Germany's final wolf pack offensive against Allied convoys in the North Atlantic. Improved Allied ASW techniques, reliable intelligence information, greater numbers of escort vessels, escort carriers, and air surveillance inflicted submarine losses on Germany that

1. Two British diesel-electric destroyer escorts, *Bayntun* (BDE 1, K 310) and *Berry* (BDE 3, K 312), crossed the Atlantic in mid-April 1943, the first DEs to arrive in Great Britain. They steamed on their own and were not part of a convoy.

2. A few individual U.S. DEs attached to various convoy screens had made transatlantic voyages beginning in late June 1943.

Cosby (K 559) and another Captains-class frigate laying a smoke screen during a training exercise off Dunoon, Scotland, in February 1944. The smoke screen was generated chemically from special canisters located between the depth charge tracks and, if necessary, could be supplemented with the ship's exhaust. A smoke screen was an effective measure to protect shipping from aircraft attack or long-range gunnery and made target selection difficult for submarines lurking on the perimeter of a convoy. (IWM A25646)

could not be sustained, and Germany was forced to withdraw its U-boats into less-contested areas of the Atlantic Ocean as it had in May 1943. German submarines and naval tactics were no longer capable of achieving the morale-breaking success that had shaken Allied shipping and military efforts in the first years of the war. Three more U-boats were sunk by diesel-electric Captains-class frigates in November 1943 northeast of the Azores: U-538 (Type IXC/40) on November 21 by *Foley* (K 474) and the sloop *Crane* (U 23); U-648 on November 23 by *Bazely* (K 311), *Blackwood* (K 313), and *Drury* (K 316); and U-600 two days later, on November 25, by *Bazely* and *Blackwood*. Prior to sinking U-648, the escorts of EG 4 had been attacked by HS 293 glide bombs

launched from Heinkel He-177s, with *Calder* (K349) and *Drury* experiencing near-misses.

In addition to escorting Mediterranean and Atlantic convoys in late 1943 and early 1944, British DEs began service as Coastal Forces control ships or as elements in support groups in home waters. The Captains class proved quite successful in the war against U-boats, S-boats (also called E-boats), and *Kleinkampfverbände*[3] in the shallows surrounding Great Britain. The British DEs would eventually sink more submarines (thirty-five) than any other type of British escort save the old V&W destroyers. This

---

3. "Small battle units": midget submarines, human-guided torpedoes, and radio-controlled explosive motorboats.

About the same time the frigate HMS *Byard* attacked another U-boat which was apparently blown to the surface by the depth charges and appeared about three cable lengths ahead of the frigate. HMS *Byard* immediately engaged with every gun which could be brought to bear and scored hits along the enemy's waterline and at the base of the conning tower. Fire from the frigate's close-range weapons, meanwhile, prevented the U-boat's crew from manning their guns. While the engagement was still in progress they abandoned ship. The U-boat sank a few minutes later. Twenty-seven survivors were picked up by HMS *Byard* and made prisoners of war.

New York Herald Tribune, December 12, 1943

total is particularly impressive because the Captains-class frigates did not enter the battle until late 1943. Their accomplishments were costly, however, with seven of their number sunk and eight severely damaged as the result of enemy action.

American DEs began operating in the Pacific in April 1943, but it was not until the end of the year that the first *Buckley*-class vessels arrived at an advance base in that theater, when *Darby* (DE 218) dropped anchor at Nouméa, New Caledonia, on December 25, 1943.[4] No destroyer escort of any class that first served in the Pacific theater was subsequently transferred to the Atlantic; all reassignments moved from the Atlantic to the

Griffin made sonar contact and went to GQ [general quarters]. I arrived on the bridge in time to see the first ship in the starboard column of the convoy— SS *Seakay*, a tanker—take a torpedo forward of midships. *Griffin* made a depth charge run on the sub, full pattern. The sub was seen to broach (conning tower and tip of bow) then sink back into the sea. *Griffin* was unable to regain firm contact due to the disturbed water conditions. The tanker did not burn, but sank bow first until 40 or 50 feet of stern remained floating vertically. Another escort sank the tanker with gunfire as *Griffin* and other escorts carried out a retiring search.

A. J. Petty, Radioman, *Daniel T. Griffin*

Pacific. The numbers of DEs ordered to the Pacific from the Atlantic Fleet increased, naturally, as the war in Europe drew to a close.

OPERATIONS IN EARLY 1944

On February 25, 1944, while on antisubmarine patrol, *Affleck* (K 462) and two diesel Captains-class frigates, *Gore* (K 481) and *Gould* (K 476), blew U-91 to the surface of the North Atlantic with repeated depth charge attacks and then sank the damaged U-boat with gunfire. Four days later, on February 29, these same ships and *Garlies* (K 475) made contact with U-358 northeast of the Azores. After more than one hundred miles of ocean traversed and twenty-nine hours of sound contacts and depth charge attacks, *Garlies* and *Gore* had to return to Gibraltar, but *Affleck* and *Gould* remained on the U-boat's trail, and nine hours later on March 1, 1944, the exhausted submarine fatally hit *Gould* with an acoustic torpedo, surfaced, and then succumbed to *Affleck*'s guns and depth charges. This was the longest continuous hunt for a U-boat in the war. A little over two weeks later, on March 16, 1944, *Affleck* had success again, destroying U-392 in the Strait of Gibraltar with the help of the destroyer *Vanoc* (H 33) and an American air patrol.

At this point in the war, British Support Groups and American HUK groups (which began incorporating DEs in February 1944) claimed more U-boats than did close convoy escorts. The Allies decided to counter any German attempt to renew an offensive against Allied shipping by aggressively deploying dedicated antisubmarine units—guided with special intelligence—along the European approaches from the Azores through the Bay of Biscay in order to destroy as many U-boats as possible before they had a chance to intercept a convoy. These groups specifically targeted Type XIV supply U-boats (*Milchkühe*, "milk cows") as a means of restrict-

4. Beginning on April 23, 1943, the *Evarts* DEs *Doherty* (DE 14) and *Austin* (DE 15) screened elements of TF 51, including *Pennsylvania* (BB 38), en route to Cold Bay, Alaska, the assembly point for forces slated to retake Attu Island in the Aleutians. This screening duty was the first military operation involving destroyer escorts in the war.

A portion of an Allied Atlantic convoy at day's end on June 25, 1943, steaming toward Great Britain. This photograph captures the magnitude, beauty, and loneliness of the ocean and sky's expanse, the realm of the combat sailor. This scene was repeated thousands of times around the globe during World War II, with critical supplies and matériel moved rapidly and in great quantities to the battlefront. The merchant ships are in careful rows as dictated by the convoy commander, while a much smaller escort vessel is at right, on guard in the event of a submarine attack. Escort vessels such as DEs would patrol the perimeter of the convoy up to several miles out, scanning the ocean's surface and depths with radar and sonar in order to detect submarines. Often, U-boats made their presence known, however, with a torpedo into the side of a merchant ship. But by mid-1943, ambushing convoys became as lethal for the attacking submarines as for the few ships unfortunate enough to be hit with a torpedo, since the Allies were able to muster large numbers of escort vessels and often aircraft at the point of an attack to either destroy the submarine or keep it in a defensive position long enough to prevent further action against the convoy. Germany was eventually unable to sustain the ratio of U-boats lost to merchantmen destroyed and had to resign itself to nuisance attacks rather than tactical blows aimed at crippling Allied supply lines. (80-G-271901)

ing the movements of U-boats at sea. As a result, fewer U-boats made their presence known through direct attacks on shipping, reducing target opportunities for the majority of American DEs, and those German submarines that were able to wage war on Allied convoys were fortunate to sink a single ship and escape unscathed. (U-311 was typical of the period: in its thirteen months of operation, it sank only the tanker *Seakay* on March 18, 1944, and was destroyed a month later, on April 22.)

The first submarine sunk by a U.S. Navy destroyer escort, in fact, occurred in the Pacific theater where the *Evarts*-class *Fair* (DE 35) helped sink I-175 on February 5, 1944, near the Marshall Islands.[5] The *Cannon*-class *Bronstein* (DE 189) was the first DE in American service credited with the destruction of a U-boat, when it sank U-603 in the wee hours of March 1, 1944,

in the North Atlantic as part of the *Block Island* (CVE 21) HUK group TG21.16. One hour later during that same "graveyard watch," the group dispatched another submarine, U-709. The first success against a U-boat for an American *Buckley*-class DE finally came on April 26, 1944, when a mixed group of DEs of the *Croatan* (CVE 25) HUK group TG 21.15 that included *Barber* (DE 161) destroyed the fuel supply submarine U-488 (Type XIV) with Hedgehog bombs and depth charges in the mid-Atlantic, 850 miles west of the Cape Verde Islands.

The intensity of the sea war increased in

5. This distinction was formerly held by *Griswold* (DE 7, *Evarts* class) for sinking I-39 on December 24, 1943, off Lunga Point, Solomon Islands, but postwar reassessment determined that no submarine was lost at that time. I-39 is now credited to the action of *Boyd* (DD 544, *Fletcher* class) on November 26, 1943, in the vicinity of the Gilbert Islands.

Our ship USS *Barber* was one of five DEs that made up a task force with the CVE-25 *Croatan* in March '44. We all spent some miserable days and nights in the North Atlantic looking for a sub that was reported to be in those waters. Whales and icebergs are numerous in that area during Spring and our sound gear zeroed on all of them, mostly during nighttime hours. We slept in wet foul-weather gear to a point where when the gear dried, salt would flake off like starch. The sea was running high the whole time, sometimes with 30-foot waves. Bad duty! After this exercise was secure we moved to the African coastal area to find another sub known as U-66 reported to be meeting with another U-boat to take on fuel. U-66 was there, but we sank the supply vessel (U-488). Our group was relieved by the *Block Island* and her escorts, one being the *Buckley*, who sank the U-66. We were in the area for awhile after being relieved, dropping depth charges on something down there, and we received play-by-play of *Buckley*'s action reports from our bridge.

Oscar E. West, Jr., Gunner's Mate, *Barber*

May 1944, as the Allies built up their forces for the cross-channel invasion of Europe and as the United States pressed its offensive through the Central and South Pacific. In the Atlantic, U-boat activity rose in response to Allied movements, and the month witnessed a frenzy of events involving DEs. On May 3, while escorting the eastbound convoy CU 22 into European waters, *Donnell* (DE 57) fell victim to an acoustic torpedo fired by U-765. The blast destroyed the DE's stern, killing twenty-nine crew members and leaving the ship dead in the water. The submarine was attacked by other escorts of the group, but it escaped unscathed.

The next day, on May 4, part of the screen from the westbound convoy GUS 38—*Joseph E. Campbell* (DE 70), *Pride* (DE 323, *Edsall* class), the French ship *Sénégalais* (ex–DE 106, a *Cannon*-class lend-lease vessel), and the British escort destroyer *Blankney* (L 30)—pinned U-371 to the bottom of the western Mediterranean after the U-boat had torpedoed their fellow convoy escort *Menges* (DE 320, *Edsall* class) in the stern, killing thirty-one. The

submarine was finally forced to surface, and under intense gunfire from the surrounding Allied ships, the crew scuttled and abandoned their battered U-boat, with *Joseph E. Campbell* picking up forty-six survivors. Just before the submarine foundered, however, U-371 fired an acoustic torpedo at *Sénégalais* and caught the DE in the stern, killing fourteen.

The destruction of U-371 was one of the few successes for convoy UGS/GUS 38; during its eastbound leg to Bizerte, Tunisia, the convoy had been savaged by Luftwaffe torpedo bombers, resulting in the loss of two merchant ships and the destroyer *Lansdale* (DD 426), but the convoy was still not free from further attacks on their westbound voyage.[6] The following day, May 5, a conventional torpedo fired by U-967 slammed into *Fechteler* (DE 157) amidships as the convoy steamed past the small western Mediterranean island of Alborán. The DE broke in half and sank, but most of the crew was saved by accompanying escorts. *Fechteler* was the first *Buckley*-class DE lost in the war. U-967, however, left the area undetected and ended up being scuttled at Toulon that August in the face of the Allied invasion of Southern France.

Twenty-four hours later and eight hundred miles to the west, in the mid-Atlantic on May 6, *Buckley* (DE 51), namesake of the class, with the help of a scouting aircraft from the carrier *Block Island*, caught U-66 (Type IXC) on the surface and proceeded to duel the submarine with gunfire. *Buckley* raced alongside and ended up ramming the sub; the ships became temporarily locked together, with some of the U-boat's crew making their way on board the *Buckley*, possibly to surrender, but their intentions were not clear to the *Buckley*'s crew. After a period of confused hand-to-hand combat between the submariners and DE sailors, the ships finally separated, and as the grenade- and shell-damaged submarine moved erratically away, it slammed into the *Buck-*

6. One of these ships was the ill-fated S.S. *Paul Hamilton* that was carrying 498 Army Air Forces personnel as well as a cargo of high explosives. The ship disintegrated in the attack with the loss of everyone aboard.

The North Atlantic in winter can be very rough indeed. When operating with some eighty-five Liberty ship freighters it was very tough to keep in formation as the Libertys were so heavily loaded and difficult to steer, and had no radar. Intervals between ships were supposed to be 1,000 yards from side to side, and 500 yards from bow to stern. On the *Robinson*, we could see the positions of the Libertys by radar, and if one was lagging behind position our usual gambit was to go alongside and signal him with flashing light (blinker tube) in Morse code, "Close up, or we cannot protect you." You could see an extra puff of smoke come out of his stack as the bridge called the engineroom for "more turns." They surely wanted our protection. I remember one afternoon going alongside a Liberty that had four steam locomotives chained to its deck, two forward and two aft, plus other freight below so that his main deck was almost awash. When he rolled toward us, we could look down his stack. I remember wondering whether he would come up again. But he always did. I did not envy the crews of those ships, but they did a tremendous job.

Lt. Cdr. Paul Campbell, Commanding Officer, *Francis M. Robinson*

July 31. Arrived in Emerau. Both DE 633 [*Foreman*] and 635 in port. The DE 635 USS *England* has six Jap subs painted on her bridge. Everyone aboard *Bowers* is a little jealous I think.

Diary of Donald Tillotson, Seaman, *Bowers*

ley once more, veered off, and then sank under a fiery wake. *Buckley* retrieved thirty-six survivors.

Also on May 6, 1944, the attack on *Donnell* was avenged by the TE Captains-class frigates *Aylmer* (K 463), *Bickerton* (K 466), and *Bligh* (K 467), when they located and sank U-765 southwest of Iceland, more than five hundred miles northwest of where the submarine had disabled *Donnell*.

On May 13, *Francis M. Robinson* (DE 220), a member of the *Bogue* (CVE 9) HUK group TG 22.2, had the distinction of sinking the Japanese submarine RO-501 in the Atlantic, five hundred miles west of the Cape Verde Islands. After obtaining a positive sonar contact, *Francis M. Robinson* quickly dispatched the submarine with a Hedgehog barrage and two patterns of depth charges. RO-501 was the ex-German submarine U-1224 (Type IXC/40), on its way from Kiel to Japan, one of a handful of U-boats transferred to the Japanese navy. *Francis M. Robinson* shared in the Presidential Unit Citation awarded to the

task group, one of five such awards *Bogue*-led HUK groups would receive for operations between March 1943 and May 1945.

On the evening of May 29, 1944, U-549 slipped through the escort screen of TG 21.11 and with three well-placed torpedoes sank *Block Island*, the only American aircraft carrier and largest U.S. Navy vessel lost in the Atlantic. In the same action, the submarine torpedoed *Barr* (DE 576) in the stern, killing seventeen and wounding fifteen. *Barr* was subsequently converted into APD 39 while undergoing repairs. Within hours of the attack, *Ahrens* (DE 575) made sonar contact with U-549 and helped guide *Eugene E. Elmore* (DE 686, *Rudderow* class) into successfully sinking the submarine with a Hedgehog pattern.

At the same time the DEs and U-boats were trading blows in the Atlantic during the month of May, halfway around the world in the Pacific the most impressive antisubmarine performance of the war was unfolding. *England* (DE 635), a recently deployed *Buckley*-class DE, along with *George* (DE 697) and *Raby* (DE 698), was directed to intercept a Japanese submarine scouting line north of the Admiralty Islands as revealed to the U.S. command through codebreaking. Over the course of twelve days (May 19–31), *England* located and sank five submarines (I-16, RO-106, RO-104, RO-116, and RO-108) with Hedgehog patterns and administered the Hedgehog coup de grâce to a sixth (RO-105), thus completely destroying the Japanese attempt to reconnoiter the movements of United States forces in the Central Pacific.[7] Although the general locations of *En-*

7. *Spangler*, *George*, *Raby*, and *McCord* (DD 534, *Fletcher* class) are credited with assisting in the destruction of RO-105, but as Samuel E. Morison notes, there is no evidence that any ship other than *England* achieved any hits on the submarine. Morison, *History of Naval Operations*, vol. 8: *New Guinea and the Marianas* (1953), 228.

Torpedo damage sustained by *Barr* (DE 576) on May 29, 1944. A T5 acoustic torpedo struck *Barr* at the starboard propeller, blowing off its fantail and buckling the stern at frame 128 near the X position. Note the 1.1-inch guns and the torpedo tubes. Casualties were high when a DE was hit in the stern because a damage control party was stationed in the emergency steering room above the rudders. Although *Barr*'s stern was destroyed, the torpedo damage did not compromise the ship's watertight integrity amidships; as a result, *Barr* was towed to an advance base and eventually returned to service as APD 39. (80-G-319603)

gland's quarry were known to the DE, the result of each action was overwhelmingly due to the expertise of the crew in handling their ship. For this achievement, *England* received the Presidential Unit Citation, the only one awarded to an individual DE during wartime.[8]

June 1944 opened with another triumph for American antisubmarine operations when the *Guadalcanal* (CVE 60) HUK group TG 22.3, which included *Jenks* (DE 665), captured U–505 (Type IXC) on June 4, off the coast of Mauritania. Material taken from U–505 included information on acoustic torpedoes, German communication codes, and the first reference to *Kurier*

("squash") communications procedures that were designed as a countermeasure to HF/DF.[9]

With the invasion of the European continent rapidly approaching and the threat from U-boats substantially reduced, an Allied victory over Nazi Germany seemed ensured. By May 1944, 288 DEs were already assigned to duty in the At-

8. In 1954, following a U.S. Navy reassessment of its World War II antisubmarine campaign, *Bronstein* was awarded a Presidential Unit Citation to acknowledge the DE's outstanding performance in the Atlantic theater. *Bronstein* single-handedly sank one U-boat and participated in the destruction of two more between March 1 and 16, 1944.

9. Hinsley, *British Intelligence*, vol. 3, part 2 (1988), 852.

lantic, including 113 of the *Buckley* class. American shipyards had been turning out DEs at an incredible rate; but even despite earlier cancellations, more than enough DEs were still under contract to supply the Navy's requirements. Therefore, in order to make the best use of the DE hull and help reduce the additional number of DE contracts that would have to be canceled, the U.S. Navy approved an alternative program for DEs. On May 17, 1944, the first fifty destroyer escort high-speed transport conversions were selected (APDs 37–86). This program eventually resulted in the conversion of ninety-four DEs into APDs. These conversions would prove quite valuable to operations in the Pacific.

D–DAY AND THE INVASION OF EUROPE

On June 6, 1944, the Allies invaded Normandy; six *Buckley*-class ships were the only American DEs assigned to specific tasks during the initial landings. *Maloy* (DE 791) was headquarters ship for TF 126, Follow–Up Force B, 29th Infantry Division; *Blessman* (DE 69), *Amesbury* (DE 66), and *Borum* (DE 790) were escorts for the assault on Omaha Beach; and *Bates* (DE 68)

> We were briefed on the night of June 5th about our part in the forthcoming landing. We then sailed for Newhaven (my hometown) where we lay off the harbour waiting for the landing craft which would convoy to the beachheads. We arrived off Sword beach about 9 am, our role being close support to the LC's; the shallow draft of the DEs were ideal for the job. We were shelled but escaped unscathed. Following the first week of the landing, *Torrington* was put on night patrols in the Channel, making forays upon enemy shipping with our MTBs which we directed with our radar, ours having a greater range. This duty was carried out continuously every night, and as the Allied Armies reached Belgium and Holland, we were moved from our Portsmouth base to Harwich on the east coast of England, so that we could operate off the Dutch coast and in the North Sea, which we did until VE day. When Germany surrendered we were sent to Norway to provide a naval "presence."
>
> Christopher Wickenden, Officer's Steward, *Torrington*

and *Rich* (DE 695) were screens for the Utah Beach bombardment group.

British DEs, including three diesel types that were converted into headquarters ships for each of the Commonwealth landing sites, were also heavily involved in the invasion. *Buckley*-type Captains-class frigates helped guide the invading forces to the French coast and protected the beachheads from submarine and torpedo boat attacks. *Halsted* (K 556) was assigned to Follow-Up Force L, *Rowley* (K 560) screened Force S (the 2nd Bombardment Squadron), and *Torrington* (K 577) escorted the first wave of landing craft to Sword Beach. During the first day of the invasion, *Stayner* (K 573), *Retalick* (K 555), and two MTBs broke up an S-boat attack on Allied landing craft near St. Vaast-la-Hougue, nine miles northwest of Utah Beach.

On June 7, *Narbrough* (K 578) pulled alongside the burning troopship *Susan B. Anthony* (AP 72), which had struck a mine on its approach to Omaha Beach. *Narbrough* was quickly joined by *Rupert* (K 561), *Blessman*, *Pinto* (ATF 90), *Mendip* (L 60), and LCI 496 in successfully evacuating all of the more than 2,200 personnel from the ship before it sank. A few hours later, *Blessman* came to the aid of another vessel that had also struck a mine, S.S. *Francis C. Harrington*, and helped transfer twenty-six injured crew to an LST equipped to handle wounded. That night, off the French coast, *Maloy* shot down a German twin-engine bomber that was attempting to attack the landing area.

The next day, June 8, 1944, *Bates* rescued 144 survivors of the destroyer *Meredith* (DD 726), which had struck a mine and had to be abandoned. The destroyer's hulk subsequently sank after being bombed by German aircraft. Later that afternoon, while attempting to aid the damaged destroyer *Glennon* (DD 620) northwest of the Saint-Marcouf Islands, *Rich* triggered three magnetic influence mines that blew off a fifty-foot section of its stern and holed the forecastle, causing the DE to sink. Ninety-one crew members perished and seventy-one were wounded. American PT boats and British coastal craft came to the aid of *Rich* and helped rescue sur-

The horrific result of a torpedo hit in the bow of *Halsted* (K 556) on June 11, 1944. This is an example of the severe punishment a DE could sustain and remain afloat, provided the crew was well trained in damage control. The explosion tore off *Halsted*'s bow from about frame 35 forward, killing thirty crew members. The force mangled the number two position, pushing it upwards and aft. According to eyewitness reports, the two ratings manning the bow chaser were blown off the ship and rescued unharmed. (Courtesy, Cdr. R. Fowler, RN, Ret.)

On the morning of the seventh of June 1944, that was D-day Normandy landing plus one, at approximately seven-thirty in the morning, we were escorting the United States transport *Susan B. Anthony* and one or two others, through a swept mine channel. *Susan B. Anthony* hit a floating mine which made a terrific amount of damage in her stern; within half an hour her engineroom was on fire, she became nearly a blazing inferno. Lt. Cdr. Muttran went alongside the *Susan B. Anthony* and HMS *Rupert* came alongside us, but *Rupert* had to go away because the securing wires were jamming, so we were left there with her standing off. We collected . . . 751 American troops, without much equipment from the *Susan B. Anthony*, transferred them across our decks partially to the *Rupert* and then eventually other landing craft came out.

Ronald Newbury, Seaman, *Narbrough*

The crew of the number three 3-inch/50 aboard *Holmes* (K 581) watching a depth charge rolled from the stern track explode on a suspicious target in the English Channel on June 7, 1944. The depth charge ready service racks with their reload hoists are clearly shown beside each K-gun. (IWM A23959)

vivors. *Rich* was the only American DE lost in the invasion force.

Mines and enemy action continued to exact a deadly toll. On June 11, *Amesbury* and several other smaller craft helped evacuate the crew and troops from LST-496, which had struck a mine off Normandy and sunk, while that night, *Halsted* had its bow destroyed by an S-boat torpedo, killing thirty crew members.

Captains-class frigates continued to challenge U-boats venturing into the Channel following the invasion. On June 25, *Affleck* and *Balfour* (K 464) were credited with sinking U-1191, although this may not have been a positive contact.[10] Later that same evening, *Bickerton* single-handedly sank U-269 off Lyme Bay with a depth charge attack, and on June 29, *Duckworth* (K 352), *Essington* (K 353), and the diesel Captains-class ships *Domett* (K 473) and *Cooke* (K 471) harried U-988 near the Channel Islands with depth charges until the submarine was destroyed.

With the Allies ashore, the beachhead was contested around the clock on land and at sea. The exhausting nighttime patrols of the coastal forces were carried out in earnest, resulting in deadly sparring with German S-boats, midget submarines, and mines. Each night scores of Allied ships, including DEs, corvettes, MTBs, MGBs, and PT boats, would move toward the continent's coast and engage enemy craft or sweep for recently laid mines. Most British DEs engaging the enemy in the Channel added a 2-pounder bow chaser fitted in the eyes of the ship so that the water close aboard could be raked with heavy automatic fire. While anchored off Sword Beach on the morning of July 8, the gun captain aboard *Duff* (K 352) used the bow chaser to smash the perspex dome of a *Neger* midget submarine that was making its way toward the DE.

In addition, the advent of the *schnorkel*—which made the detection of a U-boat from the air extremely difficult—forced Allied ships to carry out methodical searches of Channel waters to detect the presence of U-boats equipped with this apparatus. The American surface-search radar and TBS sets were particularly effective

A normal night patrol:
1600 Hands to tea.
1650 Special sea duty men to your stations.
1700 Slip and proceed to sea.
1730 Hands change into sea going rig.
1740 Action stations, test guns.
1800 Change into two-watch system (half of ships company at actions, the other half resting). Increase speed to full ahead and make for patrol area. This usually entailed steaming through a swept channel of a minefield. Also disposing of any floating mines. No 17 patrol was three miles off the coast of Belgium. Radio and radar watch would be set to check for "E" boats leaving their harbours. All engagements were short and sharp; there could be two or three engagements in one single patrol. MGBs were stationed in certain areas and the DEs, using their three-inch guns, would drive the E boats towards the awaiting gun boats, at times firing by radar only.
0600 Leave patrol area, increase to full speed.
1100 Arrive Harwich.
Fuel ship, replace used ammunition, clean ship. Each ship carried out six patrols a week, each ship taking it in turn to have one night a week in harbour.

E. H. Chivers, Boy Seaman, *Thornborough*

during the long-running battle of the narrow seas with SL and SG radars regularly acquiring diminutive targets at seven miles.

Thornborough (K 574) and *Stayner* successfully engaged S-boats off Le Havre on the night of July 3, 1944, but during a similar battle on the night of July 6–7, *Trollope* (K 575) was devastated by an S-boat torpedo that destroyed its bow, killing sixty-two crew members. *Trollope* remained afloat and was towed by *Stevenstone* (L 16) to Arromanches, France, until temporary repairs could be effected. *Balfour* severely damaged U-672 on July 18 off Portland, and the U-boat was subsequently scuttled by its crew. Three days later, *Curzon* (K 513) and *Ekins* (K 552) sank U-212 southwest of Beachy Head, and on August 4, 1944, *Stayner* and *Wensleydale* (L 86) sank U-671 off Brighton and picked up five survivors. On August 14, 1944, *Duckworth* and *Essington* sank U-618 in the Bay of Biscay.

Throughout the spring and summer of 1944, American DEs escorted convoys into the Mediterranean to support the ongoing campaign

10. See appendix D.

A view of a Coastal Forces flotilla from the deck of *Stayner* (K 573) at dawn in June 1944, following a nighttime attack on German S-boats off Cherbourg, France. The flotilla consists of British Power Boat MTBs (No. 413 is on the left), accompanied by their control ships, *Stayner*, another Captains-class frigate in the far left background, and a Hunt-class escort destroyer. The British Power Boat MTB was just under 72 feet in length overall, displaced about 50 tons, had a top speed of 39 knots and a crew of seventeen, and was armed with a 6-pounder power mount forward, two 18-inch torpedoes, and several 20mm and .303-caliber machine guns amidships. DEs, MTBs, and MGBs proved to be a lethal combination for the German Coastal Forces, with the DEs detecting S-boats on radar and driving them toward the MTBs and MGBs with 3-inch gunfire. (IWM A24046)

in Italy and the matériel buildup for the invasion of southern France, slated for mid-August. The Mediterranean theater, unlike the transatlantic convoy routes, was still contested by both U-boats and German aircraft. The hazards of air attack in this region led to the general installation of additional 40mm AA guns aboard DEs, in place of the torpedo tube mount. Two *Edsall-*class DEs—*Frederick C. Davis* (DE 136) and *Herbert C. Jones* (DE 137)—were the first DEs to undergo this modification, and it soon spread to many other Atlantic-based escorts, including *Buckley*-class ships. (*Frederick C. Davis* and *Herbert C. Jones* were also among the first vessels to be equipped with electronic countermeasures, or ECM, equipment, and were deployed off the

Bickerton (K 466, ex–DE 75) after being torpedoed on August 22, 1944, west of North Cape, Norway. Wounded are being lowered from stretchers onto boats. Note the men still on the stern around the depth charge tracks. *Bickerton* was in no immediate danger of sinking, but since the ship would have to have been towed, it was decided to scuttle the DE instead, so as not to slow the convoy and increase the possibility of further U-boat attacks. (Courtesy, Mr. A. Hammond)

The sinking of U-671 was a big success for *Stayner*. We had been exercising off Portland with American MTBs and were proceeding on patrol with six of them for the first time when we picked up the sonar "ping." The MTBs had to stand off while we went into action, which lasted six hours. In addition to the two survivors that we rescued, the destroyer *Wensleydale* rescued a few more. We landed them at Poole. Back at base in the morning, repairs had to be carried out. There were rest days in between trips, of course. Actions that took place the previous night were rarely discussed. We were just thankful that we were safe in harbour and hoped that we would survive the next trip. If I were off watch, sometimes I would stand on the stern of the ship watching the Isle of Wight dipping below the horizon and wonder if I would see it again in the morning.

John Barnes, Chief Engineroom Artificer, *Stayner*

Anzio beachhead in January 1944 to jam German radio-controlled glide bombs.)

The invasion of southern France went off as planned on August 15, 1944, with *Marsh* (DE 699) and *Haines* (DE 792) escorting the Delta force transport group, and *Frederick C. Davis*, *Herbert C. Jones*, *Currier* (DE 700), *Tatum* (DE 789), *Runels* (DE 793), and *Hollis* (DE 794) providing antisubmarine screens and landing-craft control. Five of the six French lend-lease DEs also participated in the operation. (*Sénégalais* was still undergoing repairs from the torpedo hit it sustained in May.) These thirteen ships were the only DEs specifically assigned to the invasion force.

While American DEs were engaged in the Mediterranean, the spring and summer months allowed British supply convoys to return to Russia via the Arctic routes above Scandinavia, and

Captains-class vessels were among the escorts assigned to this duty. But before these convoys could proceed with reasonable security, the Admiralty felt that the German battleship *Tirpitz*, anchored at Altenfiord, Norway, would have to be neutralized. In August 1944, *Bickerton* was reassigned from its Channel duties to accompany a carrier group on a mission against the battleship. This attack was not successful, and *Bickerton* did not return: The DE was struck in the stern by an acoustic torpedo fired from U-354 on August 22, 1944, and had to be abandoned and scuttled west of Norway. The Arctic convoys did resume, however, and following another air attack, *Tirpitz* was forced to retreat to Tromsö, Norway, in September, where it was finally destroyed in November by an RAF heavy bomber raid.

Two American DEs employed during the invasion of Normandy, *Maloy* and *Borum*, remained in the English Channel as director ships for PT boat strikes against German forces, using techniques developed by the British. Both ships were based at Cherbourg, France, and—like their British counterparts—conducted numerous patrols against enemy coastal craft in conjunction with other Royal Navy and U.S. Navy units. These ships were also called upon to rescue downed airmen, and during one such operation in August 1944, *Borum* picked up a B-17 crew within four miles of the Channel Islands but had to leave its whaleboat behind in an effort to evade heavy-caliber gunfire from shore. The airmen were saved, but three crew members of *Borum* were injured by shrapnel. *Borum* and *Maloy* continued their special duty until the end of hostilities.

Throughout the late summer the Channel remained a vicious battleground. On the night of August 23–24, 1944, *Seymour* (K 563) and three U.S. Navy PT boats sank two German ships in a convoy off Le Havre. The following night *Seymour*, the three PT boats, *Thornborough*, the French destroyer *La Combattante*,[11] and three MTBs sank four more enemy ships off Fecamp. *Thornborough* attacked German light craft evacuating Le Havre on August 23, and on August 27, *Thornborough*, *La Combattante*, and several

MTBs sank six coasters from a convoy near Cap d'Antifer, France. On the night of September 18–19, 1944, *Stayner* and two MTBs sank three S-boats and took sixty survivors prisoner.

As colder weather approached, successes against U-boats tended to decrease because of heavier seas and frequent storms; in addition, there were fewer target opportunities since the *schnorkel*-equipped U-boats were even less conspicuous during this period, as they used radar detectors and undersea topography effectively. There were occasional tragedies, however. On November 1, 1944, *Whitaker* (K 580) was torpedoed by U-483 north of Scotland, losing ninety-one crew members. The torpedo destroyed the bow and ignited the Hedgehog magazine, which contributed to the devastation. Despite the heavy damage, *Whitaker* did not sink and was towed to harbor. On December 6, 1944, *Bullen* (K 460) was less fortunate when it was torpedoed amidships by U-775 northeast of Loch Eriboll, Scotland. The ill-fated DE broke apart quickly and sank in the freezing waters, with a loss of 105. Ninety-seven of *Bullen*'s crew were rescued by the destroyer *Hesperus* (H 57). On December 20, while escorting a westbound convoy of battered LSTs that had been shot up at Normandy, *Fogg* (DE 57) was hit in the stern by an acoustic torpedo fired from U-870, killing fifteen. *Fogg* was towed to the Azores, several hundred miles to the southwest, and eventually repaired at Boston, becoming the first *Buckley*-class DE to be equipped with a 5-inch battery.

BATTLE FOR THE PHILIPPINES

Throughout 1944, United States forces had moved steadily through the archipelagoes and islands of the South and Central Pacific. DEs escorted replenishment convoys, conducted antisubmarine patrols, vectored landing craft, destroyed sea mines, and provided local gunfire support for operations in the Gilberts, the Marshalls, New Guinea, and the Marianas. The large numbers of DEs were an asset to U.S. operations in the Pacific because they allowed the Navy to

11. Lost February 23, 1945.

John C. Butler–class DEs and *Gambier Bay* (CVE 73) making smoke to conceal their formation at the start of the Battle off Samar on the morning of October 25, 1944. During this action, the DEs helped thwart the main Japanese naval thrust toward the Leyte Gulf anchorage. This battle is considered the high point of DE service during World War II. The *John C. Butler* class was the culmination of the DE design and was armed with two 5-inch/38 single enclosed mounts and had a geared-turbine power plant that could propel the ship at 24 knots. It is possible that the enclosed mounts of this class contributed to the misidentification of these ships by the Japanese. Had the escorts been a 3-inch DE class with modest open mounts, such as the *Buckley*, the Japanese may have interpreted the opposing force differently and pressed their attack. All classes of DE were employed as screens for escort carriers, since the latter used mercantile machinery and thus were similar to merchant ships in performance. (80-G-288144)

project its presence throughout the region despite the ocean's vastness and the multitude of small islands and atolls that required examination for signs of enemy occupation.

By October 1944, the United States was prepared to retake the Philippine Islands. The largest naval battle of the war, the Battle of Leyte Gulf, occurred there and garnered a place for DEs in the annals of American naval history. Twelve DEs (the "Little Wolves") were assigned as part of the escort for TG 77.4 that was embroiled in the battle off Samar, one of three distinct actions that comprised the Battle of Leyte Gulf, October 23–26, 1944. The Japanese were

attempting to devastate the American landing force at Leyte Island, which was defended only by the escort carriers, destroyers, and DEs of TG 77.4. *Coolbaugh* (DE 218) was assigned to Taffy 1, one of three escort units within the task group, and was the only *Buckley*-class ship in the battle. Taffy 3 bore the brunt of the Japanese attack off Samar on October 25, and *Samuel B. Roberts* (DE 413, *John C. Butler* class) was sunk by heavy-caliber gunfire during the engagement. This battle also saw the emergence of kamikaze suicide aircraft tactics: *Coolbaugh* rescued ninety-one sailors from *Suwanee* (CVE 27) forced overboard after the carrier was damaged by a suicide plane that crashed and exploded between the flight and hangar decks.

Air attacks were heavy around the Philippines in late October—*Manning* (DE 199) shot down an enemy twin-engine bomber on October 24 and *Lovelace* (DE 198) destroyed another on October 28 as they escorted replenishment convoys bound for the Leyte Gulf assault forces—but submarines were present as well. On October 29, 1944, *Whitehurst* (DE 634) sank the Japanese submarine I-45 (Type B2 Scout) 110 miles east of Surigao Strait in the Philippines after the submarine had fatally torpedoed the *John C. Butler*–class escort *Eversole* (DE 404) in the aft engine room earlier that day.

Although they were not large warships, DEs could attract enemy attention: During a convoy run to Leyte Gulf on November 23, 1944, *James*

E. Craig (DE 201) diverted a torpedo bomber attack on the formation it was shepherding with aggressive gunfire and maneuvering. The six Japanese bombers launched their torpedoes at *James E. Craig* instead of the supply ships; three passed close aboard to port, and another passed within five yards astern. As the bombers pulled away, gunfire from *James E. Craig* and *El Paso* (PF 41) brought down one of the planes. The convoy sustained no damage.

The campaign for Leyte Island also saw the first use of the new destroyer escort APDs. These ships became workhorses in the ensuing battles, but their duty often took them into the teeth of enemy resistance. After debarking troops at Ormoc, Leyte Island, on December 7, 1944, *Cofer* (APD 62) and *Liddle* (APD 60) came under intense kamikaze attack, and although they man-

---

October 24. Started back into port but another attack by Japs was underway so we laid down smoke and ran around for another 4 hours. Report came in that a Liberty ship was hit and sinking, and a near hit on a DD left five minor casualties. We just got into port and all hell broke out again. A Jap plane flew right over us. The oiler *Ashtabula* [AO 51] got off a few rounds but no hits. At dusk we were ordered out again. No one wants a tanker close to them in an air raid. Just after sunset at 1755 a Jap Kate torpedo bomber come in fast and low at 3,000 yds, another two were making runs on the O-51. The one on the port of us dropped his torpedo directly at us. Every gun was shooting at the planes as we waited to be hit by the torpedo but luckily it run too deep and went underneath us. The O-51 maneuvered and it was not hit either, we thought, but later learned it had been hit amidships but so low we didn't hear the explosion. No casualties and they needed no assistance. One plane exploded in a ball of flame but with so many ships shooting at it no one knew who actually shot it down. The *Ashtabula* had a 16 degree list but was doing OK on her own. We could see lots of fire on the horizon—a big battle at sea was going on. In the early morn we seen lots of ships coming in. Five cruisers and four wagons. The *Tenn* [*Tennessee*, BB 43] had been hit and had a big hole in her. Found out the DE 199 [*Manning*] took credit for one downed plane. Sunset, the raid come as expected.

October 26. The fleet come in to fuel up and take on ammo. Could count 5 BBs, 8 cruisers and many DD's. The *Calif* [*California*, BB 44] was among them, would like to talk to my uncle who is a GM2 on her. Scuttlebut is hot and heavy. Someone says we lost the *Princeton* [CVL 23, sunk October 24, 1944] and the *Denver* [CL 58] had been hit. Small battles raging beyond the horizon. Morning of Oct 27 DE 636 [*Witter*] claimed 2 enemy aircraft downed.

October 27. . . . At dusk we were ordered out to fuel up. We were attacked again. A plane come in too close and the *Calif* shot it down. Our skipper had us retrieve a wheel and tire from it. Norman bearings made in the USA were found in the wheel. Carrier [probably *Santee*, CVE 29] was seen with a large hole in its side and a heavy list. The hole is 30′ wide and 12′ long, everyone is imagining what a hit like that would do to a little DE. DE 637 [*Bowers*] is now officially listed as one of the initial wave to hit the Philippines. While escorting tonight, an F6F Hellcat tried to land on the aircraft carrier (76) [*Kadashan Bay*] and didn't make it. His motor stalled so he sat down in the water. The plane sank immediately but the pilot slipped out and surfaced where we retrieved him from the ocean. We later transferred him to a tin can with a medic. The 566 [*Stoddard*].

Diary of Donald Tillotson, Seaman, *Bowers*

January 1, 1945. Left Leyte with 75 ships. Mostly minesweepers (for Luzon), tankers, cargo ships, and four stackers. First nite out, within sight of Leyte Gulf, a bogey dropped an egg 200 yds off the fantail. We did not fire on him. Minesweepers shot us with .50 cal and shrapnel hit on deck from bomb. Next morning at 7 we were attacked by dive-bombing Vals. We got one but not the credit for it. It was within easy range of guns. P-47 shot one while he was circling looking for his buddy. Total—4 planes 1 day. GQ—average two every hour. Followed all night by bogeys. Twin motor bomber came in so low it almost hit the bow. It was hit by 20s—Betty—2 motor bomber. This morning we arrived in Mindoro (3 weeks since invaded) to find one ship smoking and several damaged. Task force shelled our beachhead on the 31st. Tonite five bogeys, 1 bomber, 4 Vals, attacked a tanker. All missed but the Betty who suicided into it. Great world! Would like to know what tomorrow holds for us.

Diary of William Johnson, Electrician's Mate, *Neuendorf*

aged to shoot down several planes, *Liddle* took a hit squarely on the bridge, resulting in the deaths of forty crew members, including the commanding officer. *Cofer* came to the aid of *Liddle* and guided the crippled transport back to safe anchorage at San Pedro Bay on the other side of Leyte. *Liddle* was repaired in the United States and returned to action before the end of the war.

DEs and APDs in the Pacific were subject to much more severe air attacks (due to kamikaze tactics) than their counterparts in the Atlantic and Mediterranean, yet very few Pacific DEs received the antiaircraft refits common to Atlantic-based DEs. Clearly, a weapon to defend against surface attacks was still deemed necessary in this theater, long after warships had been removed as a threat in the Atlantic. Pacific DEs did have a very good record in destroying aircraft despite their light automatic and (in the case of the 1.1-inch quad) outdated weapons.

As Leyte was secured, operations shifted to the west, where Mindoro was to be taken as a steppingstone to the capture of the main island of Luzon. On January 2, 1945, while escorting fleet tankers to Mindoro, *Neuendorf* (DE 200) assisted

in destroying an enemy bomber that attacked the formation, damaging *Cowanesque* (AO 79). On January 4, *Eichenberger* (DE 202) lost three crew members to an explosion while searching for survivors around the escort carrier *Ommaney Bay* (CVE 79), which was bombed south of Mindoro and subsequently had to be scuttled.

Following the establishment of a base on Mindoro, the main landings on Luzon proceeded, with troops entering Lingayen Gulf on January 9, 1945. On January 11 *Lloyd* (APD 63) destroyed a shore battery in the area, which had damaged two LSTs. Air attack was, as usual, heavy. During the three-day passage back to Leyte, *Lloyd* shot down four enemy planes that approached the ship.

Despite the small number of Japanese submarines available to operate against American forces, constant ASW patrols and surveillance bore what successes could be wrought. On January 23, *Raby*, along with the *John C. Butler*–class escorts *Corbesier* (DE 438) and *Conklin* (DE 439), sank the Japanese submarine I-48 (Type C2 Attack) twenty-five miles northeast of Yap, Caroline Islands. I-48 had been modified to carry four *kaiten* suicide torpedoes, but it is not clear whether the submarine was able to launch any of them before being sunk.[12] *Thomason* (DE 203), with the assistance of *Neuendorf*, was credited with destroying the Japanese submarine RO-55 (K6 Medium) lurking off Luzon on February 7, 1945, but postwar reassessment concluded that RO-55 escaped *Thomason*'s attack only to be torpedoed and sunk two days later by *Batfish* (SS 310), which acquired its target by homing in on the Japanese submarine's radar signal.[13]

U.S. forces now prepared to shift their attention to the islands of Iwo Jima and Okinawa, but as these assaults were planned and undertaken, the Third Reich began to collapse under the weight of Russian, British, and American pressure.

12. Dorr Carpenter and Norman Polmar, *Submarines of the Imperial Japanese Navy* (Annapolis, Md.: Naval Institute Press, 1986), 56.

13. See appendix D.

Christmas 1944 was I think the worst one of my life. There were lots of good ships being torpedoed, escorts and troopships alike. I remember one, the *Leopoldville*, in which hundreds of US army engineers were trapped below and drowned despite every effort to beach her. At this time the U–486 had us in her sights, but the *Affleck* had just received orders to proceed to a different position and turned round to go to the rear of us. As she passed us she got the torpedo which was meant for us. It took her stern off. As I was watching, a poor fellow was blown out of the rear steering compartment about fifty feet in the air; I learnt later he was a petty officer who was checking the steering at the time.

Harold Bird, Signalman, *Hotham*

GERMANY'S FINAL MONTHS

As 1944 came to a close, action continued in the English Channel. *Ekins* sank a *Seehund* midget submarine on December 24, 1944, off Ostend. On Christmas Day, *Dakins* (K 550) struck a mine in the same vicinity, but managed to return to Harwich under its own power. On December 27, U–486 torpedoed and sank the diesel-electric DE *Capel* (K 470) north of Cherbourg, with a loss of seventy-seven, and disabled *Affleck* with an acoustic torpedo in the stern, killing eight crew members. (The possibility of using the stern section of *Whitaker* to repair *Affleck* was considered, but the lack of personnel and congested shipyards were the deciding factors in letting the ship remain laid up until it was sold.) On December 28, 1944, *Hargood* (K 582), the destroyer *Brilliant* (H 84), and the French frigate *L'Escarmouche* rescued survivors of the troopship *Empire Javelin*, which was torpedoed and sunk thirty-four miles southeast of the Isle of Wight.

The German army in western Europe staged a last-ditch counteroffensive through the Ardennes in December 1944, catching the Allies off guard. The German attack was beaten back, but its brief success lengthened the ground war by several months. The offensive had been aided by U-boats that supplied weather information so that the German formations could attack when

flying conditions were unfavorable. One of these submarines, U–248, fell victim on January 16, 1945, to the HUK group TU 27.1.1 consisting of *Otter* (DE 210), *Hubbard* (DE 211), *Hayter* (DE 212), and *Varian* (DE 798). U–248 was the first German submarine sunk in the new year.

Destroyer escorts proved invaluable during this much less heralded, though critical, final phase of the Atlantic sea war, when U-boats were armed with acoustic torpedoes and refitted with *schnorkel* devices that allowed them to operate under diesel power while remaining almost completely submerged. *Schnorkel*-equipped U-boats were extremely difficult to detect from the air, even with radar; therefore, with air surveillance compromised, it was up to the vigilance and endurance of surface ships (many times aided with special intelligence) to rout the submarines from the depths.[14]

In the last year of the war, U-boats in European waters were deployed individually to lurk off the coasts of Great Britain and the Iberian Peninsula in order to ambush convoys, while in April and May 1945 a group of *schnorkel*-equipped U-boats attempted to reproduce earlier U-boat successes in the mid-Atlantic and along the U.S. Eastern Seaboard. Both strategics failed: the U-boats around Great Britain and the continent were flushed and sunk one by one, while the movements of those approaching the United States were revealed through codebreaking, allowing the U-boats to be systematically intercepted and destroyed by DE and escort carrier HUK group barriers. Without the great numbers of DEs in both British and American service to scour the shallows and stormy seas with sonar, surface-search radar, and lookouts, however, the final U-boat efforts would have proven far more deadly to the Allied cause.

The elimination of U-boats continued in 1945. On January 26, ten days after TU 27.1.1's

---

14. The magnetic anomaly detector (MAD), carried by low-flying U.S. aircraft off Gilbraltar in early 1944, showed promise as a means of detecting *schnorkel* U-boats, but its short range and the lack of a suitable airborne weapon to prosecute a contact reduced its effectiveness. Roskill, *The War at Sea*, vol. 3, part 1 (1960), 246–47.

In January 1945, DE K 568 HMS *Manners* was on passage in the Irish Sea when she was hit by two torpedoes. She remained afloat and managed to gain contact with her asdic on the U-boat, which was laying on the sea bed. DEs *Bligh*, *Bentinck*, *Calder*, and our ship dropped depth charges and forced her to the surface. Our captain gave the order to ram the U-boat 1051 because of the danger of firing torpedoes at our ships. We struck the submarine aft of the conning tower; the impact was severe, and we were stuck fast to the sub. As she filled with water our bows were so low in the water it seemed she was going to take us down with her but at the last moment she broke free, taking some of our bows with her.

David Regan, Seaman, *Aylmer*

After putting into Belfast on the 3rd April 1945 (flying our "Jolly Roger"), the 21st Escort Group was met and congratulated by the C. in C. Belfast. The ships were refueling and storing and shore leave was granted to the off-duty watch. This didn't last long as a general order went out to all ships' companies to report back to their ships without delay. Eight hours later the group left harbour in darkness and, on clearing the harbour, set out at full speed heading for the southwest coast of Ireland. They reached their projected point on the 6th April in the morning. It had been reported that a pack of U-boats was operating in this area. HMS *Fitzroy* made the first positive contact at 1500 hours. Assisted by *Byron* and *Conn* it was now a case of playing "cat and mouse" game, which lasted 48 hours. Incidentally, *Conn* was now armed with 1-ton depth charges. It was *Fitzroy* that administered the "coup de grâce" to U-1001. . . . There were no survivors. Five days later the U-1001 washed ashore off Wolf Rock badly damaged.

Norman Howgego, Signalman, *Conn*

success, *Aylmer*, *Bentinck* (K 314), and *Calder* were led to the location of U-1051 by *Manners* (K 568), a diesel-electric Captains-class frigate which had been torpedoed in the stern by the submarine two hours earlier. *Manners* remained afloat and was able to maintain sonar contact with the U-boat, which had failed to leave the area. A depth charge barrage by *Calder* succeeded in driving U-1051 to the surface, where it was rammed by *Aylmer* and sank with all hands. The next day, *Bligh*, *Tyler* (K 576), and *Keats* (K 482) sank U-1172 in the Irish Sea off Cahore Point, Ireland. On February 3, 1945, elements of the 10th EG—*Braithwaite* (K 468), *Bayntun* (K 310), and two Loch-class frigates—shared in the destruction of U-1279 northwest of the Shetland Islands, and eleven days later in the same vicinity, these same vessels sank U-989. Three days later, on the 17th, *Bayntun* located and sank U-1278. Ahead-throwing weapons accounted for all three sinkings. On February 24, *Duckworth* and *Rowley* sank U-480 southwest of Land's End. (*Fowler* [DE 222] was credited with sinking U-869 [Type IXC/40] on February 28, 1945, west of Casablanca, but it is now certain that no submarine was sunk at the time.)[15]

German small craft would remain a menace until the entire northwest European coast was secured. *Cubitt* (K 512) drove off six S-boats attempting to lay mines in the Channel on January 30, 1945. On March 1, *Seymour* helped destroy an S-boat, and with *Ekins* and *Retalick*, thwarted an S-boat flotilla attack along the Thames–Scheldt shipping route on March 9. Two days later, on March 11, *Torrington* destroyed a *Seehund* midget submarine off Ramsgate, and on March 13, it sank another off Dunkirk. On the night of March 24–25, *Riou* (K 557) and the Polish destroyer *Krakowiak* broke up a mine-laying excursion by two German S-boat flotillas.

Late March 1945 was particularly successful for Captains-class frigates. On March 26, *Duckworth*, leader of the 3rd EG, obtained sonar contact and single-handedly sank U-399 in the English Channel. The next day, as the 21st EG patrolled the northern and southern entrances of the Minches shipping route in two three-ship divisions, *Redmill* (K 554) destroyed U-722 at the southern entrance between Eriskay and the Isle of Skye with the assistance of *Byron* (K 508) and *Fitzroy* (K 553), while their cohort *Conn* (K 509) sank U-905 that same day at the northern end of

15. See appendix D.

A rare photograph of destroyer escorts in action, taken by Chief Sonarman Roger W. Cozens of the *Flaherty* (DE 135, *Edsall* class) on April 24, 1945, during Operation Teardrop. *Hubbard* (DE 211, in the right foreground) has just unleashed a depth charge attack on U-546 (Type IXC/40) using sonar bearings provided by *Flaherty*; *Neunzer* (DE 150, *Edsall* class) stands by in the background. The large splash was caused by a depth charge that had been inadvertently left on a shallow hydrostatic setting instead of the ordered magnetic setting. The magnetically fused charges were designed to explode when they neared a submarine's hull and were very effective against deep-diving submarines. Deep-exploding depth charges had little surface effect. The U-546 had torpedoed and sunk *Frederick C. Davis* (DE 136, *Edsall* class) earlier that day, and after a lengthy hunt in which *Flaherty*, *Varian* (DE 798), and other DEs managed to track the U-boat and damage it with magnetic-fused depth charges, U-546 was finally forced to come up several hundred feet. Squarely in its sonar beam, *Flaherty* was then able to deliver its Hedgehog projectiles to the target, bringing the U-boat to the surface. The submarine fired a last-ditch torpedo at its attacker, which missed, and finally sank under a barrage of 3-inch and automatic gun fire from the surrounding ships. The DEs managed to rescue thirty-three members of the crew, including the CO. (Courtesy, Mr. R. Cozens)

the Minches with assistance from *Deane* (K 551) and *Rupert* (K 561). *Duckworth* and *Rowley* were credited with destroying U-246 on March 29, 1945, in the English Channel, but reexamination of German documents revealed that the submarine could not have been U-246, but may have been U-1169.[16] *Rupert*, however, with the assistance of *Deane* and *Conn*, positively sank U-965 on March 30 off Point of Stoer, Scotland.

Hedgehog was used with positive results in all of these attacks.

The Allied offensive continued into April 1945, and the resistance from German channel forces and U-boats, although still deadly, waned. *Byron* and *Fitzroy* sank U-1001 on April 8 south-

16. R. M. Coppock, Ministry of Defence, correspondence with author August 22, 1995. See appendix D.

west of Ireland. Later that same day, *Bentinck* and *Calder* sank U-774 in the Southwest Approaches, near Ireland, and that night, *Rutherford* picked up survivors from two S-boats that collided at high speed and sank while evading its 3-inch gunfire. *Cranstoun* (K 511) helped *Loch Killin* (K 391) sink U-1063 on April 15 west of Land's End. A week later, on April 21, *Bentinck* and two diesel-electric Captains-class frigates, *Bazely* and *Drury*, sank U-636 northwest of Ireland, the last U-boat to be sunk by surface vessels in the approaches around Great Britain. That evening, *Retalick* destroyed four *Linsen* radio-controlled explosive motorboats operating twenty-eight miles off Ostend, the Netherlands.

American DEs remained vigilant against U-boats operating far afield from European waters, and on April 19, *Buckley*, with the assistance of *Reuben James* (DE 157) and *Scroggins* (DE 799), dispatched the *schnorkel*-equipped U-548 (Type IXC/40) with a Hedgehog barrage 550 miles east of Boston. The most important U.S. ASW activity in April and May 1945 was Operation Teardrop, the CVE and DE barrier force deployed to intercept six *schnorkel* U-boats (Group "Seewolf") attempting to infiltrate the Western Atlantic as a pack. On April 24, while screening the escort carrier *Bogue* at the height of this operation, *Frederick C. Davis* was torpedoed amidships and sunk by U-546 (Type IXC/40) in the Newfoundland Basin. *Frederick C. Davis* was the last major American warship lost in the Atlantic theater. *Hayter* and *Otter* rescued survivors, while *Flaherty* (DE 135, *Edsall* class), with the assistance of seven other DEs including *Hubbard* and *Varian*, sank its attacker, capturing thirty-three prisoners.

Operation Teardrop was an important success. Four of the six U-boats were destroyed (U-518, 546, 880, and 1235), while the remaining two submarines, U-805 and 858, ended up surrendering at the Portsmouth Navy Yard. Days before this operation, President Roosevelt died. "One regrets," Samuel Morison wrote, "that he could not have been spared at least another week to hear about the brilliant fight that followed, where a type of naval vessel in which

The U-546 had just torpedoed and sunk one of our sister ships, the *Frederick C. Davis*, DE 136, with a huge loss of life. When we arrived at the scene, carnage and debris covered the water and I could only feel bitter hatred toward those responsible for such a terrible deed. We were ordered to join three other DEs who also had arrived at the scene, and begin an organized search for the U-boat. After several hours, we located the U-boat, forced it to surface with depth charges and Hedgehogs, and sealed its fate with deck guns from all four DEs. The *Varian* picked up twelve Germans from the water, and the following day transferred twenty-one additional prisoners of war from the other DEs involved. When the surviving Germans climbed up our rescue nets, which had been lowered over the side of our ship, I saw them as human beings—very tired, very scared, and very happy to be alive. We gave them hot showers, Red Cross survival kits that included dry clothes, toiletries, etc., and subsequently fed them the first food they had eaten in more than twenty-four hours. Twenty-two of their shipmates had gone down with their ship, so the survivors knew they were lucky to be alive. The following day, I learned that one of the survivors was the captain of the U-boat. I ordered him to my stateroom so I could interrogate him about the events of the prior two days. I expected him to be older than I was (I was 28 years old at the time), a mean and arrogant Nazi, and a more experienced seafarer than I. During our first meeting, I learned that we were within six months of the same age, we were both married with two children, neither of us had seen our wives for many months, and we were both very homesick.

Lt. Cdr. L. A. Myhre, Commanding
Officer, *Varian*

he had taken particular interest, the destroyer escort, broke up the last German threat to the United States."[17]

While Operation Teardrop played out in the western Atlantic, the final U-boat attacks were sustained in European waters. On April 27, 1945, *Redmill* was disabled by an acoustic torpedo from U-1105 off the northwest coast of Ireland. The torpedo wrecked the stern and killed twenty-nine crew members. *Rupert* took the damaged ship in tow until being relieved by

17. Morison, *History of Naval Operations*, 10:346.

the tug HMS *Jaunty*. On April 29, as the last wartime Arctic convoy left Russia, a pack of U-boats prepared to challenge the departing merchant ships and their escorts. In the ensuing action, *Loch Shin* (K 421), with assistance from *Cotton* (K 510) and *Anguilla* (K 500), sank U-286 in the Kola Inlet, while *Goodall* (K 479), a diesel-electric DE, was torpedoed and sunk by U-968 in the same icy waters, the last DE to be lost in the European theater.

Two Type IXC/40 U-boats were sunk by DEs on May 6, 1945—U-881 by *Farquhar* (DE 139, *Edsall* class) in the western Atlantic and U-853 by *Atherton* (DE 169, *Cannon* class) and the frigate *Moberly* (PF 63) off Rhode Island. These were the last two German submarines credited to the action of surface vessels in the war. The complete collapse of Nazi Germany was now just days away.

THE ADVANCE ON JAPAN

In the Pacific, February through April 1945 saw the most intense action of the war for DEs and APDs. During the assault on Iwo Jima, APDs landed advance parties at different points along the tiny volcanic island, while DEs escorted replenishment convoys and screened the beaches from submarines. On February 18, 1945, while on a reconnaissance mission prior to the main landings on Iwo Jima, the recently converted high-speed transport *Blessman* (APD 48) was bombed from the air, destroying the crew area amidships. The explosion killed forty-seven (including nineteen members of UDT 15) and wounded sixteen. The fate of *Blessman* was not a common occurrence during the Iwo Jima campaign, fortunately, because of American air and sea superiority. The real horror was on land, and U.S. Marines fought for the island foot by foot until it was declared secure on March 16. With Iwo Jima available to American forces, B-29s had an airfield for emergency landings to and from their bombing missions over Japan.

The systematic advance of the United States military then turned to Okinawa Gunto, an archipelago immediately south of Japan that includes the small islands of Kerama Retto and Ie

> The SL and I think the SA radars were on when the *Blessman* was bombed at night at Iwo Jima. The bomber, presenting a much smaller target than a ship on the radar, came in at a very low altitude, approximately at mast height, and was able to avoid detection.
>
> Robert G. Wagoner, Radio Technician, *Blessman*

Shima. It would be necessary to secure Okinawa Gunto as a staging area for any further operations against Japan. Off Okinawa, the attack from the sky would be the most devastating of the war.

Because of the intensity of the enemy air raids and the vulnerability of ships in the transport area, DEs and APDs were frequently assigned to help screen the main landing force at Okinawa. The screen consisted of several defensive layers, beginning with the radar picket stations located around the archipelago about fifty to seventy miles from the transport area, followed by an outer antisubmarine screen ten miles from the main anchorage, and culminating with an inner antisubmarine screen adjacent to the landing site. HUK groups and other patrols operated between the various screens. Ships on screening duty were charged with providing early warning of enemy plane movements as well as countering, when possible, enemy air attacks. At this point in the war, these attacks were usually mass kamikaze raids. More than ninety DEs and APDs were assigned to the screens around the island of Okinawa between March 17 and June 30, 1945, and because DEs and APDs did not have the antiaircraft firepower of fleet destroyers, these ships were usually attached to the outer antisubmarine screen. Ships patrolling this area had to be vigilant for suicide motorboats in addition to submarines and aircraft.

Screening duty was perhaps the most harrowing assignment for a DE, since it placed the lightly armed ships directly in the path of numerous enemy aircraft. Ships in the screen ended up becoming victims themselves because kamikaze pilots often attacked the first target encountered (or one that offered resistance) instead of continuing on to the main fleet anchorage. DEs were easily overwhelmed by multiple aircraft attacks; therefore, during the campaign, the structure of the screening station was revised so that more ships were assigned to each station in order to provide additional firepower if the station were besieged. Thirty-two DEs and APDs reported significant damage from enemy aircraft during the battle, and one ship subsequently sank; 232 U.S. Navy personnel were killed in action aboard these ships.

A survey of the action involving *Buckley*-class DEs and *Charles Lawrence*–class APDs will alone illustrate the unrelenting ferocity of the Okinawa campaign as a whole and why, when it came time to consider the invasion of Japan itself, the United States dreaded a similar, desperate confrontation. *Foreman* (DE 633) was among the ships of TF 54's gunfire and covering force that arrived off Okinawa on March 25, 1945, before the main invasion; the DE destroyed one plane during the initial air attacks but was knocked out of action for eight weeks when an air-dropped bomb passed through the ship's hull and exploded. *Hopping* (APD 51) destroyed or assisted in destroying seven suicide planes between March 29 and April 2. On March 29, *Bunch* (APD 79) sank two suicide motorboats and five days later rescued sixty-one survivors of *Dickerson* (APD 21, ex-flush-decker), which had been sunk by a kamikaze.

The late afternoon and evening of April 6, 1945, saw one of the largest kamikaze raids of the war. That afternoon, *Bunch* destroyed one attacking Japanese aircraft and *Willmarth* (DE 638) tore another diving kamikaze apart with 3-inch and 1.1-inch gunfire, forcing it to crash twenty yards off the port side (*Willmarth* managed to remain the only ship of CortDiv 40 not hit by a kamikaze in the campaign; see appendix F). Later that afternoon a kamikaze broke off the radar antenna of *Fieberling* (DE 640) and exploded alongside, leaving a wing on board aft of the bridge; the plane caused no fatalities, but the ship would have to put in for repairs. Still on that fateful day, *Daniel T. Griffin* (APD 38) downed two enemy planes and, along with *Bates* (APD

We were on the western side of the island [Okinawa] in the anchorage where all the ships were, and we had a report that there was a bogey, which is a kamikaze plane, closing in on our starboard bow. The first report we got was the plane was about ten miles away. We went to general quarters, what they call GQ. I was up in the forward 20mm gun, gun captain, on the port side. The next report we got from the captain was it was closing in, it was seven miles away, then five miles away, then we were told by the captain and the exec over the PA system that all hands be on the lookout on the starboard bow for the enemy aircraft, kamikaze. When he came into view all our guns that could train at the plane, at the bogey, commenced firing. I tapped my gunner on the shoulder and he opened fire with the twenty; all the twenties on the starboard side were firing at him, plus the three inch. That son-of-a-gun was so close to us you could see the bullets going through the plane and you could see the pilot, the whites of his eyes. As soon as he was hit, the pilot leaned forward and the plane made a dive into the sea, about fifty feet away from our ship. When that happened, we stood frozen until he went under. Then we came to our senses, we knew we got him.

E. J. Sikora, Gunner's Mate, *Paul G. Baker*

47), aided *Morris* (DD 417) after that destroyer was struck by a kamikaze, killing thirteen. *Witter* (DE 636), in the vicinity of *Morris* southeast of Okinawa, was simultaneously attacked by two suicide planes; while maneuvering evasively at 23 knots, *Witter* shot down one and damaged the second, but the wounded aircraft managed to crash into the ship on the starboard side amidships, killing six. Seventeen U.S. warships were struck by kamikazes on April 6, the most of any single day in the war.

On April 9, *Hopping* lost two persons—a crew member and a member of UDT 7—to a shore battery, but the APD was able to return fire with its 5-inch/38 and destroy the gun emplacements. On April 12, *Whitehurst* was attacked by three enemy dive bombers in quick succession; two were destroyed by the DE's gunfire, but the third plane hit the ship in the pilothouse. Forty-two died in the resulting explosion and gasoline fires.

Bowers (DE 637) destroyed three planes while

The burnt remains of the Nakajima Ki 43 Oscar that crashed into *Bowers*'s (DE 637) bridge on April 16, 1945. This pilot did as instructed—something the majority of kamikazes could not accomplish—and hit the ship at its nerve center, but the fact that even a small DE could withstand a direct hit and ultimately return to service exposed the futility and ineffectiveness of these tactics. Suicide aircraft were the most terrifying weapon faced by the United States Navy in World War II and served only to increase American resolve to force Japan into an unconditional surrender. (80-G-315256)

operating off Okinawa between April 3 and April 16, 1945, but on that latter date, *Bowers* was struck in the bridge by a fourth kamikaze, killing sixty-five and wounding forty-three in a fiery explosion. *Gendreau* (DE 639) is credited with shooting down four aircraft and assisting in destroying a fifth while on picket duty during the month of April 1945. (*Gendreau* ended up escaping harm from the air, but was struck in the number one fire room by a shore battery off Okinawa in June, killing two crew members.) On April 22, *Paul G. Baker* (DE 642) rescued seventy-eight survivors of the mine sweeper *Swallow* (AM 65),

They were very accurate on their kamikaze attacks and ramming their planes with bombs into our vessels. One—late one afternoon or early evening—we watched one kamikaze flying not far away from our ship. He sighted a small ship [*Swallow*, AM 65], and I watched every second of it. He took a dive at a forty-five degree angle; he hit that ship amidship and blew it up. That evening, right after this happened, we picked up over eighty—I would say close to seventy-five or eighty—survivors along with some officers.

E. J. Sikora, Gunner's Mate, *Paul G. Baker*

April 6 Japanese plane (Kate) was shot down by DE 639 [*Gendreau*] with us getting an assist.

April 7 At dawn alert a contact was made on an incoming plane distance 14 miles and closing. Finally spotted at 5,000 yds coming in very low and fast. At 2,000 yds we opened fire as it flew past our port side. As it banked, all guns opened up and it went down in flames. Our first kill. It was a Kate torpedo bomber. Also got word DE 638 [*Willmarth*] shot down an attempted suicide plane. I believe this makes every ship in our division registering a kill. Destroyed a floating mine.

April 11 DE 634 [*Whitehurst*] took a suicide hit. Many ships in our area are taking hits as the Japanese become more desperate each day.

April 14 We all stood on deck and witnessed a real dog fight very close to our ship. What a sight. One plane blew up in a total explosion and two spiraled into the ocean. Couldn't tell who was who. One parachute was sighted. The night before fourteen enemy planes were shot down in this immediate area.

April 15 Tonight we are patrolling what is called "suicide row" for a very good reason. At dawn we splashed our second Jap airplane coming in the haze to inside 2,000 yds. It splashed about 500 yds off our port beam. They seem to be getting closer and closer. We were hit by his machine guns with one slug entering after steering and lodging in a battle lantern. No casualties.

* * *

April 21? We are tied up alongside a repair ship. They tell us we were one of ten ships hit the 16th. Our casualties were staggering. I remember most of it in a haze. My best friend Robert Thornberg looked in real bad shape—one leg and arm very shot up. Out of the torpedo crew Elberson and I are the only two not hit. The radio, bridge crew, signalmen, and quartermasters took a beating. The USS *Hope* has many of our crew. One of the hardest things I'll ever do is helping to identify bodies of close friends so they can be tagged. The 24th we are due to start the long, sad trip stateside. I've been assigned as a helmsman—tough place to stand watch. Burned flesh and battle odors give me an eerie feeling. Every time GQ is sounded I get a real sick feeling in the pit of my stomach.

May 1 In Ulithi—raining. We got a big steel plate welded over the hole in the superstructure. Got other holes patched and the mast reinforced. Our next stop should be Majuro. With us are the DMS *Hobson* and the DD 661 [*Kidd*].

May 6 Underway, supposed to arrive in Eniwetok today; next stop Pearl Harbor. During April we had 477 hours underway, logging over 5,000 miles.

May 9 VE Day—8th at home. We celebrated it two days in a row as we crossed the international date line.

May 15 Arrived in Pearl Harbor.

May 16 Got our first fresh milk in over a year. Nothing ever tasted so good. Ship was thrown a free beer party in appreciation by locals. Lots of unwinding and tears flowed, but trying now to put it behind us, but no one who ever went through this can ever put it out of their minds forever.

Diary of Donald Tillotson, Seaman, *Bowers*

---

which capsized and sank after being holed on the starboard side by a suicide plane.

Almost a year after its spectacular antisubmarine success in the central Pacific, *England*, the decorated Nimrod, was severely damaged at the base of the bridge by a kamikaze on May 9, 1945, northwest of Kerama Retto, Okinawa, killing thirty-seven, wounding twenty-five, and putting the venerable DE out of the war. The next day, *Yokes* (APD 69) shot down an attacking Japanese aircraft. On May 11, *Barber* (APD 57) transferred fifty-four wounded from the kamikaze-damaged destroyer *Hugh W. Hadley* (DD 774) to a hospital ship. *Chase* (APD 54) was hit by a kamikaze on May 20, ripping open its hull on the starboard side and jamming the steering gear, but no one was killed. *Chase* ended up being declared a total loss, however, and was scrapped after returning to the United States.

Loy (APD 56) fought off numerous air attacks during the Okinawa campaign and assisted LSM(R) 188 on March 29, when that rocket-armed landing craft was hit by a suicide plane, and *Barry* (APD 29, ex-flush-decker) when it was hit in the bridge and set ablaze by a kamikaze on May 25. *Loy* tore a suicide plane apart with gunfire on May 27, but it exploded close aboard, killing three and wounding fifteen.

Bates (APD 47) burning off Ie Shima after being attacked by three Japanese suicide aircraft simultaneously on May 25, 1945. The stricken APD sank a few hours later. (NH 66450)

The ship had to put in for temporary repairs at Kerama Retto (splashing another kamikaze on the way), and then it steamed out of the battle zone. *Loy* destroyed seven kamikazes between March 26 and May 28, 1945. *Sims* (APD 50) is credited with destroying four kamikazes in May 1945, including three that inflicted light damage to the ship. *Sims* also aided *Barry*. On May 24 and 25, *William C. Cole* (DE 641) used 3-inch and automatic gunfire to destroy two suicide planes that attempted to crash into it.

On the morning of May 25, 1945, two miles south of Ie Shima, Okinawa, *Bates* was attacked by three enemy aircraft. One dropped a bomb close aboard and then crashed into the ship's starboard fantail, another slammed into the pilothouse, and the third dropped a bomb along the port side amidships that exploded, rupturing the hull. Twenty-three crew members were killed and thirty-seven were wounded during the attack. *Bates* was towed away from the action to a secure harbor at Ie Shima, but the APD continued to burn and eventually capsized and sank that evening. *Bates* was the only destroyer escort APD lost to enemy action during the war.

While anchored off Ie Shima, *Vammen* (DE 644) assisted in destroying an attacking Japanese aircraft on May 28 during the last large-

scale kamikaze raid of the campaign. The following evening, *Tatum* (APD 81) was attacked by four suicide aircraft at the same time. As the first plane was shot down, its underslung bomb came loose, skipped across the water, and penetrated *Tatum*'s hull. Had the bomb not been a dud, *Tatum* may have been destroyed. *Tatum* continued repelling the second, third, and fourth attacks, splashing all three remaining aircraft while sustaining limited damage and no fatalities.

Pavlic (APD 70) operated as a special rescue vessel in the Okinawa area between May 18 and June 27, 1945, and aided numerous ships damaged throughout the campaign, including *Oberrender* (DE 344, *John C. Butler* class), *Thatcher* (DD 514), and *Rednour* (APD 120, *Crosley* class). *Pavlic* was credited with shooting down an attacking aircraft on May 27 and, along with *Yokes*, rescued survivors from *Drexler* (DD 741), sunk on May 28 by two suicide aircraft. The next day, *Pavlic* rescued almost two hundred survivors from the kamikaze-damaged destroyer *Shubrick* (DD 639). Like *Pavlic*, *Frament* (APD 77) was assigned to rescue duty, and on June 10, 1945, the high-speed transport and other ships safely evacuated the entire complement of *William C. Porter* (DD 579), which sank after a

The German submarine U-1009, flying a black flag from its periscope, surrendering to the lend-lease *Buckley*-class destroyer escort HMS *Byron* (K 508, ex–DE 79) on the morning of May 10, 1945. The British Admiralty broadcast orders on May 8, 1945, that required all U-boats remaining in the eastern Atlantic and North Sea to surface, radio their positions, hoist a black surrender flag, and steam to Loch Eriboll, Scotland. Nine U-boats were intercepted at sea on May 9, but U-1009 became the first German submarine to approach Loch Eriboll as directed, where it was closed by escorts of the 21st EG. (IWM A28521)

downed suicide aircraft unexpectedly exploded beneath the ship, causing irreparable damage.

In the midst of this hellish battle, servicemen learned that the Nazi regime in Germany had been defeated.

END OF THE WAR IN EUROPE

As the Okinawa campaign moved into its final phase, the war ended for Germany. On May 8, 1945, with Hitler dead and Berlin in ruins, Germany capitulated. The following day the Channel Islands were returned to British control, with *Narbrough* and *Bulldog* (H 91), designated Lib-

eration Force 135, accepting the surrender of the German garrison and its eight ships (six mine sweepers, two patrol craft) at Guernsey, and *Cosby* (K 559), *Borum*, and *Maloy* escorting the advance party into St. Helier, Jersey.

Byron and the other DEs of EG 21 had the honor of delivering the first surrendered U-boat into a British anchorage as ordered by the Admiralty when they led U-1009 into Loch Eriboll on the morning of May 10, 1945. As its final act of the war, *Varian* (DE 798) accepted the surrender of U-805, one of the two surviving submarines from the ill-fated Group Seewolf, on May 12 off

Cape Race, Newfoundland, and escorted the U-boat to the Portsmouth Navy Yard, Kittery, Maine. During the second week of May, while under tactical control of the Royal Navy, *William T. Powell* (DE 213), *Spangenberg* (DE 223), *Alexander J. Luke* (DE 577), and *Robert I. Paine* (DE 578) helped escort U-boats to Lochalsh, Scotland, and then participated in surrender ceremonies.

More than five and a half years of sea battles—the last year and a half with full participation of destroyer escorts—had finally come to an end. Most captured German submarines were subsequently scuttled north of Malin Head under escort from Allied ships, including DEs, during Operation Deadlight, conducted between November 1945 and January 1946.

END OF THE WAR IN THE PACIFIC

The battle in the Pacific was also nearing its conclusion in mid-1945. Okinawa was declared secure on June 21, 1945. Between April and July, the southern islands of the Philippines were systematically wrested from Japanese control, with landings on Palawan, Zamboanga, Panay, Cebu (where *Newman*, APD 59, may have sunk a Japanese army transport submarine), and Mindanao. The final major wartime operation involving DEs and APDs was the reconquest of Borneo between May and July 1945; during this period, *Cofer* rescued the remaining crew of *YMS 481* that had been sunk by a shore battery, as well as *Salute* (AM 294) and *YMS 50* that had been sunk by mines. The invasion of Balikpapan, Borneo, the last hostile amphibious landing of the war, began on July 1, 1945, with the high-speed transports *Newman*, the recently repaired *Liddle*, *Kephart* (APD 61), *Lloyd*, and *Schmitt* (APD 76) assisting the main assault force of Australian troops.

Despite optimism that the war was coming to an end, action at sea remained deadly. On July 24, 1945, several hundred miles northeast of Luzon, *Underhill* (DE 682) rammed a midget submarine, perhaps unaware that it was actually a *kaiten* suicide torpedo launched by the Japanese submarine I-53. The explosion blew off the

A few minutes later, a sub was sighted on the surface in the area where the *PC-804* had dropped charges. The *Underhill* set a course to ram, but the sub was diving and the command was changed to drop depth charges. A thirteen-charge pattern was laid on top of the diving sub, and explosions brought up oil and debris. *Underhill* reversed course, reloaded K-guns and passed through debris. Sonar picked up another contact. The depth charges had brought to the surface a *kaiten* on the port side and one on the starboard side (these *kaitens* were about 35 feet long and carried the equivalent explosive charge of two torpedoes). The *kaiten* at starboard was too close in range for the main battery or the 20mm or 40mm to bear on target. The captain ordered all hands to "stand by for a ram." (*Kaitens* are capable of speeds to 45 knots.) After ordering flank speed, and a course change to come to a collision course, the *Underhill* rammed the port side *kaiten*. After a few seconds, there were two explosions—one directly under the bridge and magazine area, the second one forward of the bridge area and more to starboard—which ripped the *Underhill* apart. The entire forward part of the ship was blown off forward of the stack. The stern section aft of the stack remained afloat. The bow, sticking straight up, was floating off to starboard. There was no panic among surviving crew members.

Stanley Dace, Chief Boiler's Mate, *Underhill*

bow and bridge, killing 113 crew members, including the ship's commanding officer. PC-803 and PC-804 rescued 125 survivors, and the remaining hulk was sunk by gunfire from PCE-872. *Underhill* was the last destroyer escort lost in World War II.

After delivering components for the atomic bombs to Tinian, the cruiser *Indianapolis* (CA 35) was torpedoed and sunk between Leyte and Guam on July 30, 1945, by the Japanese submarine I-58. Due to a series of communications breakdowns, the loss of the cruiser was not realized until August 2. Rescue aircraft and vessels were immediately dispatched, including *Bassett* (APD 73), the *John C. Butler*–class DEs *Alvin C. Cockrell* (DE 366), *French* (DE 367), *Cecil J. Doyle* (DE 368) and *Dufilho* (DE 423), and the *Crosley*-class transports *Register* (APD 92) and *Ringness* (APD 100). Of the 318 *Indianapolis*

On the morning of August 28, 1945, Lt. Cdr. E. P. Clayton, commanding officer of UDT 21, received the first sword surrendered to an American force on the Japanese home islands. The sword was presented by a Japanese army coast artillery major (*center,* wearing a white armband) on the Futtsu Saki Peninsula outside of Tokyo Bay. Lieutenant Commander Clayton is speaking to an interpreter. Note the characteristic .50–caliber machine guns mounted on the LCP(L)s, the radio whip antennas, and the American flags. UDT 21 had disembarked from *Burke* (APD 65). (NH 71599)

crew members who survived the ordeal (about one quarter of the cruiser's complement), 151 were rescued by *Bassett.*

Following the atomic bombing of Hiroshima (August 6) and Nagasaki (August 9), Japan finally agreed to the Potsdam Declaration on August 14, 1945, and Emperor Hirohito announced that Japan had ceased fighting. On August 22, the destroyer escort *Levy* (DE 162, *Cannon* class) accepted the surrender of Mili Atoll, Marshall Islands—the first Japanese garrison to capitulate in the wake of the emperor's broadcast. On August 26, *Currier* (DE 700) and *Osmus* (DE 701) accepted the surrender of the Japanese garrison on Rota, Mariana Islands, and on the morning of August 28, UDT 21 disembarked from *Burke* (APD 65) to the Futtsu Saki Peninsula outside of Tokyo Bay and received the first sword surrendered to an American force on the Japanese home islands.

On September 1, *Reeves* (APD 52) transported 149 prisoners of war, including Maj. Gregory "Pappy" Boyington and Cdr. Richard O'Kane, CO of the submarine *Tang* (SS 306), to the hospital ship *Benevolence* (AH 13). *Hollis* (APD 86), *Reeves,* and *Major* (DE 796) were present in Tokyo Bay on September 2, 1945, for the main Japanese surrender ceremony aboard the *Missouri* (BB 63). That same day, *George* and *Osmus* were present for the Japanese surrender on Truk Island, and on September 4, 1945, *Levy* presided over the return of Wake Island to U.S. Marine Corps forces, after almost four years of Japanese occupation.

Nearly one thousand British and American servicemen lost their lives while serving aboard *Buckley*-class ships in World War II. Six *Buckley* DEs were sunk due to enemy action (one of which was scuttled by its own task force after

Frybarger (DE 705) in September 1945, standing by to support the U.S. Marine landings at Chinwangtao, China. The occupation of the town was accomplished without resistance from the remaining 1,600 Japanese troops. An American military presence in several key areas of northern China served to counter any sudden communist Chinese movements in the wake of the Japanese surrender. The campaign served only as a delaying action, however, as the communist forces inexorably gained control of the mainland, forcing the United States to abandon its assistance to the nationalist Chinese. The flags on the LCVPs were used to coordinate and guide the landing craft to their designated beach locations. (80-G-349372)

losing its propellers to a torpedo) and twelve more were damaged beyond repair (see appendix E).

The Postwar Period

Following the war, a few *Buckley*-class DEs and APDs remained in the Far East or conducted brief tours of duty in the American occupation zone. Between October and December 1945, *Haines* (APD 84) and *Reeves* transported members of the Strategic Bombing Survey to several destinations in Japan for data collection. *Lee Fox* (APD 45), *Ira Jeffery* (APD 44), *Gantner* (APD 42), and *Blessman* all landed UDTs at various points in Japan to reconnoiter beaches prior to the full-scale United States occupation, while *George W. Ingram* (APD 43), *Laning* (APD 55), *Newman, Liddle, Kephart, Lloyd, Weber* (APD 75), and *Bunch* ferried occupation troops to Korea and China between September and November 1945. *Gantner* was part of the American presence in Chinese ports during the last phase

of the civil war between Nationalist and Communist forces, from February to April 1949.

Most DEs and APDs of all classes, however, were placed into the inactive reserve or disposed of by 1948. Immediately following hostilities, all but one of the forty-four *Buckley*-class ships loaned to Great Britain that survived the war (two had been sunk) were returned to the United States or, in the case of damaged ships, to U.S. custody, and sold to ship breakers. (The one exception, *Hotham*, remained in British possession to undergo an experimental refit with English Electric EL60A gas turbine engines in 1949, but these modifications did not proceed and *Hotham* was finally returned to the U.S. in 1956 for disposal.) Of the forty-five *Buckley*-class DEs and forty-one *Charles Lawrence*-class APDs placed into the U.S. reserve fleet after World War II, thirty-six of the DEs and thirty-five of the APDs were never recommissioned into the U.S. Navy. Sixteen of the APDs were eventually transferred to foreign countries, while the rest of

In early 1951, we had a five month overhaul in the Portsmouth navy yard where the bridge was cut down and all new guns and computerized control systems were installed. Our 5-inch/38s in the forward and aft turrets were not changed except for the fire control systems. The turbines, switch gear, boilers, etc. in the engineering spaces were completely overhauled also. We then went to Guantanamo Bay navy station for ten weeks of retraining. On the way down to Cuba we conducted all kinds of sea trials. On the way from Key West to Portsmouth [on the return trip] we conducted what was called a structural test run. We were steaming at five knots with all hands at general quarters when we dropped a depth charge from all depth charge tracks and from every K gun onboard. The depth charges were set shallow. Now I don't have to tell you that normally when dropping depth charges the ship is steaming at flank speed. I was at my general quarters station on the throttles in the after engine room. I was standing in front of a fresh air blower with my phones on and my hands on the throttles. When the depth charges exploded, the lights in the engine room were shattered, the glass in the steam gauges was blown out and the hands on the gauges vanished and all the rust in the blower came loose and hit me in the back. It was as if I had been shot with a shotgun. But we only had one leak and that was in the forward engine room on the port side of the ship. Of course it was hell trying to change speeds without hands on the steam gauges.

Charles Keys, Electrician's Mate, *Coolbaugh*

the ships were gradually sold off and scrapped or destroyed as military targets.

One active *Buckley* DE was accidentally lost on April 30, 1946. *Solar* (DE 221) was torn apart by a series of explosions that occurred while the ship was unloading its Hedgehog bombs and 40mm and 3-inch rounds at the Leonardo Pier I of the Naval Ammunition Depot in Earle, New Jersey. Seven crew members and 158 dockworkers were killed in the blast, and sixty-five others were wounded. The DE's hulk was scuttled on June 9, 1946, about 100 miles east of New York City.

Twelve *Buckley*-class ships were the only DEs that remained in active commission by the end of 1948. The group consisted of two TEGs (59 and 699), one DER (213), six 5-inch TEs (217, 679, 696, 697, 698, and 700) and three 3-inch TEs (220, 791, and 800). These ships ended averaging more than thirteen and a half years of post–World War II active service. *Buckley*-class DEs were chosen for the active fleet because of the preference for steam turbine driven ships over diesel-powered varieties and the generally favorable review of the open bridge compared to the enclosed bridge of the other steam turbine classes. The advantages of the high, open conning position diminished, however, with the increased reliance on electronic sensors. The control of the ship shifted to the CIC (combat information center), bringing the CO and helm in closer proximity. Some *Buckley*-class ships did end up having their bridges cut down and enclosed in the ensuing decade. But by the time the Korean War began in 1950, all but one of the 5-inch *Buckley*-class ships had been replaced as first-line escorts in favor of recommissioned *John C. Butler*–class ships. The *John C. Butler* class was a more recent DE design that incorporated a 5-inch main battery and enclosed bridge from the start and had a slightly more powerful and efficient geared drive compared to the *Buckley*-class turboelectric power plant.

Another valuable use for DEs emerged after World War II and took on greater significance in the 1950s: that of training naval reservists. *Weeden* (DE 797), one of the first ships selected for this duty, served as a naval reserve training ship with the 11th Naval District, San Diego, from November 1946 until November 1957. Eventually, eleven more *Buckley*-class DEs and three *Charles Lawrence*–class APDs, along with seven *Cannon*, three *Edsall*, six *Rudderow*, seven *Crosley*, and twenty-six *John C. Butler*–class ships participated in this important service between 1950 and 1969. Thousands of American reserve servicemen learned seamanship and ASW tactics aboard these vessels.

The Korean War

The Korean War erupted in June 1950, and ninety DEs and APDs were recommissioned into active service over the course of the three-year

Foss (DE 59) at anchor at Hungnam, Korea, December 1950. *Foss* was "wired in" to provide electrical power for the port facilities during the evacuation of the Tenth Corps. (Courtesy, Mr. K. White)

conflict. Seventeen DEs (six *Buckley* class, eleven *John C. Butler* class) and five APDs (all *Crosley* class) served in Korea, while the remaining commissioned ships conducted training exercises and patrolled U.S. and international waters.

Conditions during the Korean War were quite different from those of World War II because there was almost no naval opposition, nor was any expected. Most of the ships assigned to the United Nations forces focused on keeping the seas secure around the Korean Peninsula and providing support to troops ashore with gunfire and carrier strikes. Mines and coastal batteries were the primary enemies. Amphibious operations such as the Inchon landing drew upon World War II experience, but the massive evacuation of the 10th Corps from Hungnam in December 1950 had no World War II precedent.

The Korean War did not require the services of the general DE, since supply convoys were not threatened and there was no significant submarine opposition. In addition, with the advent of jets, the antiaircraft weapons carried aboard DEs became obsolete. Two variants of the destroyer escort, however—the floating power supply ships (TEGs) and the high-speed transports—were well suited to the littoral nature of the Korean sea war. Both types were integral to amphibious operations and were deployed immediately: *Marsh*, a power supply unit, was the first DE and *Horace A. Bass* (APD 124, *Crosley* class) was the first APD to enter the war zone. The remaining three *Buckley*-class TEGs—*Foss* (DE 59), *Whitehurst*, and *Wiseman* (DE 667)— saw considerable service in Korea, as did *Currier*, the only 5-inch-armed *Buckley*-class ship to fire its guns in anger, and *Vammen* (DE 644).

The four TEGs were deployed along the Korean Peninsula at various locations, which shifted with the exigencies of the war. *Marsh*

The First Marine Division had been cut off and surrounded by Chinese troops and they were battling to reach the coast in the area of Hungnam. Our mission was to go to Hungnam and provide electricity to the evacuation port. As we proceeded south at night through a maze of small islands, the weather was bitterly cold. I recall that, enroute to Hungnam, I came off the bridge with about four inches of snow on my shoulders. Upon reaching the harbor at Hungnam, we were ordered to moor alongside a very fine wharf which extended along the waterfront. During this period, Lt. Gen. [Edward M.] Almond, commander of Xth Corps, had his headquarters "across the street from *Foss*." General Almond and some of his staff, with khaki colored towels across their arms, would come over for a welcomed opportunity to take a hot shower. While we were moored, the cruiser *St. Paul* [CA 73] came in and anchored. She fired salvo after salvo over us into the hills. We could see aircraft from our carriers off Hungnam, diving down into the hills in the distance, strafing and bombing enemy troops pursuing the marines. After weeks of fighting the frigid cold, the mountainous terrain, and the hordes of Chinese troops, the marines made it to Hungnam, with the bodies of their fallen comrades lashed to their vehicles and tanks. The marines were transported from the beach to waiting transports. About December 23rd or 24th, army engineers went along the dock and with a telephone-type auger drilled holes in the wharf every 100 feet or so. (We later learned that these holes were filled with explosives.) On December 25th, we once again reeled in our electrical line, pulled away from the dock, and headed out to sea where we formed up with other ships constituting the evacuation fleet.

Lt. (jg) Kimber L. White, Executive Officer, *Foss*

supplied ship-to-shore power at Pusan and Masan between September 1950 and March 1951. *Foss* supplied power to shore installations at Chinnampo, Inchon, Hungnam, and Ulsan Man and also assisted in the transport of army troops from Chinnampo to Inchon (December 4–6, 1950) and marines from Hungnam to Pusan (December 9–24, 1950). *Wiseman* supplied electrical power to the city of Masan for ten months, from November 1950 to August 1951. But these power supply vessels were still warships: On October 2, 1952, during its second tour of duty,

Marsh, along with HMCS *Iroquois*, destroyed a shore battery in the vicinity of Songjin, Korea, which had damaged the Canadian destroyer. On February 18, 1953, also on its second tour of duty, *Wiseman* captured five North Koreans off Chongjin and destroyed their sampan.

Currier used its 5-inch guns on July 3–4, 1952, to provide counter-battery fire that allowed the mine sweepers *Current* (ARS 22), *Zeal* (AM 131), and *Symbol* (AM 123) to escape harm from land-based guns along the eastern shore of North Korea. *Vammen* conducted two tours of duty in 1952, patrolling off the port of Wousan. No *Buckley*-class vessels were damaged during the war, but three *John C. Butler* DEs were hit by shore batteries that killed crew members on two of the ships.

Final Disposition

With a truce declared in Korea in July 1953, and the fighting suspended, most DEs and APDs were decommissioned or returned to their role as naval reserve training ships. The most important program involving DEs during the mid-1950s and early 1960s was the conversion of thirty-six reserve DEs into radar pickets (DERs) for duty along the distant early warning (DEW) line, but no *Buckley*-class vessels took part in this program.

The few *Buckley*-class and *Charles Lawrence*-class units that remained in active service into the 1950s and early 1960s were called upon for various assignments, as when *Bassett* was sent to aid flood victims around Tampico, Mexico, in the aftermath of Hurricane Janet in October 1955.

The Berlin Crisis of 1961–62 was the last time DEs and APDs were recommissioned in numbers. Twenty-one DEs and three APDs were recommissioned during this period, including the *Buckley*-class DEs 218, 219, 634, 644, 667, 679, 680, and 699, and the *Charles Lawrence*-class APD 60. The crisis occurred when the Soviet Union began building a wall between East and West Berlin in August 1961 and threatened to sign a separate treaty with East Germany in its attempt to retain a buffer between Western and Eastern Europe. Presi-

Eichenberger (DE 202) mothballed at Stockton, California, in October 1972, more than twenty-six years after it decommissioned. The ship's long period in the inactive reserve would end two months later when the ship was struck from the U.S. Navy Register. *Eichenberger* was sold for scrap in November 1973. More than two hundred other DEs and APDs were similarly preserved after World War II and never recommissioned, and all were eventually sold, scrapped, or used as targets. *Eichenberger* has been stripped of all its armament and electronics except for the 3-inch main battery, which has been sealed under protective dehumidifying domes. Mothballed ships were periodically inspected and repainted. An unidentified APD with a stub mainmast is inboard. (Courtesy, The Mariners' Museum, Newport News, Virginia, Ted Stone Collection)

dent John F. Kennedy decided to de-emphasize the threat of nuclear retaliation and instead ordered the activation of conventional military forces, including reserve army, air force, and navy units. Kennedy felt a conventional military response in conjunction with negotiations would create the atmosphere for resolution. Some of the tension was diffused, but the crisis would come to a head in October 1962 when the Soviet Union attempted to arm Cuba with nuclear missile sites. DEs and APDs patrolled extensively around Cuba during this period.

Two escort divisions of *Buckley-* and *John C. Butler*–class DEs that had been recommissioned during the Berlin Crisis (CortDivs 71 and 72)

were ordered to Vietnam in early 1962 and conducted training exercises with the nascent South Vietnamese navy for several months. These were the last two DE escort divisions deployed.[18]

The final *Buckley*-class DE to decommission was *Maloy* on June 1, 1965. *Maloy* had the longest continuous active service of any destroyer escort, remaining in commission for twenty-one years, five months, and fifteen days, primarily as a platform for sonar experiments. The final *Charles Lawrence* APD to decommis-

18. CortDiv 71: *Walton* (DE 361), *McGinty* (DE 365), *Edmonds* (DE 406), *Whitehurst** (DE 634); CortDiv 72: *Alvin C. Cockrell* (DE 366), *Charles E. Brannon* (DE 446), *Vammen** (DE 644), *Wiseman** (DE 667), *Marsh** (DE 699). **Buckley* class.

The Mexican frigate *Coahuila* (B 07) in July 1993. The ship—the former high-speed transport *Barber* (APD 57)—was renamed *Vincento Guerro* in 1994 and was still serving as a training vessel for cadets in 1998. The ship was mothballed in May 1946 at Green Cove Springs, Florida, where it remained until purchased by Mexico more than two decades later, in February 1969. It has now served the Mexican nation for nearly thirty years. The ship is virtually unchanged from its final World War II appearance: it would be worthwhile to preserve this ship, the last of the great *Buckley* class and possibly the only World War II–era high-speed transport afloat. (Courtesy, Leo Van Ginderen)

sion from active service was *Liddle* on March 18, 1967. A few *Buckley*-class ships remained in service in reserve as training ships until 1971. *Gunason* (DE 795), placed in the inactive reserve in 1948, was the last World War II destroyer escort still classified as a DE on the United States Navy register; it was struck on September 1, 1973, and subsequently destroyed as a missile target.

There are no *Buckley*-class DEs in existence today. One *Charles Lawrence* APD (ex–APD 57) is still in foreign service (Mexico's training ship *Vincento Guerro*, E-21), although it may no longer be active. The only surviving examples of

destroyer escorts in the United States are two museum ships: *Slater* (DE 766, *Cannon* class) in Albany, New York, and *Stewart* (DE 238, *Edsall* class) in Galveston, Texas. A *Cannon*-class DE loaned to Brazil during World War II, *Bauru* (Be-4, the former *McAnn* DE 179), is also preserved as a museum exhibit. In addition, two *Cannon*-class, three *Edsall*-class, and four *Crosley*-class APDs are still listed on foreign naval registers (1998). However, most of these ships are probably now out of service and are slated for disposal. Like the *Buckley*-class DE, no example of the *Evarts*, *Rudderow*, or *John C. Butler* class remains.

Part Two

PICTORIAL HISTORY

5   *The Photographic Record*

All 154 *Buckley*-class DEs are presented below in ascending order of hull numbers, beginning with *Buckley* (DE 51) and ending with *Jack W. Wilke* (DE 800). Ships loaned to Great Britain are listed in proper order but with the Royal Navy pennant numbers beside their names, followed by the original United States Navy hull numbers in parentheses.

Each entry consists of the ship's name, designation and hull number, other designations and numbers if a ship was reclassified, its former name and number (when applicable), its nickname (when known), a statement of the ship's namesake, and a photograph and explanatory caption. Camouflage patterns and colors are discussed, but the analysis in some instances is limited or open to interpretation due to the difficulty of drawing conclusions from black-and-white photographs; this is particularly true with British camouflage schemes, since they exhibited a greater variety of colors and patterns than American warships.

Photographs credited as 19-N, 19-LCM, BS, 80-G, and 428-N are official United States Navy photographs held at the Still Picture Branch (NNSP), National Archives. Those marked with 80-G and 428-N are from the Department of Navy, while those beginning with 19-N, 19-LCM, and BS are from the former Bureau of Ships (BuShips). Photographs identified with the prefix NH are held at the Navy Historical Center, Washington Navy Yard. The prefix IWM indicates the photograph is the property of the Imperial War Museum, London, and includes photographs previously held by the Ministry of Defence (MoD). NMM identifies photographs held at the National Maritime Museum, Greenwich, England. All other photographs are credited to the collection or the name of the individual owner.

The photographs, both official and nonofficial, vary in quality. Negatives for several photographs in the United States National Archives have been lost, and prints had to be duplicated from existing exposures, while a few negatives in the collection are in poor shape due to age and rough handling over the years. In many of these cases, an effort has been made to reproduce the photographs as clearly as possible, eliminating scratches, fingerprints, and blotches electronically. This may be the last time some of these photographs will be reproduced from the original negatives, since it may not be possible to arrest their steady deterioration.

Photographs have been selected to show different views and time periods. In some cases, a poorer quality photograph was chosen over a better one because of the former's historical interest; in a few instances, the photograph is the only known picture of a particular ship.

Buckley DE 51 DER 51

Named for: Aviation Ordnanceman John Daniel Buckley, killed December 7, 1941, at Kaneohe Bay, Oahu, Hawaii

Buckley as commissioned in April 1943. The ship is built to the original class specifications that called for portholes on either side of the sound room, a 40mm twin mount in the X position, and only four 20mm gun positions—two forward of the pilothouse and two in tubs on either side of the aft fire room uptake. The ship also lacks observation posts at the forward corners of the flying bridge. The blast shield for the Hedgehog is visible immediately aft of the number one gun and the torpedo handling crane is amidships, just forward of the director station. By June, four more 20mm guns would be added, two in sponsons on either side of the bridge at the 01 level and two in tubs abreast the stack, raised and forward of the original gun positions. Observation posts were also added to the bridge and the sound room portholes were covered over. All U.S. Navy *Buckley*-class ships commissioned before July 1943 were retrofitted to include the full battery of 20mm guns and the alterations to the bridge structure. A censor has removed the SA and SL radars from the mast in the photograph. *Buckley* is wearing Measure 22, a common wartime camouflage scheme of navy blue and haze gray introduced in June 1942. The designation "DE" was originally painted before the hull number at the shipyard and removed soon after the ship finished its trials and entered fleet service, but by early 1944 this convention lapsed and only the hull number appeared on newly built ships. *Buckley* was allocated for conversion into a DER on May 14, 1945, and the conversion was completed in October 1945 at the New York Navy Yard. (80-G-44378)

Bentinck K 314 (ex-*Bull* DE 52)

Named for: Capt. William Count Bentinck (1764–1813), commanded *Phaeton* during The Glorious First of June

Bentinck, the first *Buckley*-class DE transferred to Great Britain, oiling at Lisahally, Northern Ireland, on September 23, 1943, before proceeding to Greenock, Scotland, to undergo light repairs and Admiralty-sanctioned modifications. *Bentinck*, like the original *Buckley*, has portholes in the sound room, no observation posts at the forward corners of the open bridge, and only four 20mm guns (two forward of the pilothouse and two in tubs on either side of the aft fire room uptake). A crow's nest has been fitted above the yard, just beneath the prominent SL radome. An FH4 HF/DF antenna has also been substituted for the SA radar at the masthead. The camouflage scheme is a Western Approaches pattern of pale blue fields over a white background. Most Captains-class ships left the United States with a variation of this camouflage (which appears to have been designed specifically for the Captains class), although the pattern was usually changed after arriving in the United Kingdom in favor of simplified or disruptive schemes, or the Admiralty standard pattern adopted in 1944 (examples are noted below). *Bentinck* served the SO (senior officer) of the 4th EG. *Bentinck* began conversion into a fighter director ship for the British Pacific Fleet at Belfast on June 25, 1945, but the conversion was canceled on August 23, 1945, due to the end of the war and left incomplete. (IWM A19460)

Charles Lawrence DE 53 APD 37

Named for: Aviation Motor Machinist's Mate 2/C Charles Lawrence, killed December 7, 1941, at Kaneohe Bay, Oahu, Hawaii

Charles Lawrence, following its conversion into an APD in mid-January 1945. Even though *Charles Lawrence* was the namesake of the new class of high-speed transport, photographs of the ship as an APD are rare. A single 5-inch/38 enclosed base-ring mount and a 40mm Mk1 twin mount with Mk51 director have replaced the two 3-inch/50s and Hedgehog apparatus forward of the bridge. The superstructure sides have been moved outboard, flush with the hull to make room for the extra troops and equipment. Davits holding four LCVPs and a lattice cargo derrick have been added aft of the stack. Two 40mm Mk1 twin mounts are on either side of the derrick. All K-guns have been removed, but the depth charge tracks remain on the stern. The conversion of a DE into an APD took about ten weeks. *Charles Lawrence* was flagship for CortDiv 6, the first American escort division composed entirely of DEs to cross the Atlantic. (Courtesy, Mr. G. Stewart)

Daniel T. Griffin DE 54 APD 38
The Danny T

Named for: Aviation Machinist's Mate 1/C Daniel Thornburg Griffin, killed December 7, 1941, at Kaneohe Bay, Oahu, Hawaii

An overhead shot of *Daniel T. Griffin* off the New York Naval Air Station on April 17, 1944. The layout of DE armament and equipment is clearly shown, including the lookout stations and rounded observation posts on either side of the open bridge, the four 20mm gun tubs abreast the aft uptake, the triple torpedo tube bank amidships (with one torpedo withdrawn), the 1.1-inch quad machine gun in the X position, and the eight K-guns with their ready service racks outboard along the aft end of the ship. Two 20mm guns have been added in a gallery forward of the depth charge tracks. This was a common refit for DEs, and by March 1944, it was incorporated into the *Buckley*-class design. A similar stern 20mm gallery was part of the design of the last two DE classes, *Rudderow* and *John C. Butler. Daniel T. Griffin* was transferred to Chile in November 1966 and operated as a training vessel until 1993, when it was taken out of service and discarded. (80-G-224739)

Byard K 315 (ex-*Donaldson* DE 55)

Named for: Capt. Sir Thomas Byard, commanded *Windsor Castle* at Toulon (1793)

Byard sliding down the ways on a snowy March 6, 1943, at the Bethlehem-Hingham shipyard. DE 55 was originally assigned the name *Donaldson*, which was canceled and reassigned to another DE on April 26, 1943, when it was decided that a number of *Buckley*-class DEs under construction or scheduled to be laid down in spring 1943 would be transferred to Great Britain in place of the majority of their original fifty-ship order, which had been taken over by the U.S. Navy and renamed the *Evarts* class. Note the prefix "BDE" now painted before the hull number. A photograph of *Byard* in service has yet to be located by the author. The only wartime photograph found so far that is purported to be *Byard* is actually a shot of *Hotham* (K 583) with *Byard*'s hull number added to the print. The same shot was used to represent various *Buckley*-type Captains-class ships with the simple manipulation of the hull number, and these photographs were distributed at the end of the war to crew members as keepsakes. During the summer of 1945, *Byard* was converted into a Coastal Forces control ship for the East Indies Fleet but did not steam to the Pacific due to the end of the war. (19-N-81621)

Donnell DE 56 IX 182

Named for: USS *Enterprise* pilot Ens. Earl Roe Donnell, Jr., killed February 1, 1942, near the Marshall Islands

"I can still see her, dead in the water, her after-end curled like a scorpion's tail, up and toward the 1.1 guns."—A. J. Petty, radioman, *Daniel T. Griffin*. *Donnell* as damaged by a T5 acoustic torpedo fired from U-765 on May 3, 1944, 280 miles southwest of Cape Clear, Ireland. Twenty-nine crew members were killed and twenty-five were wounded. The Germans introduced the T5 (*Zaunkonig*) acoustic torpedo in September 1943. It was designed specifically to attack the convoy escort by homing in on the sound of the ship's propellers. Once the escort screen was broken, the U-boat would have clear access to the merchant ships. The T5 was limited to a speed of about 25 knots so that its own noise would not interfere with the sound detection mechanism, which meant that it could be evaded by faster ships. On the other hand, the torpedo could not acquire a target traveling under 10 knots due to the lack of sufficient noise at those speeds. Effective countermeasures were quickly introduced, such as Foxer and FXR, which consisted of clanging metal rods towed by the ship in order to produce a sound louder than the ship's propellers, and the similar CAT (Canadian anti-acoustic torpedo) device. If a T5 struck an escort, the results were often devastating: Of sixteen DEs hit, eight were sunk outright and a ninth was scuttled at the scene. The T5, however, suffered from mechanical unreliability; this, combined with countermeasures, reduced the success rate of the weapon to an unsatisfactory level. After it was hit, *Donnell* was towed into Dunnstaffnage Bay, Oban, Scotland, arriving May 12, 1944. *Donnell* served as an accommodations ship at Lisahally, Northern Ireland, until being reclassified IX 182 on July 15, 1944. The former DE was then towed to Plymouth, and in August, to Cherbourg, France, where it was installed as an offshore electric generator. In February 1945, *Donnell* was taken back to England and then towed to the United States, arriving at the Philadelphia Navy Yard on July 18, 1945, for disposal. (Courtesy, Mr. L. Grasek)

Fogg DE 57 DER 57

Named for: USS *Enterprise* pilot Lt. (jg) Carleton Thayer Fogg, killed February 1, 1942, near Kwajalein

Fogg at Boston Harbor, May 12, 1945, with a new stern and heavily modified armament. *Fogg* was the first *Buckley*-class ship to be rearmed with 5-inch guns. *Fogg* was hit with a T5 torpedo on December 20, 1944, about 700 miles northeast of the Azores. The torpedo tore off the stern aft of frame 125, killing fifteen crew members. As reconstructed, two 5-inch/38 Mk30/69 single enclosed mounts have replaced *Fogg*'s number one and number three 3-inch guns. The Hedgehog is now in the number two position, flanked by two 40mm single guns in extended sponsons. Two 40mm twin mounts and six 20mm guns are amidships, while a 40mm quad has been added in the X position. A stub mainmast has been added to support the HF/DF antenna and the K-guns have been moved forward to accommodate the 5-inch gun near the stern. SU surface-search radar has replaced the SL above the yard on the foremast and a Mk52 director has been added on top of the bridge. While undergoing these repairs, *Fogg* was allocated for conversion into a DER, which was accomplished at the Philadelphia Navy Yard between June and October 1945. (BS 120973)

Calder K 349
(ex-*Formoe* DE 58)

Named for: Adm. Sir Robert Calder (1745–1818), commanded *Prince of Wales* at Calder's Action

Calder off Belfast in November 1943, with its guns trained toward the camera, wearing the Captains-class Western Approaches camouflage pattern. The frigate has additional life rafts amidships, a 40mm twin mount in the X position, extra depth charge racks outboard toward the stern, and a crow's nest above the yard. *Calder* came equipped with a torpedo crane (just visible at this angle in front of the X position director station), even though *Calder*, like all Captains-class frigates, never carried torpedo tubes. *Calder* was one of only eight *Buckley* DEs transferred to Great Britain with a 40mm twin mount fitted. Note the porthole at the side of the sound room and lack of observation posts at the forward edge of the open bridge. The mast supports an HF/DF antenna, SL radome, and TBS antenna on the port side of the yard. *Calder* was converted into a Coastal Forces control frigate for the East Indies Fleet at Belfast between May and July 1945, but its orders to proceed to the Pacific were canceled in August. (IWM FL 7395)

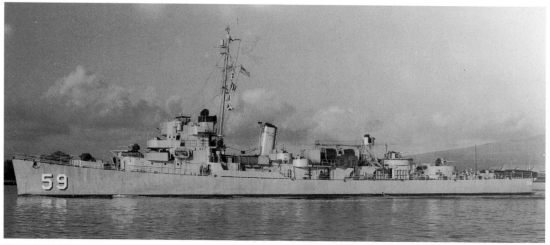

Foss DE 59

Named for: Ens. Rodney Shelton Foss, killed December 7, 1941, at Kaneohe Bay, Oahu, Hawaii

Foss on January 20, 1953, at Pearl Harbor. A transformer and cable reels have replaced the 40mm battery amidships that had, in turn, replaced the torpedo mount during World War II. The ship still has all of the 20mm positions it had as an escort, although they are now Mk24 twin mounts instead of the original single guns. The X position director station is raised to clear the cable reels, and a Mk52 director is under cover atop the bridge. *Foss* is painted in Measure 13, haze gray overall (this measure would be renamed US 27 in March 1953). (80-G-630973)

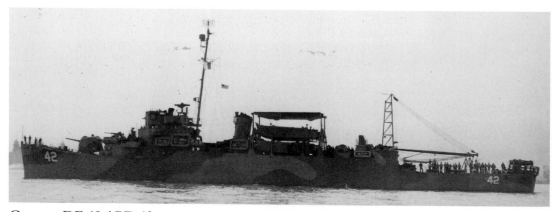

Gantner DE 60 APD 42

Named for: Boatswain's Mate Samuel Merritt Gantner, killed December 7, 1941, aboard the USS *Nevada*

Gantner preparing to depart the New York Navy Yard for amphibious warfare training in the Chesapeake Bay on May 13, 1945, following its conversion into a high-speed transport. Like the majority of *Buckley*-class ships selected to be converted into APDs, *Gantner* first served as an Atlantic convoy escort. The ship is wearing a Measure 31 pattern of large irregular patches of dark and lighter green hues. Hull numbers on APDs began to be painted larger and in white by early 1945, compared to the small, usually subdued, hull numbers on the first APDs deployed in the Philippines in late 1944 (see *Bates*, below). *Gantner* retains the fire control and radar systems it carried as a DE, with an optical range finder and Mk51 director atop the bridge and SL and SA on the mast. Each of the three 40mm Mk1 twin mounts—one forward of the bridge and two abreast the derrick aft—are equipped with a Mk51 director. *Gantner* arrived at Japan within days of the formal surrender ceremony and operated in Japanese waters for several weeks before returning to the United States. The transport deployed to the Far East for a second time in 1949, when it took station at various ports along the coast of China at the end of the Chinese Civil War, in support of retreating Nationalist Chinese forces. (19-N-85814)

Duckworth K 351 (ex-*Gary* DE 61)

Named for: Adm. Sir John Thomas Duckworth (1748–1817), commanded *Orion* during The Glorious First of June

Duckworth at Belfast on April 11, 1945. *Duckworth* served the SO of the 3rd EG; the black band around the top of the funnel indicates the SO's ship, while the four red and five white squares below the band is the insignia of the 3rd EG, adapted from the signal flag for the number three. The insignia is also on the Jolly Roger hoisted next to the SL radome, which denoted a successful attack on a U-boat. *Duckworth* exhibits several Captains-class alterations, including an oiling bumper on the edge of the hull near the bow and a spray shield with illumination rocket rails on the number two gun. The mast supports an HF/DF aerial on top, a Type 244 IFF antenna immediately below, an SL radome, and a crow's nest. *Duckworth* has extra life rafts stowed amidships on racks and a 40mm twin gun in the X position. The ship's bridge has retained the original *Buckley*-class porthole layout, with two portholes on either side of the sound room and three in front of the pilothouse, although observation posts, like those found on ships that were refitted to the later design standard, have been added to the forward edge of the open bridge. On most early units that were refitted, the portholes on the sound room were covered over at the same time that the observation posts were installed, and two more portholes were added in front of the pilothouse. The ship is painted in the standard pattern camouflage adopted in 1944 of overall light or medium gray with a light or dark sea blue panel amidships, depending on the season. The black boot topping was also reintroduced with this pattern. *Duckworth*'s scheme appears to be the winter variation, which used the lighter shades of gray and sea blue. *Duckworth* was converted into a Coastal Forces control ship for the East Indies Fleet at Belfast from June to August 1945, but its orders to the Pacific were canceled. (IWM A28186)

George W. Ingram DE 62 APD 43

Named for: Seaman 2/C George Washington Ingram, killed December 7, 1941, at Kaneohe Bay, Oahu, Hawaii

George W. Ingram off New York City on July 22, 1944, following its fifth round-trip transatlantic convoy escort. Prior to its fourth voyage, the DE had its torpedo tubes replaced with four 40mm Army-type Mk3 single guns. The replacement of the torpedo tube battery with 40mm single guns was the most significant AA refit to Atlantic Fleet DEs. These weapons were manually operated; therefore, pipe guards were added around each tub so that crews could not inadvertently train the guns into the ship while following a target. *George W. Ingram* is the quintessential World War II Atlantic escort: an HF/DF antenna atop the mast, numerous automatic AA guns along the compact superstructure, a heavy battery of depth charges, Hedgehog, and smoke generators at the fantail. The rafts outboard of the bridge and the X position director station were designed to slide into the water in the event the ship was sinking. The original negative for this photograph, like the one for *Ira Jeffery* below, is deteriorating with age, resulting in a loss of contrast between the sky, ship, and the sea. (80-G-235917)

Ira Jeffery DE 63 APD 44
The Ira J
Named for: Ens. Ira Weil Jeffery, killed December 7, 1941, aboard the USS *California*

A view above *Ira Jeffery*'s bow on July 22, 1944, in the same formation with *George W. Ingram*, above, following CortDiv 12's fifth round-trip transatlantic voyage. Four 40mm Mk3 single guns have replaced the torpedo tubes, and two 20mm guns have been added to the stern. The portholes on either side of the sound room have been removed, but *Ira Jeffery* retains the original *Buckley*-class design's three portholes in front of the pilothouse, later expanded into five. Each sky lookout station on either side of the open bridge contained two crew positions, one to scan the sky and one to scan the horizon; it was critical for the lookouts to be disciplined so that no area around the ship was without a pair of eyes. High-powered binoculars and alidades were available to each lookout. (80-G-235858)

Duff K 352 (ex-*Lamons* DE 64)
Figgy; The Plum Pudding Cruiser; Pudding Class Cruiser
Named for: Capt. George Duff (1764–1805), commanded *Mars* at Trafalgar

Duff, probably at Portsmouth in the summer of 1944. Although this picture—one of the few wartime photographs of *Duff*—is rather blurry, a MkVIII 2-pounder with spray shield is visible on the bow, a 40mm twin mount is in the X position, and extra depth charge racks are outboard along the quarterdeck. The mast supports an HF/DF antenna on top, an SL radome, and a crow's nest. *Duff* is wearing an intermediate-tone Admiralty disruptive pattern of dark gray, sea blue, and light gray that was designed for use in the English Channel. *Duff*'s nicknames are references to "figgy duff," a steamed suet pudding with figs. (NMM N22104)

Lee Fox DE 65 APD 45

Named for: Ens. Lee Fox, killed December 7, 1941, at Kaneohe Bay, Oahu, Hawaii

Lee Fox in 1944, wearing camouflage Measure 32/3D, the initial dazzle pattern authorized for Atlantic Fleet DEs. The pipe guards are quite prominent around the 40mm gun tubs added amidships. The MF/DF loop antenna is on a ledge just aft of the bridge and mast. This direction-finder loop, which can be seen on most American DEs, was used to verify the ship's position by triangulating the signals from two fixed transmitters, a precursor to the LORAN system established during the war. (80-G-1175145)

Amesbury DE 66 APD 46

Named for: USS *Ranger* pilot Lt. Stanton Morgan Amesbury, killed November 9, 1942, over North Africa

Amesbury in an undated photograph, but possibly September 4, 1945, when the ship made a stop at Okinawa before continuing on to Korea. This may be the only photograph of *Amesbury* in service. The ship is at anchor and is taking on supplies. All of its LCVPs have been released, with one LCVP standing by along the aft end of the ship. The cranes are in operation with a large load on the stern. *Amesbury* carried occupation troops to Korea and China in September and early October 1945. (Courtesy, Mr. J. Rettke)

Essington K 353 (ex–DE 67)

Named for: Capt. William Essington (1753–1816), commanded *Triumph* at Camperdown

Essington at Belfast in January 1944, with its guns trained to port. *Essington* is equipped with a 40mm twin mount in the X position. The ship is painted in the intermediate simplified pattern of overall gray-green, although the former Western Approaches camouflage is still visible underneath. The 3rd EG insignia is emblazoned on the funnel. Admiralty alterations include the 27-foot whaler added portside, depth charge stowage outboard along the stern, davits adjacent to the K-guns, and a crow's nest fitted below the SL radome on the mast. *Essington* has an SA aerial at the masthead, while most Captains-class frigates substituted an HF/DF antenna for this radar. *Essington* was converted into a Coastal Forces control ship for the East Indies Fleet at Belfast from May to July 1945, but did not proceed to the Pacific due to the end of the war. (IWM FL 11758)

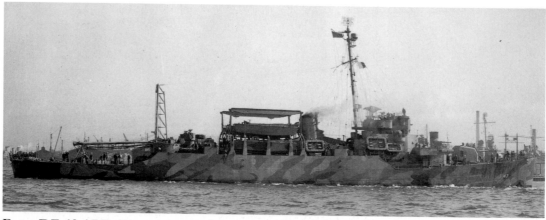

Bates DE 68 APD 47

Named for: Ens. Edward M. Bates, killed December 7, 1941, aboard the USS *Arizona*

Bates at the New York Navy Yard on October 28, 1944, following its conversion into an APD. *Bates* is painted Measure 31/20L, designed specifically for DE high-speed transports. The application of this mottled pattern of greens, brown, and black varied between ships; a concurrent pattern used much larger irregular areas of greens and brown. *Bates* has retained its SA air-search antenna on top of the mast and the SL surface-search radome immediately below. The hull sides of the APD were extended upward and outboard amidships to increase the internal volume of the ship. The cargo derrick's lattice kingpost was a distinctive feature of the *Charles Lawrence* class. Two 40mm twin mounts and their directors are on either side of the derrick, and four LCVPs with davits are amidships. During a frenzied attack on May 25, 1945, off Ie Shima, Okinawa, *Bates* was severely damaged by several aerial bombs and a kamikaze. The burning ship was towed to a safe anchorage by *Cree* (ATF 84), but it continued to burn until it eventually capsized and sank. In 1957, *Bates*'s hulk, along with other sunken wrecks around Okinawa, was donated to the government of the Ryukyu Islands for their maintenance or disposal. (BS 74100)

Blessman DE 69 APD 48

Named for: USS *Marblehead* pilot Lt. Edward Martin Blessman, killed February 4, 1942, during the Battle of the Java Sea

Blessman leaving Mare Island Navy Yard on August 4, 1945, following battle repairs and conversion into the flagship for UDRon 1 (Underwater Demolition Squadron One). A short communications mainmast has replaced the original lattice cargo derrick aft of the LCVP davits, and a 40mm quad has been added to the stern. *Blessman* was scheduled to receive an SU radar set but none was available; therefore, the original SL was retained. *Blessman* is painted Measure 21, overall navy blue. By early 1945, as American forces moved toward Japan, Measure 21 became a more common paint scheme for APDs, replacing the mottled Measure 31 jungle camouflage patterns that had been used during the initial destroyer escort APD deployment around the Philippine Islands. Three Japanese aircraft are painted on the side of *Blessman*'s bridge as a reminder of the action it had already seen. *Blessman* was sold to Taiwan on July 3, 1967, where the ship operated as a customs service patrol ship until it was struck in May 1995. (19-N-88316)

Joseph E. Campbell DE 70 APD 49

Named for: Ens. Joseph Eugene Campbell, pilot, killed August 9, 1942, in the Pacific

Joseph E. Campbell on June 3, 1944, wearing Measure 32/3D. The arrangement of the DE's heavy depth charge battery is visible toward the stern. Alterations to *Joseph E. Campbell* include a 20mm gallery added forward of the depth charge tracks, four single 40mm gun tubs fitted amidships, and a stub mainmast carrying an HF/DF antenna. The replacement of the torpedo bank with 40mm guns was an excellent solution to increasing the antiaircraft firepower of the DE within the constraints of the ship's compact upper deck, although two 40mm twin mounts with directors, when available, were preferred to the four single guns. Pacific Fleet *Buckley*-class DEs, however, did not have their torpedo tubes replaced with 40mm guns despite the heavy presence of enemy aircraft in this theater. (80-G-233053)

Affleck K 462
(ex-*Oswald* DE 71)

Named for: Adm. Sir Edmund Affleck (1723–88), commanded *Bedford* during the American War of Independence

Affleck in October 1943, during its work-up in Bermuda. There are no Admiralty alterations evident, except for the FH4 HF/DF antenna at the masthead. It is not likely that the paint on *Affleck*'s hull has been badly scoured; instead, it appears that a fake bow wave has been added to the Western Approaches camouflage scheme, perhaps for trial purposes. Reports from several former Captains-class crew members indicate that fake bow waves were added to the hulls of their ships during wartime. Black smoke resulted from incomplete combustion due to too little air in the air/fuel oil mixture and was usually avoided except in the few instances when a heavy smoke screen was requested. Black smoke could be produced in several circumstances: new crews learning to balance the air and fuel oil mixture; a sudden request for speed; a change between firing off one boiler and firing up the other when the ship was running on one boiler; or a ship blowing its tubes to clean soot from the updraft, something it needed to do every four or five days, usually at night if in a war zone. *Affleck* would eventually serve the SO of the 1st EG and receive a dark band around the top of its funnel. Note the empty X position and its director station. *Affleck* was eventually sold to a Portuguese company in 1947 and renamed *Nostra Senora de la Luz*. The ship was used as a mercantile hulk and power supply station at Tenerife, Canary Islands, and continued to provide electricity to the shore establishment for several decades. (Courtesy, Mr. K. R. Macpherson)

Aylmer K 463 (ex-*Harmon* DE 72)

Named for: Adm. Lord Matthew Aylmer (d. 1720), commanded *Royal Katherine* at the Battle of Beachy Head

Aylmer at speed in the Mediterranean, December 1944. The dark band on the top of the funnel indicates the SO of the 5th EG. *Aylmer*'s captain became the senior officer following the loss of *Bickerton* (K 466) in August 1944. *Aylmer* has many Admiralty alterations, including the 27-foot whaler on the port side, a crow's nest (note the lookout on station), and a spray shield with illumination rocket rails on the number two gun. An HF/DF aerial is at the top of the mast, followed by a Type 244 interrogator and the characteristic parabolic antenna of the 10cm SG surface-search radar. The sea blue camouflage panel along the middle of the hull is just discernible; the winter variation of the standard pattern camouflage had lighter tones than the summer pattern, which used a sea blue panel on a medium gray background. If only one spray shield was fitted, which was often the case with Captains-class frigates, it was always on the number two gun since this position was the ready gun while at cruising stations. (Courtesy, Mr. L. Gomersall)

Balfour K 464 (ex-*McAnn* DE 73)

Named for: Capt. George Balfour (d. 1794), commanded *Conqueror* at the Battle of the Saintes

Balfour on August 11, 1944, off the Devon coast. The ship is wearing a light simplified camouflage scheme that is reminiscent of U.S. Measure 12, since the darker color on the hull follows the sheer line of the main deck. The British camouflage was a combination of medium greenish-gray on the hull and light gray, while the U.S. Measure 12 was composed of sea blue and lighter grays above the sheer line. The X position and its director station are empty, but a crow's nest has been added to the mast and extra depth charge racks have been fitted outboard along the aft end of the ship; a spray shield has been added to the number two gun as well. SG surface-search radar has replaced the SL. (IWM FL 1338)

Bentley K 465 (ex-*Ebert* DE 74)

Named for: Vice Adm. Sir John Bentley (d. 1772), commanded *Warspite* at Gibraltar

Bentley at Cardiff, Wales, during its reconfiguration into a fighter director ship for the British Pacific Fleet in the summer of 1945. Photographs of Captains-class ships undergoing conversion to specialized vessels are uncommon. All 20mm guns and tubs have been removed at this point, a shield has been added to the number one gun, and a 40mm twin mount has replaced the number two 3-inch/50. A compartment has been added to the upper deck aft of the funnel, as well as two platforms for heavy AA guns. *Bentley* was to have received late-model air-search and warning radar. *Bentley*'s orders to the Pacific were canceled on August 23, 1945, and the ship was returned to the United States with the conversion left incomplete. (Courtesy, Mr. C. Dick)

Bickerton K 466 (ex-*Eisele* DE 75)

Named for: Vice Adm. Sir Richard Bickerton (1727–92), commanded *Terrible* at Ushant

Bickerton at sea during its last operation in August 1944, escorting an aircraft carrier force to bomb the German battleship *Tirpitz* at Altenfiord, Norway. At this time, *Bickerton* was under the command of Cdr. Donald Macintyre, SO of the 5th EG, who while in charge of the destroyer *Walker* (D 27) gained renown for sinking U-99 and capturing its captain, the U-boat ace Otto Kretschmer, in March 1941. *Bickerton*'s mast supports an HF/DF antenna at top, an IFF antenna, SG radar, and a crow's nest. The davits associated with each K-gun are visible on the stern. The cruiser HMS *Kent* and the escort aircraft carrier *Trumpeter* are in the background. *Bickerton* was damaged by an acoustic torpedo on August 22, 1944, west of North Cape, Norway, and had to be scuttled. *Bickerton* is wearing a Western Approaches scheme; the slightly contrasting color in the darker areas is due to water and weather and is not another shade of gray. (IWM A25406)

Bligh K 467
(ex-*Liddle* DE 76)

Named for: Capt. William Bligh (1754–1817), commanded *Glatton* at Copenhagen; also, *Bounty*

Bligh along "The Wall" at Belfast, Northern Ireland, in November 1944. Belfast was the home port for the Captains-class escort groups responsible for protecting the Western Approaches. The HF/DF is barely visible on top of the mast, and a crow's nest has been fitted beneath the SL radome. Additional rafts have been secured to frames amidships with extra depth charge racks immediately below. The X position and director station are empty. *Bligh* is wearing a Western Approaches scheme; compare this pattern (as well as *Bickerton*'s, above), with its sharp lines, to the broad curved band painted on most Captains-class frigates that received a Western Approaches scheme at the building yards in the United States. *Bickerton*'s and *Bligh*'s pattern is typical of this scheme; the curved band appears to have been used only on Captains-class frigates upon their completion. (Courtesy, Mr. L. Gomersall)

Braithwaite K 468 (ex-*Straub* DE 77)

Named for: Capt. Samuel Braithwaite (1725–1805)

Braithwaite late in the war, along a snow-covered landscape, possibly the northern Scottish coast. Although it is a grainy photograph, it is an uncommon example of a Captains-class camouflage scheme that called for the stern to be painted a light color as a means of disguising the aft portion of the ship. The rest of the camouflage consisted of a dark band from the boot topping to the sheer line of the main deck, followed by a medium color along the upper forward portion of the hull and the first tier of superstructure, and then the light color for the rest of the superstructure. The scheme was quite successful from this photograph. Spray shields have been added to all three guns of the main battery. The number three shield, like the stern, is painted in a light color. *Braithwaite* began conversion into a fighter director ship for the British Pacific Fleet at Southampton from May to August 1945, but its orders to the Pacific were canceled on August 23, 1945, and the conversion was suspended. (Courtesy, Mr. K. R. Macpherson)

Bullen K 469 (ex–DE 78)

Named for: Capt. Sir Charles Bullen (1768–1853), commanded *Britannia* at Trafalgar

Bullen at St. George's, Bermuda, in November 1943. The ship has an FH4 HF/DF antenna atop the mast and an SL surface-search radome below. The dark material tied to the searchlight railing at the 02 level acted as a spray and wind screen. An FM12 MF/DF antenna is mounted on the face of the bridge. This antenna was the British counterpart to the American MF/DF loop antenna and was used for obtaining navigational bearings. Typically, the Western Approaches scheme was applied over the entire boot topping, instead of just where the darker color extends to the load waterline. Some *Buckley*-type Captains-class vessels left the United States with schemes that left the entire boot topping intact, and none had the boot topping completely covered. (NMM N6367)

Byron K 508 (ex–DE 79)

Named for: Adm. the Honorable John Byron (1723–86), circumnavigated the globe in *Dolphin*

Byron under way in the Irish Sea on May 26, 1945. The ship exhibits the final appearance of Captains-class frigates deployed as escorts and submarine hunters. Two 20mm guns have been added to the X position and its director station, spray shields are fitted to all three 3-inch guns, and a crow's nest is above the yard. SG surface-search radar has replaced the SL. Extra Carley life rafts fill out the upper deck aft of the stack, and additional depth charge racks line the sides of the ship outboard toward the stern. Two single 20mm guns have been added amidships on the "torpedo deck" and are visible amongst the life rafts, giving *Byron* a total of twelve 20mm guns. A British whaler is on the port side and an observation shelter has been added to the aft end of the open bridge. The shelter allowed the CO to be on call close to the sound room during long depth charge attacks. *Byron* is painted in the standard pattern of overall light gray with a sea blue panel amidships, although the constant sea wash and lack of proper scuppers has produced streaks along the hull sides. (Courtesy, Mr. A. Hope)

Conn K 509 (ex–DE 80)

Named for: Capt. John Conn (1764–1810), commanded *Dreadnought* at Trafalgar

Conn, the SO's ship of the 21st EG, arriving at Belfast on April 3, 1945, following the group's third successful encounter with a U-boat in the space of four days. The occasion is marked with a makeshift Jolly Roger flying from the mast; the symbol of the division, a gold key, is also displayed on the Jolly Roger (the key symbolized the social key one receives at the age of twenty-one). Spray shields have been added to all three 3-inch guns, including illumination rocket rails on the number two mount. An oiling bumper is just aft of the anchor. An HF/DF antenna is atop the mast with a Type 244 IFF aerial immediately below, followed by the SL radome and the crow's nest. A narrow spray shield similar to the type used with the 2-pounder MkVIII automatic gun is at the bow. Although *Conn* is not carrying a gun in this position, it had, like *Byron*, one fitted when it was assigned to the Nore command during the Allied invasion of Europe in June 1944. An observation shelter has been added to the aft end of the open bridge. (IWM A28197)

Cotton K 510 (ex–DE 81)

Named for: Capt. Sir Charles Cotton (1753–1812), commanded *Majestic* during The Glorious First of June

Cotton at Vaenga Bay, Kola Inlet, USSR, on April 28, 1945, as an escort with the last convoy to Murmansk. This is one of the few photographs of *Cotton*. The White Ensign is flying above the quarterdeck just forward of the number three gun, and the ship's boat is alongside the stern. The XIX emblem of the 19th EG is painted on the funnel, although it is difficult to make out on the photograph. The mast supports an HF/DF antenna at top, an SG radar, and a crow's nest. The number two mount has a spray shield and rails for illumination rockets. A generous number of life rafts are stowed amidships, since contact with the cold water was deadly. *Cotton* began conversion into a fighter director ship for the British Pacific Fleet at Liverpool from June to August 1945, but the conversion was left incomplete. (Courtesy, Mr. S. J. Ballard)

Cranstoun K 511 (ex–DE 82)

Named for: Capt. James Lord Cranstoun (1755–96), commanded *Belliqueux* at St. Kitts

Cranstoun at Bermuda in November 1943. An SL surface-search radar radome is above the yard but there is no antenna on top of the mast. The photograph has not been censored: Several ships during this period were transferred without an SA air-search radar in anticipation of being fitted with an HF/DF antenna. In the Atlantic theater in early 1944, air-search radar was not as important as surface-search radar or HF/DF for escort and antisubmarine vessels, since U-boats—and not aircraft—were the major threat to Atlantic shipping at this time. SL was ideal for monitoring ships in convoy and could pick up surfaced submarines as they approached within striking range, while HF direction-finding was the best means for detecting and locating submarines at a distance. A MF/DF antenna is mounted on the face of the bridge. *Cranstoun* does not have a weapon in the X position. (NMM N6373)

Cubitt K 512 (ex–DE 83)

Named for: Capt. Joseph Cubitt, commanded *Tulip* at the First Battle of the North Foreland

Cubitt at Bermuda during its work-up period in January 1944. The black ball suspended above the bridge, just forward of the mast, indicates the ship is at anchor. Depth charge arbors are mounted along the aft superstructure and on the sides of the X position and number three mount. Compare the starboard side pattern of this Western Approaches camouflage scheme on *Cubitt* with its portside appearance on *Cranstoun*. The only known photographs of *Cubitt* and several other Captains-class ships were taken at the British Naval Station, St. George's, Bermuda, during their work-ups. (NMM N6377)

Curzon K 513 (ex–DE 84)

Named for: Capt. the Honorable Henry Curzon (1765–1846), commanded *Elizabeth* at Tagus

Curzon at Chatham in April 1945, following an availability to increase its antiaircraft capabilities. Although this kind of refit was desirable, *Curzon* may be the only Captains-class ship to have actually undergone these modifications before the end of hostilities in Europe. Two 40mm guns have replaced the 20mm guns in front of the pilothouse and three 20mm guns have been added amidships (part of a tub and their gun barrels are visible). *Curzon* was transferred with the 40mm twin mount in the X position. Its antiaircraft battery now consisted of four 40mm and nine 20mm automatic guns. An observation shelter has been added to the aft end of the open bridge, and illumination rocket rails are on either side of the number two mount, although no spray shields have been fitted to the 3-inch guns. (IWM A30320)

Dakins K 550 (ex–DE 85)

Named for: Rear Adm. George Dakins, commanded *Worcester* at the First Battle of the North Foreland

Dakins at Bermuda in December 1943. *Dakins* does not have an HF/DF aerial mounted on the masthead but would eventually receive one. The collapsible windscreen on the open flying bridge is in the raised position. The navigational FM12 MF/DF is mounted forward of the bridge. The anchor light is attached to a pole rising above the 20mm battery at the 01 level, and a loudspeaker is on the 01 level balcony, facing the number two position. The anchor light was illuminated when the anchor was dropped. *Dakins*'s Western Approaches camouflage, both white and pale blue, is neatly edged by the black boot topping instead of extending to the load waterline (compare *Cranstoun*, above). (NMM N6386)

Deane K 551 (ex–DE 86)

Named for: Adm. Richard Deane (1610–1653), commanded *Resolution* at the First Battle of the North Foreland

Deane at Loch Eriboll in May 1945. Few photographs of this ship exist. A spray shield with illumination rocket rails has been added to the number two mount, davits for a British whaler are on the port side amidships, and two 20mm guns are in the X position and its director station. Extra depth charge racks are outboard along the stern. The insignia of EG 21, a gold key, is painted in the box toward the top of the stack, although it cannot be made out in this photograph. The spray shield at the bow is a vestige of when *Deane*, like other ships in its escort group, had a 2-pounder bow chaser fitted. The mast supports the standard arrangement of electronics aboard a Captains-class vessel: HF/DF at the top, followed by a Type 244 interrogator, and an SL surface-search radar radome. A crow's next is above the yard. (Courtesy, Mr. A. Hope)

Ekins K 552 (ex–DE 87)

Named for: Adm. Sir Charles Ekins (1768–1855), commanded *Defence* at Copenhagen

Ekins at Harwich on November 12, 1944, operating as a Coastal Forces control ship. A 2-pounder MkVIII automatic gun is at the bow. This weapon was often added to the bow of ships that engaged light enemy craft in the Channel because this position gave the gun a broad field of fire and enabled the ship to rake the water at shorter ranges where low, fast S-boats and midget submarines operated. The vertical dipole attached by two brackets forward of the mast and immediately below the SL radome is a "headache" antenna used to monitor local German radio transmissions. Illumination rocket rails have been added to the number two position and 20mm guns have been fitted in the X position and its director station. *Ekins* also has an observation shelter added to the aft end of the open bridge. Note the shelter abaft the number three gun position to protect the depth charge crews from heavy weather, and extra chemical smoke generators atop the depth charge tracks. The ship is wearing an intermediate simplified scheme of medium gray-green along the hull up to the sheer line and a lighter gray above. The stack, X position, and number three gun tub appear to be painted an even lighter shade of gray. (IWM A26398)

Fitzroy K 553 (ex–DE 88)

Named for: Vice Adm. Robert Fitzroy (1805–65), commanded *Beagle* during Charles Darwin's voyages

Fitzroy, escorting a Type VIIC U-boat into Loch Eriboll, Scotland, in May 1945, following the surrender of Germany. It is possible that the submarine is U-826, the first U-boat boarded by members of *Fitzroy*'s crew on May 11, 1945. *Fitzroy*'s hull is streaked because it lacked the proper scuppers that would have allowed the sea wash to run off the main deck more efficiently; a similar effect can be seen on other Captains-class ships.

Fitzroy has spray shields at the bow and on the forward two 3-inch guns; an oiling bumper is also present and extra depth charge racks have been added outboard toward the stern. The mast supports a crow's nest, HF/DF aerial, and SL radome. Two 20mm guns are installed in the X position and its director station. The four humps toward the bow of the submarine are pressurized containers for inflatable life rafts. *Fitzroy* began conversion into a fighter director ship for the British Pacific Fleet at Belfast from June to August 1945, but was left incomplete due to the end of the war. (Courtesy, Mr. S. Pell)

Redmill K 554 (ex–DE 89)

Named for: Capt. Robert Redmill (d. 1819), commanded *Polyphemus* at Trafalgar

Redmill after being hit by an acoustic torpedo from U-1105 on April 27, 1945, twenty-five miles northwest of Blacksod Bay, Ireland. Twenty-nine crew members were killed. Without propellers or rudders, *Redmill* has dropped anchor to keep the ship from drifting erratically. *Rupert* (K 561) is preparing to assist *Redmill*, after having first secured the area from further U-boat attacks. Both ships have spray shields on their number two guns; the open-backed design of the shield is noticeable on *Redmill*. Depth charge racks line the quarterdecks of both vessels. *Rupert* towed *Redmill* until being relieved by the rescue tug HMS *Jaunty*, which then brought *Redmill* into Londonderry on April 29, 1945. (Courtesy, Mr. K. R. Macpherson)

Retalick K 555 (ex–DE 90)

Named for: Capt. Richard Retalick, commanded *Defiance* at Copenhagen

The launching of *Retalick* at the Bethlehem-Hingham shipyard in the early morning of October 9, 1943. As with the case of *Byard* (K 315), no photograph of *Retalick* in wartime service has been located, which is disappointing since Stephen W. Roskill in the final volume of his *War at Sea* concluded that *Retalick* was "[one] of our most successful ships" for its role in the pitched battles with German coastal forces in the Channel. The photograph does show that shipyards operated around the clock. (80-G-216402)

Halsted K 556 (ex–HMS *Reynolds*, ex–DE 91)

Named for: Adm. Sir Lawrence William Halsted (1764–1841), commanded *Namur* at Trafalgar

Halsted departing the Bethlehem-Hingham shipyard on November 10, 1943, exactly thirty days after its keel was laid. *Halsted* is flying a signal flag hoist of its pennant number while the forecastle and wire handling parties have fallen in. This is the traditional Royal Navy salute to acknowledge a senior officer at a shore establishment or on another ship. The SA radar array has not been fitted to the top of the mast in anticipation of the ship receiving an HF/DF antenna. Both *Halsted* and *Cosby* (K 559/DE 94, see below) were renamed to avoid confusion with recently commissioned U.S. DEs with the same names. (Courtesy, Cdr. R. Fowler, RN, Ret.)

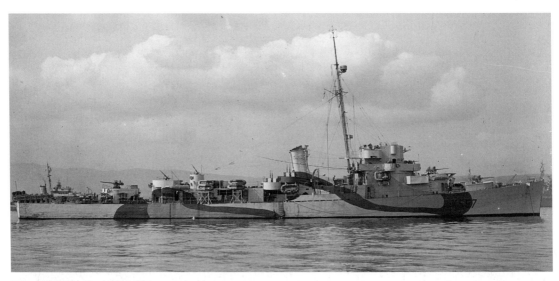

Riou K 557 (ex–DE 92)

Named for: Capt. Henry Riou (1758–1801), commanded *Amazon* at Copenhagen

Riou anchored at Greenock on May 22, 1944. The ship is wearing a light disruptive camouflage scheme of dark blue-gray (the darkest color), pale gray (the lightest color), and two other shades of light and medium bluish-gray. The most noticeable British additions are the 20mm guns in the X position and its director station, and the life rafts stowed amidships. Depth charge ready racks have not been fitted outboard along the quarterdeck. An HF/DF antenna is atop the mast with the SL radome below, but a crow's nest is absent. (IWM A23703)

Rutherford K 558 (ex–DE 93)

Named for: Capt. William Gordon Rutherford (1764–1818), commanded *Swiftsure* at Trafalgar

Rutherford in February 1944, at speed off Dunoon, Scotland. The graceful and proportional lines of the *Buckley*-class design are readily apparent. No major Admiralty alterations have been carried out, but the ship would eventually receive spray shields for its main battery and 20mm guns in the X position and its director station. The Royal Navy's antisubmarine school was relocated from Portland to Dunoon in the summer of 1940. Dunoon offered a facility capable of being expanded and was further removed from enemy action, which after the fall of France placed Portland in jeopardy. *Rutherford* began conversion into a fighter director ship for the British Pacific Fleet at Greenock, Scotland, from June to August 1945, but the conversion was suspended due to the end of the war. (IWM A25641)

Cosby K 559 (ex–HMS *Reeves*, ex–DE 94)

Named for: Capt. Phillips Cosby (1727–1808), commanded *Robust* during the American War of Independence

Cosby at St. George's, Bermuda, in February 1944, toward the end of its work-up period. All Captains-class ships had their pennant number painted on the sides of the hull, as well as the stern. Like the majority of Captains-class ships, *Cosby* was transferred without any gun in the X position. (NMM N6372)

Rowley K 560 (ex–DE 95)

Named for: Vice Adm. Sir Joshua Rowley (1730–90), commanded *Monarch* at Ushant

Rowley at anchor, probably at Spithead in mid-1944. During this period, *Rowley* was engaged in nighttime combat with German coastal forces. A 2-pounder MkVIII automatic gun with spray shield has been added to the bow, and the barrels of the 20mm guns placed in the X position and its director station are just visible. *Rowley* began conversion into a power supply ship at Portsmouth from August to October 1945, but the refit was canceled and left incomplete. (NMM N22103)

Rupert K 561 (ex–DE 96)

Named for: Prince Rupert (1619–82), commander-in-chief in the Third Dutch War

Rupert on October 10, 1945, arriving at Plymouth. The anchor is "walked forward," indicating that the ship is prepared to dock. The number two gun has a spray shield and illumination rocket rails, and 20mm guns have been added to the X position and its director station. A British life boat has been substituted for the original American whaler on the starboard side. (World Ship Society)

Stockham K 562 (ex–DE 97)

Named for: Capt. John Stockham (d. 1814), commanded *Thunderer* at Trafalgar

Stockham anchored offshore near Belfast in early 1945. The anchor chain is visible on the port side. *Stockham* has an oiling bumper near the bow, a spray shield on the number two gun, a crow's nest, and 20mm guns in the X position and its director station. *Stockham* was to be converted into a power supply ship for the East Indies Fleet, but the conversion was canceled. (Courtesy, Mr. C. Dick)

Seymour K 563 (ex–DE 98)

Named for: Vice Adm. Lord Hugh Seymour (1759–1801), commanded *Leviathan* during The Glorious First of June

Seymour in early 1945. The color breaks of the Admiralty light disruptive scheme are quite distinctive. The ship is painted overall pale gray, with light bluish-gray fields, outlined with dark blue gray. A 2-pounder MkVIII automatic gun with spray shield is fitted to the bow, and 20mm guns have been added in the X position and its director station. (Courtesy, Mr. D. W. Evans)

Reuben James DE 153 DER 153

Named for: Boatswain's Mate Reuben James (c. 1776–1838); also, *Reuben James* (DD 245), sunk October 31, 1941, the first U.S. Navy warship lost to enemy action in World War II

Reuben James on April 17, 1943, off Norfolk, Virginia, during its evaluation trials. *Reuben James* was the first *Buckley*-class ship to commission, the eighth destroyer escort overall. The ship has been built to the original *Buckley*-class specifications with only two 20mm gun tubs amidships and two 20mm guns forward of the pilothouse. The clean and simple layout of the long-hulled DE is evident, as well as the ample deck space aft that was eventually used for two more 20mm guns. The X position contains a 40mm twin mount. *Reuben James* and *Buckley* (DE 51) were the only American *Buckley*-class DEs to commission with 40mm twin mounts. Note that the whaleboat is turned out in the position for launching. *Reuben James* was allocated for conversion into a DER on May 15, 1945, and converted by the Brown Shipbuilding Corp., Houston, from July to November 1945. (80-G-62412)

Sims DE 154 APD 50

Named for: Adm. William S. Sims (1858–1936); also, *Sims* (DD 409), sunk May 7, 1942, in the Coral Sea

Sims cruising along the U.S. Atlantic coast in August 1944. The ship is painted Measure 22, haze gray and navy blue. *Sims* exemplifies the light escort destroyer as conceived in the early 1940s, with its mixture of antiaircraft guns, depth charge projectors, and torpedo tubes to provide both air and sea protection for a convoy. By 1944, however, most of *Sims*'s armament was obsolescing or already obsolete. The 1.1-inch quadruple machine gun in the X position and the 20mm Oerlikons did not have the power necessary to counter mid-1940s aircraft— let alone planes used for suicide tactics. Furthermore, its modest 3-inch main battery was not automatically director-controlled or power-operated, making rapid target selection difficult. Note the HF/DF antenna at the masthead. (80-G-282693)

Hopping DE 155 APD 51

Named for: USS *Enterprise* pilot Lt. Cdr. Hallsted Lubeck Hopping, killed February 1, 1942, above Roi, Marshall Islands

Hopping during the assault on Okinawa in April 1945. All four of its LCVPs have been launched. Once an APD released its troops, the ship would provide fire support, both ground and antiaircraft, and continue screening the beach where the troops landed. *Hopping* is wearing Measure 31/20L, a mottled pattern of varying greens, browns, and black. An LCI(L) is in the foreground, and the battleships *New York* (BB 34) and *Idaho* (BB 42) are in the background. (U.S. Naval Institute)

Reeves DE 156 APD 52

Named for: Electrician's Mate 3/C Thomas James Reeves, killed December 7, 1941, aboard the USS *California*

Reeves on April 17, 1944, off New York City. The ship has an HF/DF antenna atop its mast and an SL surface-search radar radome below. A 20mm gallery has been added forward of the depth charge tracks on the stern. Like *Sims* (DE 154), *Reeves* kept its torpedo tubes until it was converted into an APD, beginning in September 1944. (80-G-224699)

Fechteler DE 157

Named for: Lt. Frank Casper Fechteler, killed September 18, 1922, in a plane crash near Detroit, Michigan

Commissioning ceremonies aboard *Fechteler*, July 1, 1943, at the Norfolk Navy Yard. Note the civilians on the starboard side and the band—including a sousaphone player—within the number three gun tub. The chemical smoke generators and empty depth charge tracks are clearly shown, as well as the ship's name on the fantail. *Fechteler* began its career as a convoy escort in September 1943; eight months later, the ship was sunk. This is the only official photograph of *Fechteler* still recorded, and no other photograph of the ship beyond this date may exist. *Fechteler* was torpedoed by U-967 on May 5, 1944, near the island of Alborán in the western Mediterranean. The hull was blown open at the number two engine room, and the ship sank about ninety minutes later. Twenty-nine crew members were killed and twenty-six wounded. *Fechteler* was the first *Buckley*-class destroyer escort lost during World War II, the third DE sunk overall. (NH 79827)

Chase DE 158 APD 54

Named for: Adm. Jehu Valentine Chase (1869–1937)

Chase off New York City on June 1, 1944. Its torpedo tubes have been replaced by four 40mm single guns and a 20mm gallery has been added to the stern. *Chase* carries an SA air-search radar antenna atop its foremast and an HF/DF antenna on a stub mainmast. SA air-search radar was originally intended to be carried on top of the DE's single mast, but the British ended up replacing the SA radar on most of their DEs with an HF/DF antenna because HF radio direction-finding was a much more effective means of submarine detection at the time. Once the United States began antisubmarine operations in earnest the Navy also replaced the SA radar on many of its Atlantic-based DEs with an HF/DF antenna. As the relative tactical value of SA radar increased, the antenna arrangement on *Chase* became common, with SA returned to the top of the original mast and HF/DF added to a stub mainmast. In the last nine months of the Atlantic war, DEs ended up relying on radar for locating surfaced submarines more often than radio detection since German countermeasures diminished the ability of HF/DF receivers to get a sufficiently accurate bearing on the radio source. (80-G-233044)

Laning DE 159 APD 55 LPR 55

Named for: Adm. Harris Laning (1873–1941)

Laning engaged as a reservist training ship in the mid-1950s. *Laning*'s appearance has changed very little from the time the ship was converted into a UDT flagship at the end of World War II. The 20mm gun stations forward and aft of the LCVP davits are still in place, but the 20mm sponsons at the 01 level on either side of the bridge were removed prior to *Laning*'s recommissioning during the Korean War. As part of its conversion into a UDT flagship, *Laning* had its cargo derrick replaced with a communications mainmast and a 40mm twin mount with director added to the stern. Two K-guns have now been added just forward of the depth charge tracks at the stern. A Mk52 director is on the top of the bridge under a protective covering. The foremast supports SA and SU radar. *Laning* was reclassified LPR 55 on January 1, 1969. (428-G-1045355)

Loy DE 160 APD 56

Named for: Gunner's Mate 3/C Jackson Keith Loy, killed November 12, 1942, aboard the USS *San Francisco*

Loy on April 9, 1944, steaming with Task Group 21.16 in the North Atlantic. This photograph was taken from the escort carrier *Core* (CVE 13). TG 21.16 monitored shipping lanes between the Azores and Africa from April 3 to May 29, 1944. Destroyer escorts were sometimes criticized for their excessive pitching and rolling since it could make weapon handling difficult and life aboard ship uncomfortable, but these same ships were equally praised when their inherent liveliness enabled DEs to endure heavy weather better than other ships. Following the devastating storm off the Philippines in December 1944, Samuel E. Morison wrote, "Most successful in riding out the typhoon were the destroyer escorts. They rode the seas more easily than the destroyers, and were well handled by their young officers and men." Almost every DE has a story about taking a roll of 60 degrees or greater during a storm. (80-G-269006)

Barber DE 161 APD 57 LPR 57

Named for: Malcolm, Randolph, and Leroy Barber, brothers killed December 7, 1941, aboard the USS *Oklahoma*

The fast transport *Barber* secured and under way in the Pacific in 1945, probably off Okinawa toward the end of the APD's tour of duty around the island in July. A sailor on the forecastle is retrieving a line, most likely following a personnel transfer between *Barber* and another ship from the division. Although similar lines were used during refueling at sea, the fact that only the colors are flying from the mast, and not the signal flag Baker (for "dangerous cargo—no smoking"), indicates that the ship was not taking on fuel. The ship is painted Measure 31/20L. A range finder is on top of the bridge, and the cargo booms are tied down to keep them from swinging while not in use. Wartime photographs of destroyer escort APDs at sea are rare. *Barber* was reclassified LPR 57 on January 1, 1969, and sold to Mexico in February of that year. *Barber* is the only ship of the entire class remaining as of 1998. (Courtesy, Mr. O. E. West, Jr.)

Lovelace DE 198
The Lucky Lady

Named for: USS *Yorktown* pilot Lt. Cdr. Donald Alexander Lovelace, killed June 2, 1942, near Midway Island

Lovelace oiling from the tanker S.S. *Acme* at Nouméa, New Caledonia, on February 19, 1944. Antisubmarine netting is stretched across the anchorage. *Lovelace* is wearing Measure 32/13D and has two of its hull numbers outlined on the bow in an uncommon fashion (see *Manning*, below, in contrast). Note the HF/DF antenna at the top of the mast. This was quite unusual for a Pacific theater ship and indicates that *Lovelace* was originally intended for Atlantic service. Pacific DEs rarely carried the HF direction-finding antennas common on Atlantic escorts because Japanese submarines were not coordinated by shortwave radio like German U-boats and were under general orders to maintain radio silence. Japanese submarines were usually detected with radar on the surface and then sonar once the submarine submerged. Often the general locations of Japanese submarines were disclosed through codebreaking. *Lovelace* did not receive SA air-search radar until almost a year later, in January 1945. (19-LCM-DE198-4)

Manning DE 199

Named for: Aviation Machinist's Mate Milburn A. Manning, killed December 7, 1941, at Kaneohe Bay, Oahu, Hawaii

Manning anchored at Nouméa, New Caledonia, on February 19, 1944. Nouméa was a major United States Navy sea and air base in the South Pacific and was the site of the South Pacific Area Command at this time. *Manning* is wearing Measure 32/13D. There is an SA array atop its mast and an SL radome immediately below. The anchor ball is suspended between the mast and the bridge. *George* (DE 697), wearing Measure 21, is in the background, having just arrived in Nouméa as an escort for a convoy from Norfolk, Virginia, to New Caledonia. (19-LCM-DE199-1)

Neuendorf DE 200

Named for: Seaman 1/C William Frederick Neuendorf, Jr., killed December 7, 1941, aboard the USS *Nevada*

Neuendorf at Nouméa, New Caledonia, in August 1944. The ship is painted in Measure 32/14D. The Hedge-hog projector forward of the number two position is loaded with bombs. A small loop antenna for MF direction-finding is just abaft the mast at bridge height. This antenna, which was fitted on most American DEs, was used to calculate the ship's position by determining the direction of radio signals from two fixed transmitters and then plotting their intersection. (The Floating Drydock)

James E. Craig DE 201
The Jim Easy

Named for: Lt. Cdr. James Edwin Craig, killed December 7, 1941, aboard the USS *Pennsylvania*

A weatherworn *James E. Craig* in an undated photograph, probably in the Philippines in mid-1945. The ship's whaler has been dispatched and a movie screen is set up on the fantail. The ship is being repainted Measure 21, overall navy blue. The bow has been completed and a sailor is working on the hull right above the waterline amidships. This is one of the few photographs of this ship. (Courtesy, Mr. A. Dzurinda)

Eichenberger DE 202
The Fighting Ike

Named for: USS *Saratoga* pilot Ens. Charles Emil Eichenberger, Jr., killed September 12, 1942, over the Solomon Islands

Eichenberger entering San Diego Harbor upon its return to the United States on October 23, 1945, after twenty-two months and over 120,000 miles at sea. The ship is painted Measure 21, overall navy blue, although the corrosiveness of the sea is evident along the boot topping, where the lighter undercoat has been revealed. The sun is gleaming from the intricate pipe guards surrounding the 20mm guns around the bridge and the number two 3-inch gun. The protective railing prohibited the guns from being trained into the ship, since they were not power-operated or automatically directed. (Courtesy, Mr. H. Smith)

Thomason DE 203
The Terrible T

Named for: Marine Sgt. Clyde A. Thomason, killed August 17, 1942, on Makin Island

Thomason at the Charleston Navy Yard on February 17, 1944, wearing a striking dazzle pattern, Measure 32/16D, of light gray, ocean gray, and black. *Thomason* has undergone its shakedown cruise and is preparing to embark for the South Pacific. A Mk51 director is underneath the hood on the top of the bridge just forward of the optical range finder. (19-N-60770)

Jordan DE 204

Named for: Lt. Julian Bethune Jordan, killed December 7, 1941, aboard the USS *Oklahoma*

Jordan under way in the Atlantic on May 3, 1944. *Jordan* shows the slender lines of these ships, accentuated by the high bridge and angled exhaust uptakes. The gracefulness of the *Buckley* class is characteristic of American warship design of the period, which included the *Fletcher*-class destroyers, *Baltimore*-class cruisers, and *Iowa*-class battleships. A 20mm gallery has been added forward of the depth charge tracks. *Jordan* collided with the freighter S.S. *John Sherman* on September 18, 1945, and sustained structural damage. The DE was subsequently decommissioned and eventually sold for scrap. (80-G-229655)

Newman DE 205 APD 59

Named for: Machinist's Mate 3/C Laxton Gail Newman, killed December 7, 1941, at Kaneohe Bay, Oahu, Hawaii

Newman in the same convoy as *Jordan* (above), also on May 3, 1944. These nearly identical escort vessels illustrate the high degree of complexity that multiple ship production achieved during World War II. On May 12, *Newman* and its five division mates joined eight other escorts to shepherd a 105-ship convoy of merchant and naval vessels from Norfolk, Virginia, to Bizerte, Tunisia. The departure from the Mediterranean would be *Newman*'s last task as a DE: the ship was selected for conversion into an APD, which began upon its return to New York on June 29, 1944. (80-G-229646)

Liddle DE 206 APD 60

Named for: Pharmacist's Mate 3/C William Porter Liddle, Jr., killed August 19, 1943, on Guadalcanal

Liddle at Mare Island Navy Yard on February 19, 1945, following repairs from the kamikaze damage received near Ormoc, Philippine Islands, on December 7, 1944. Circles surround specific alterations. The 20mm guns on either side of the bridge are equipped with Mk14 gunsights. Bins containing floater nets are welded to the gun tub forward of the pilothouse, which supports a 40mm twin mount and a Mk52 director, circled, under a protective hood. Note the open hatches on the face of the 5-inch gun's blast shield, which allowed access to the mount's gearboxes. *Liddle* had an active postwar career and was the last ship of either the *Buckley* or the *Charles Lawrence* class to be decommissioned from the regular navy, on March 18, 1967. (19-N-83401)

Kephart DE 207 APD 61
The Mighty K

Named for: USS *Wasp* pilot Lt. (jg) William Perry Kephart, killed October 14, 1942, over Guadalcanal

An outstanding view of *Kephart* off the New York Navy Yard on May 3, 1944, prior to its next convoy assignment to the Mediterranean. Following this voyage, *Kephart* would begin conversion into an APD. The lifelines surrounding the main deck are clearly visible, as are the distinctive exhaust uptakes of the *Buckley* class. A gallery for two 20mm guns has been added to the stern, but the DE still retains its original torpedo bank. The hinged spoon extension on each tube is folded back along the barrel for access to the torpedo; these would be dropped forward should the torpedoes be launched. At least two *Buckley*-class DEs fired torpedoes at submarines during the campaign in the Atlantic, but neither attack was successful. The tripod stub mainmast added to support the HF/DF antenna straddles the X position director station. *Kephart* would go on to have active duty as a high-speed transport during the liberation of the Philippines and Indonesia. (80-G-229621)

Cofer DE 208 APD 62

Named for: Seaman 1/C John Joseph Cofer, killed November 13, 1942, aboard the USS *Aaron Ward*

The newly completed fast transport *Cofer* off New York City on September 22, 1944. The ship is painted in a camouflage pattern of large irregular patches of greens, brown, and black designed for the Philippine Islands environment; this was an alternative pattern to design 20L, which used smaller blotches of the same colors. Note the 20mm gun positions forward and aft of the LCVP davits. (80-G-282445)

Lloyd DE 209 APD 63

Named for: Ens. William Rees Lloyd, killed May 6, 1942, aboard the USS *Oahu*

Lloyd on June 25, 1951, after recommissioning during the Korean War. The major alterations to the ship from its World War II appearance are the removal of the two 20mm gun sponsons on either side of the forward 40mm position, the replacement of the SL surface-search radar with SU, and a Mk52 fire control director added to the top of the bridge. *Lloyd* is painted overall haze gray. (19-N-137882)

Otter DE 210

Named for: Lt. Bethel Veech Otter, killed May 6, 1942, on Corregidor

Otter preparing to get under way at the New York Navy Yard on May 28, 1944. *Otter* exhibits two major Atlantic Fleet destroyer escort modifications: the HF/DF stub mainmast added just forward of the X position, and the four 40mm single guns in tubs that replaced the torpedo tubes. The foremast carries an SA antenna on top and an SL radome below. The navigational MF/DF loop antenna is on a small platform at the bridge level, aft of the foremast. The ship is painted Measure 22. (19-N-69445)

Hubbard DE 211 APD 53

Named for: Cdr. Joseph Charles Hubbard, killed November 13, 1942, aboard the USS *San Francisco*

Hubbard at the Charleston Navy Yard on March 13, 1944, one week after commissioning. The DE is painted Measure 22. Despite the fact that many active *Buckley*-class vessels in the Atlantic Fleet were now undergoing refits to replace their torpedo banks with 40mm guns, all *Buckley*-class ships completed as DEs had a torpedo bank amidships upon delivery to the Navy. The final *Buckley*-class DE was completed in July 1944, long after torpedo tube replacement became commonplace. The number three gun exhibits the upper range of elevation for the Mk22 high-angle mount. *Hubbard* has an HF/DF antenna array atop the mast, with the IFF ski pole antennas visible outboard on the yard, along with a T-shaped TBS antenna on the port side. The T-shaped TBS antenna superseded the earlier radiating dipole array. *Hubbard* began conversion into an APD following the end of the war in Europe but was not completed until August 14, 1945, the day before Japan surrendered. (19-N-62203)

Hayter DE 212 APD 80

Named for: Lt. Cdr. Hubert Montgomery Hayter, killed November 30, 1942, aboard the USS *New Orleans*

Hayter off Charleston, South Carolina, on May 19, 1944, following the replacement of its torpedo battery with four 40mm single guns and the addition of two 20mm guns on the stern. An HF/DF antenna is at the masthead, with an SL radome below. Two 12-inch signal lights and a Mk51 director and 2.5-meter range finder (both under protective coverings) are visible on the bridge. (NH 91555)

William T. Powell DE 213 DER 213
The Mighty Willie T

Named for: Gunner's Mate 2/C William Thomas Powell, killed November 12, 1942, aboard the USS *San Francisco*

William T. Powell at New York City in July 1947. The ship was reclassified as DER 213 on March 18, 1949, but returned to DE 213 on December 1, 1954, with the introduction of better-equipped and longer-ranging *Edsall*-class DER conversions. The major features of the *Buckley*-class DER conversion consisted of rearming the ship with 5-inch/38 guns and installing a tripod main mast to support radar and ECM equipment. In this photograph, *William T. Powell* is almost unchanged from the time it was converted into a DER during the autumn of 1945. The most noticeable differences are the lack of the 40mm twin mount in the number two position and the Mk63 director with corresponding Mk34 radar added to the 40mm quad in the X position. *William T. Powell* was the only *Buckley*-class radar picket ship to recommission after World War II and helped to train navy reservists between 1950 and 1958. (Courtesy, The Mariners' Museum, Newport News, Virginia, Ted Stone Collection)

Scott DE 214
(APD 64, canceled)

Named for: Machinist's Mate 1/C Robert R. Scott, killed December 7, 1941, aboard the USS *California*

Scott on June 9, 1944, off the New York Naval Air Station. For a full year, beginning in October 1943, *Scott* crossed the Atlantic sixteen times without incident. The ship has four 40mm single guns amidships in place of its bank of torpedo tubes, a 20mm gallery added to the stern, and a stub mainmast carrying an HF/DF antenna. The foremast supports an SA aerial and an SL radome. *Scott* was supposed to be converted into APD 64, but the conversion was canceled due to the end of the war and the ship was never officially reclassified. (80-G-235201)

Burke DE 215 APD 65

Named for: Lt. Cdr. John Edward Burke, killed November 15, 1942, during the Battle of Guadalcanal

Burke on April 24, 1945, following its conversion into a fast transport. *Burke* is painted Measure 31/20L, a camouflage pattern of small blotches of greens, brown, and black. The lattice frame derrick is flanked by two 40mm twin mounts and supports twin cargo booms, clearly shown in this photograph. The booms were capable of lifting five tons each, or ten tons combined. Destroyer escort APDs were capable of carrying fuel for vehicles, something the older flush-decker APDs could not. (80-G-316763)

Enright DE 216 APD 66

Named for: Ens. Robert Paul Francis Enright, killed June 6, 1942, aboard the USS *Hammann*

Enright at speed in the Atlantic, around June 1944, following repairs to the hull. This is one of the few photographs of *Enright*. On April 16, 1944, *Enright* collided with an errant Portuguese tanker that tore a 65-foot gash along the port quarter, killing one crew member. At the same time *Enright* underwent repairs at the Brooklyn Navy Yard, the torpedo tubes were replaced with four single 40mm guns. A HF/DF antenna was not added, however. The ship is painted Measure 22. (Courtesy, Mr. A. DiRienzo)

Coolbaugh DE 217

Named for: Lt. (jg) Walter Wesley Coolbaugh, killed December 19, 1942, in an aircraft accident

Coolbaugh at sea in August 1958. *Coolbaugh* exhibits the final configuration of the *Buckley*-class escort vessel. The ship has two 5-inch single enclosed mounts, a Mk15 trainable Hedgehog projector in the number two position, an open bridge (now covered with a tarpaulin) around the pilothouse, one 40mm twin mount with director on the port side amidships, a 40mm quadruple mount with Mk63 director in the X position, six depth charge projectors, and a single depth charge track on the starboard side of the stern. *Coolbaugh* no longer carries any 20mm guns. *Coolbaugh*'s mast supports an SPS-5 antenna near the top and an elongated SU radome below. Following World War II, most DEs remaining in service, both active and reserve, were used as training, experimental, or patrol ships, predisposing DEs to a reduction in their military capabilities. This was particularly evident by the end of the 1950s. (428-N-1038488)

Darby DE 218

Named for: Lt. Marshall Eugene Darby, Jr., killed December 7, 1941, aboard the USS *Oklahoma*

Darby serving as a training ship for the Fleet Sonar School, Key West, Florida, on May 9, 1952. *Darby* still has its complete complement of antisubmarine weapons, including a Mk15 trainable Hedgehog in the number two position, eight depth charge projectors outboard along the stern, and two depth charge tracks on the fantail. The starboard side 40mm twin mount has been removed, however, as well as the ship's entire 20mm battery. Destroyer escorts were ideal for training reservists because of their comparatively simple machinery. *Currier* (DE 700) is in the background. *Darby* was the first *Buckley*-class DE to arrive in the Pacific war zone, dropping anchor at Nouméa, New Caledonia, on December 25, 1943. (80-G-443644)

J. Douglas Blackwood DE 219

Named for: Cdr. James Douglas Blackwood, killed August 9, 1942, aboard the USS *Vincennes*

J. Douglas Blackwood in March 1956, making smoke with its chemical smoke generators located on the fantail. Until the advent of radar, smoke was the primary means of obscuring targets from aircraft and surface ships. Smoke was used, for example, to shield the transport area off Okinawa from nighttime air attacks, since kamikazes did not regularly use radar for target selection. *J. Douglas Blackwood* was one of eleven *Buckley*-class ships that underwent availability in late 1945 to have its main battery upgraded. The DE received a 5-inch/38 single gun forward, followed by a fixed hedgehog projector in the number two position. All 20mm guns around the bridge were removed, and two 40mm single guns were added in extended sponsons on the 01 level. The sonar room was enlarged and now slightly overhangs the pilothouse. A Mk52 director is on top of the bridge just forward of the mast. *J. Douglas Blackwood* retains its original SA radar on top of the mast and the SL radome below. Amidships, the 20mm guns remain around the stack, but the torpedo tubes have been replaced by two 40mm twin mounts with directors on the port and starboard sides. Two additional 20mm tubs have been added abreast of the director station for the 40mm quadruple mount added in the X position. The ship has another 5-inch/38 single gun near the stern and the standard complement of eight K-guns and two depth charge tracks, although the former have been moved slightly forward to accommodate the 5-inch gun. A gallery with two 20mm guns is just forward of the depth charge tracks. This arrangement was the most firepower approved as a general refit for destroyer escorts. The advent of missile technology during the 1950s, combined with the narrowing tactical role of the DE, led to the removal of the 40mm guns around the bridge and one of the 40mm twin mounts amidships. Eventually all of the 20mm guns, four of the K-guns, and one of the depth charge tracks were also removed, and the bridge was cut down to the 02 level and enclosed. *J. Douglas Blackwood* was mobilized as an antisubmarine patrol and training ship during the Korean War period and continued to serve in this capacity until 1970. (80-G-689135)

Francis M. Robinson DE 220 EDE 200
Rockin' Robbie

Named for: Cdr. Francis Martin Robinson (1883–1942)

Francis M. Robinson on June 25, 1948, at Miami, Florida, where the ship was deployed as a training and experimental vessel from February 1947 to June 1960. During this period, *Francis M. Robinson* underwent a succession of structural changes. The ship's first postwar refit, as shown in this photograph, included the replacement of the torpedo battery with two 40mm twin mounts and the 1.1-inch guns in the X position with a

40mm quadruple mount. The sound room was also enlarged and extended forward. The ship has an SA radar array atop its mast instead of the HF/DF antenna it carried in that position during its initial deployment in World War II. The DE is painted in the standard postwar camouflage scheme of overall haze gray. In the mid-1950s, *Francis M. Robinson*'s 20mm guns and tubs were removed, the bridge was cut down to the 02 level and enclosed, and two Hedgehog projectors were added abreast the number two position. (Courtesy, The Mariners' Museum, Newport News, Virginia, Ted Stone Collection)

Solar DE 221

Named for: Boatswain's Mate 1/C Adolfo Solar, killed December 7, 1941, aboard the USS *Nevada*

Solar in Boston Harbor on October 1, 1944. The ship is painted in an unidentified pattern of Measure 32. Dozens of camouflage patterns were designed for DEs during World War II, and the variations of application can make positive identification difficult in some instances. *Solar*'s torpedo mount has been replaced with four 40mm single guns, and a 20mm gallery has been added forward of the depth charge tracks. On April 30, 1946, *Solar* was destroyed by an accidental internal explosion while unloading its ammunition at the Naval Ammunition Depot, Earle, New Jersey. The DE's hulk was subsequently scuttled. (80-G-382841)

Fowler DE 222

Named for: Lt. Robert Ludlow Fowler III, killed October 11, 1942, aboard the USS *Duncan*

Fresh from the Philadelphia Navy Yard, *Fowler* gets under way down the Delaware River after commissioning on March 15, 1944. *Fowler*'s Measure 22 camouflage is in immaculate condition. The ship is equipped with the standard *Buckley*-class weapons and sensors of the period: three 3-inch dual-purpose guns, ten 20mm guns, a 1.1-inch quadruple machine gun, two depth charge tracks, eight K-guns, an SA radar at the masthead, and an SL surface-search radar radome immediately below. In early 1944, the *Buckley*-class design was revised to include two more 20mm guns forward of the depth charge tracks, increasing the 20mm battery from eight to ten guns. (Courtesy, Mr. G. S. Forde)

Spangenberg DE 223 DER 223

Named for: Gunner's Mate 3/C Kenneth Jerome Spangenberg, mortally wounded November 13, 1942, aboard the USS *San Francisco*

Spangenberg undergoing an inclining experiment at the New York Navy Yard on September 20, 1945, toward the end of its conversion into a radar picket ship. The ship had been allocated to become a DER on May 15, 1945. The tripod mainmast supports radar detection and jamming equipment, as well as an SP radar dish, while the foremast supports an SC-2 antenna in place of the former SA air-search set, an SL radome, and a DBM radar direction-finder beneath the yard. A Mk52 fire-control director is underneath the hood on top of the bridge. Two of the four Mk24 20mm twin mounts are visible, one at the side of the bridge and another near the stack. (19-LCM-DE223-1)

Spragge K 572 (ex–DE 563)

Named for: Adm. Sir Edward Spragge (1629–73), commanded *Loyal London* at Solebay

Spragge on June 27, 1945, just prior to an availability period at Portsmouth, where the ship would take on electrical equipment to become a floating power station. *Spragge* has a 2-pounder MkVIII automatic gun at the bow and a spray shield with illumination rocket rails added to the number two gun. Other modifications include the whaler mounted on the port side and 20mm guns added to the X position and its director station. Extra life rafts are stowed amidships and depth charge racks line the sides outboard toward the stern. The ship is painted overall dark blue-gray. Following its conversion into a power supply ship, *Spragge* provided electricity to Hong Kong from November 1945 through January 1946. The ship was returned to United States custody at the Subic Naval Base, the Philippines, on February 28, 1946. (IWM FL 19273)

Stayner K 573 (ex–DE 564)

Named for: Adm. Sir Richard Stayner (d. 1662), commanded *Foresight* at the First Battle of North Foreland

Stayner at anchor on June 12, 1944, following a nighttime engagement with German S-boats. *Stayner* acted as a control ship for Coastal Forces that included motor launches, MTBs, and MGBs. The ship has a 2-pounder bow chaser with spray shield, extra life rafts amidships, and 20mm guns in the X position and its director station. The ship does not have an HF/DF or air-search radar antenna, but the SL surface-search radome is on the mast, while the TBS radiating dipole aerial is on the port side of the yard. The latter two electronic devices became integral to Coastal Forces operations. *Stayner* is painted in an Admiralty disruptive scheme. Like most Coastal Forces ships, *Stayner* engaged light German navy vessels, usually at night, on numerous occasions throughout 1944 and early 1945. *Stayner* was quite successful and is credited with assisting in the destruction of a U-boat and several S-boats and foiling an enemy attack on Allied landing craft during the invasion of Normandy. Note the plaque with the ship's name aft of the 24-inch searchlight station on the bridge. (IWM A24049)

Thornborough K 574 (ex–DE 565)

Named for: Adm. Sir Edward Thornborough (1754–1834), commanded *Latona* during The Glorious First of June

Thornborough in February 1944, off Dunoon, Scotland; the ship had recently arrived from its work-up at Bermuda. An HF/DF antenna is at the masthead with an SL radome below. The TBS antenna is on the port side of the yard and is now T-shaped instead of the earlier radiating dipole array. (IWM A25640)

Trollope K 575 (ex–DE 566)

Named for: Adm. Sir Henry Trollope (1756–1839), commanded *Russell* at Camperdown

Trollope berthed along the southwest wall, Portsmouth Dockyard, between the diesel-electric Captains-class frigate *Lawford* (K 514) and LST 302 on May 26, 1944, in preparation for the D-Day landings. Photographs of *Trollope* are rare: *Trollope*'s bow was destroyed by an S-boat's torpedo off the coast of France six weeks later, on the night of July 7, killing sixty-two of its crew and putting the frigate out of action for the duration of the war. Remarkably, the ship remained afloat and was towed back to Great Britain. *Lawford* suffered a similar fate during the invasion, when it was bombed and sunk by German aircraft on D-Day plus two, with the loss of thirty crew members. *Lawford* has been refitted as a headquarters ship for Assault Group Juno 1 and offers an interesting contrast with *Trollope*. The original DE design (*Evarts* class) has a single 20mm forward of the pilothouse, compared to the *Buckley* class, which has two of these weapons in this position (under hoods). *Trollope*'s mast supports a crow's nest, a TBS antenna on the port yard, and an SL radome, while *Lawford*, due to its special mission as a headquarters ship, has enhanced electronic capabilities consisting of a Type 271 centimetric surface-search radar (the squat cylindrical object abaft the open bridge), Type 291 search radar at the masthead, an SL radome, IFF, and multiple radio antennas streamed along the mast from two yardarms. The ship has had a short mainmast added (just visible beyond the taller foremast) toward the stern to support additional communications equipment. Although not apparent in this photograph, an enlarged deckhouse and multiple 20mm single guns have been added amidships. Note *Lawford*'s darker paint scheme (including the blackened masts), intended as a means of blending with the variegations of surf and sky encountered just offshore from the assault area. (NMM N25507, detail)

Tyler K 576 (ex–DE 567)

Named for: Adm. Sir Charles Tyler (1760–1835), commanded *Tonnant* at Trafalgar

Tyler at anchor in Lough Foyle in March 1944, not long after its first transatlantic voyage. No Admiralty alterations are apparent. The X position and its director station are empty, and the top of the mast has yet to be fitted with an HF/DF antenna. The White Ensign is flying from the flag staff. *Tyler* began conversion into a power supply ship at Portsmouth in August 1945, but the conversion was canceled and left incomplete. (NMM N32106)

Torrington K 577 (ex–DE 568)

Named for: Adm. George Byng, Viscount Torrington (1663–1733), commanded *Ranelagh* at Gibraltar

Torrington off Dunoon, Scotland, in February 1944, wearing the Western Approaches camouflage pattern applied in the United States upon the ship's completion. *Torrington* exhibits the standard layout of Captains-class ships following their arrival in Great Britain. No major Admiralty alterations have been carried out at this point except for the HF/DF antenna fitted to the top of the mast and the MF/DF apparatus on the face of the bridge. Lifelines are visible along the empty torpedo deck amidships. The fully armed Hedgehog is clearly shown aft of the number one mount, as well as the two portside K-guns along the stern and the depth charge tracks overhanging the fantail. (IWM A 25637)

Narbrough K 578 (ex–DE 569)

Named for: Adm. Sir John Narbrough (1640–88), commanded *Henrietta* in the Mediterranean

Narbrough at anchor near Bilbao, Spain, in July 1945. According to its log book, *Narbrough* was ordered to escort two German (ex-Dutch) tankers across the Bay of Biscay to Plymouth. Although the war in Europe officially ceased in May 1945, there were many operations that still had to be performed, including the consolidation of former enemy shipping. This is one of the few photographs of *Narbrough*. If this photograph was indeed taken at the end of the war and not during its work-up, it is unusual that the ship has retained the paint scheme applied in the United States and lacks any discernible Admiralty alterations. (Courtesy, Mr. F. G. Froud)

Waldegrave K 579 (ex–DE 570)

Named for: Adm. William Waldegrave (1753–1825), commanded *Barfleur* at the Battle of Cape St. Vincent

Waldegrave at speed, probably near Portsmouth. This rare, possibly unique photograph appears to have been taken sometime after its arrival in Great Britain, perhaps in early 1945, because several Admiralty alterations have been carried out. The ship has a 2-pounder automatic gun with spray shield fitted at the bow and two 20mm single guns in the X position and its director station. A British whaler is on the port side and additional life rafts are stowed amidships. Note the oiling bumper just abaft the bow at the main deck level. The SL surface-search radome is visible above the yard, but the HF/DF antenna atop the mast is indistinguishable from the overcast sky. *Waldegrave* is painted overall light gray. (Courtesy, Mr. P. Phelps)

Whitaker K 580 (ex–DE 571)

Named for: Adm. Sir Edward Whitaker (1660–1735), commanded *Dorsetshire* at Gibraltar

Whitaker in an undated photograph, possibly the only photograph of the ship during its service. Two 20mm guns have been added to the X position and its director station, and additional life rafts are fitted amidships. The HF/DF antenna appears as two blurred points on top of the mast. *Whitaker* was torpedoed in the bow by U-483 on November 1, 1944, off Malin Head, near Lough Swilly, Ireland. Ninety-two crew members were killed. The torpedo caused an additional explosion in the Hedgehog magazine, which compounded the damage. *Whitaker* was towed by *Gore* (K 277) until *Gore* was relieved by the rescue tug HMS *Earner*. The tug took *Whitaker* to Moville, Ireland, and then to Belfast, arriving on November 3, 1944. (Courtesy, Mr. P. Phelps)

Holmes K 581 (ex–DE 572)

Named for: Adm. Sir Robert Holmes (1622–92), commanded *St. Michael* against the Dutch Smyrna fleet

Holmes in July 1944, at the time of the Normandy invasion. A 2-pounder MkVIII automatic gun without a spray shield is mounted at the bow. A portrait of the ship's unofficial namesake, Sherlock Holmes, is painted on the bridge. *Holmes* fought German coastal forces, but despite its sleuthing, no U-boat was credited to the ship. Two 20mm guns have been added in the X position and its director station. Extra depth charge ready racks are outboard toward the stern, parallel with the number three gun position. An FH4 HF/DF antenna is atop the mast, with a Type 244 IFF antenna between it and the SL radome; a crow's nest has not been added, however. *Holmes* is painted in the Admiralty light disruptive scheme; all four colors of the scheme are clearly visible as varying shades of gray amidships, just aft of the pennant number on the hull. The differences between these colors are not always discernible in photographs, since some of their subtle variations are lost in changing light conditions. (IWM A24652)

Hargood K 582 (ex–DE 573)

Named for: Adm. Sir William Hargood (1762–1839), commanded *Belleisle* at Trafalgar

Hargood at Portsmouth in 1945. The ship has a 2-pounder automatic gun without spray shield mounted at the bow and 20mm guns added in the X position and its director station. *Hargood* is painted in the Admiralty standard pattern; the sea-blue panel along the hull appears particularly dark in this photograph and stands out against the rest of the ship's pale gray paint. (Courtesy, P. A. Vicary)

Hotham K 583 (ex–DE 574)

Named for: Adm. Sir William Hotham (1772–1848), commanded *Britannia* at Genoa

Hotham at Malta in July 1948. The ship was converted into a floating power station at Portsmouth between June and September 1945. The ship is disarmed except for the depth charge tracks on the stern. Electrical terminals appear to be located forward of the X position director station, at the 01.5 level next to the stack, and forward of the pilothouse. Portholes have been added along *Hotham*'s hull. This was an approved Admiralty alteration for Captains-class ships but was not often carried out. The long pennant signifies the imminent payoff of the crew. *Hotham* ended up being the only Captains-class ship to have a career that extended beyond the end of the war and subsequent demobilization. The British retained possession of the ship and planned to use it as a test bed for a gas turbine engine trial, but this never materialized and *Hotham* was finally returned to United States custody in 1956 for disposal. (Wright & Logan)

Ahrens DE 575

Named for: Marine Pvt. Edward Henry Ahrens, killed August 8, 1942, on Guadalcanal

Ahrens, photographed from the deck of *Bogue* (CVE 9) on May 13, 1944, in a calm Atlantic Ocean near the Cape Verde Islands. *Ahrens* is painted Measure 22 and has an HF/DF aerial on top of the mast and an SL surface-search radar radome below it. *Ahrens* did not operate with *Bogue* but was part of TG 21.11 built around *Block Island* (CVE 21). The *Bogue* group (TG 22.2) relieved the *Block Island* group on this date, which is what brought the two ships into such close proximity. *Ahrens* began operations with the *Block Island* antisubmarine hunter-killer group on April 22, 1944. Five weeks later, on May 29, 1944, *Block Island* and *Barr* (DE 576) were torpedoed by U-549 (Type IXC/40) 250 miles northwest of the Canary Islands. *Ahrens* rescued 673 men from the sinking escort carrier. Later that same day, *Ahrens* helped the *Rudderow*-class *Eugene E. Elmore* (DE 686) locate and successfully destroy U-549. (80-G-266487)

Barr DE 576 APD 39

Named for: Marine Pfc. Woodrow Wilson Barr, killed August 7, 1942, on Tulagi Island

Barr on October 31, 1944, near the Boston Navy Yard following its conversion into a high-speed transport. *Barr* was converted into an APD after it was torpedoed in the stern by U-549 on May 29, 1944. (80-G-382873)

Alexander J. Luke DE 577 DER 577

Named for: Marine Sgt. Alexander Joseph Luke, killed August 7, 1942, on Tulagi Island

Alexander J. Luke at New York City on June 1, 1946. The inboard ship is *Reuben James* (DER 153). Each ship has an SC-2 air-search radar antenna atop its foremast, an SL radome immediately below, and a DBM radar direction-finder just beneath the yard. A Mk24 20mm twin mount is visible in the sponson at the 01 level on the starboard side of the bridge. The tripod mainmast holds an SP air-search dish antenna and YE radar beacon on top, and a TDY radar jammer with a second DBM radar direction-finder below. The yardarm holds two derby-type radar signal interceptors and two sword-type interceptors closer in. *Alexander J. Luke* is still wearing its wartime Measure 22 paint scheme. A third DER is in the background. (NH 79724)

Robert I. Paine DE 578 DER 578

Named for: Marine Pvt. Robert Ignatius Paine, killed August 7, 1942, on Tulagi Island

Robert I. Paine at speed in July 1944. The ship has a quadruple 1.1-inch mount in the X position and four 40mm single guns that replaced the triple torpedo tube bank amidships. Four single 40mm guns were often installed on *Buckley*-class DEs refitted for greater AA firepower because the more desirable 40mm multiple mounts were allocated to higher priority programs, including the 5-inch DE classes. Ammunition ready lockers are inboard between the 40mm gun tubs. *Robert I. Paine* has a stub mainmast supporting an HF/DF antenna, and an SA air-search radar atop the foremast with an SL radome immediately below. *Robert I. Paine* rescued 279 survivors of *Block Island* (CVE 21), sunk by U-549 on May 29, 1944, and assisted the damaged escort *Barr* (DE 576). The vessel was converted into a radar picket at the Brown Shipbuilding Corp. yard in Houston from June to December 1945. (80-G-237139)

Foreman DE 633

Named for: Ens. Andrew Lee Foreman, killed November 30, 1942, aboard the USS *New Orleans*

An excellent study of *Foreman* on November 13, 1943, standing to during its shakedown cruise. *Foreman* was the first DE built by the Bethlehem–San Francisco shipyard. The ship is painted Measure 21, overall navy blue and deck blue, designed to help blend the ship with the sea when viewed from the air, but in this photograph the brilliant sunlight has captured many details of the *Buckley*-class design and layout. Note the alternative stowage of the life rafts amidships outboard from the X position director station, as compared to the frames installed on some ships that allowed the raft to slide directly into the water. The SA air-search radar antenna rotated at speeds of 2.5 and 5 rpm. (19-N-200662)

Whitehurst DE 634

Named for: Ens. Henry Purefoy Whitehurst, Jr., killed August 8, 1942, aboard the USS *Astoria*

Whitehurst cruising Philippine waters in the spring of 1962. Electrical cable reels are under a protective cover amidships. All the automatic guns have been removed except the 40mm quad immediately aft of the cable reels. Two fixed Hedgehogs are on a platform at the 01 level forward of the bridge. A covered Mk52 director is on top of the bridge. *Whitehurst*'s mast supports an SPS-5 surface-search radar near the top and a World War II–era SC air-search radar below and forward. An insignia of the Seventh Fleet is painted on the funnel. *Whitehurst* was converted into a power supply ship at Pearl Harbor from May to July 1945, after having suffered considerable damage from a kamikaze hit on April 12, 1945. The DE subsequently provided electricity for the city of Manila from August to October 1945. (NH "L" file)

England DE 635 (APD 41, canceled)

Named for: Ens. John Charles England, killed December 7, 1941, aboard the USS *Oklahoma*

The proud but battle-scarred *England* arrives at the Philadelphia Navy Yard on July 21, 1945, to undergo a planned conversion into a high-speed transport. *England* was hit by a kamikaze at the base of the bridge on May 9, 1945, northwest of Kerama Retto, Okinawa. Thirty-seven crew members were killed and twenty-five were wounded. *England* epitomizes the World War II DE: slight, open-ocean escorts, oftentimes ordered to perform duties that were beyond their intended capabilities but were nevertheless executed with alacrity and unexpected ruggedness. The ship's record of six submarines destroyed, the Presidential Unit Citation, and two planes shot down are painted on the side of the bridge. The damage from the kamikaze is not readily evident; a temporary steel plate is bolted to the forward base of the bridge where the plane hit, but the interior of the pilothouse and CIC were completely gutted by fire. *England* has an early version of the TDY radar-jamming antenna on top of its bridge. Beginning in late 1944, most ships of DE size and greater were authorized to carry ECM gear capable of disrupting Japanese search radar. *England*'s conversion into an APD was canceled due to the end of the war. (80-G-336947)

Witter DE 636 (APD 58, canceled)

Named for: Ens. Jean Carter Witter, killed November 13, 1942, aboard the USS *San Francisco*

Witter undergoing trials off San Francisco on January 11, 1943. The ship is painted Measure 21, overall navy blue. *Witter*, like *England*, was damaged by a kamikaze at Okinawa and selected to be repaired as an APD; its planned conversion too was canceled due to the end of the war. (80-G-216244)

Bowers DE 637 APD 40

Named for: Ens. Robert Keith Bowers, killed December 7, 1941, aboard the USS *California*

Bowers as completed, in San Francisco Bay, February 6, 1944. This is a clear view of the Hedgehog projector and blast shield just forward of the number two gun position. The ship's boat is secured to davits and tightly stowed on the starboard side. A kamikaze crashed into the face of the bridge on April 16, 1945, off Okinawa. *Bowers* was converted into an APD (the only Pacific-based DE to undergo conversion into an APD), but it was finished too late for further wartime service. (80-G-216256)

Willmarth DE 638

Named for: Ens. Kenneth Willmarth, killed August 9, 1942, aboard the USS *Vincennes*

Willmarth in San Francisco Bay, March 27, 1944, during its shakedown cruise. *Willmarth* was the first *Buckley*-class DE to commission with two 20mm guns forward of the depth charge tracks on the stern, for a total of ten 20mm guns. The ship is painted Measure 21, overall navy blue. *Willmarth* was the only ship of CortDiv 40 that was not hit by a suicide plane. (19-N-105677)

Gendreau DE 639

Named for: Capt. E. Alfred M. Gendreau, killed July 21, 1943, aboard LST 343 at Rendova, Solomon Islands

Gendreau as commissioned on March 17, 1944, painted in Measure 32/11D. Unlike their Atlantic theater counterparts, *Buckley*-class DEs assigned to the Pacific never had their torpedo tubes replaced by additional antiaircraft guns even though aircraft were the primary threat to these ships from October 1944 to the end of the war. *Gendreau* retained its torpedo tubes and 1.1-inch gun throughout the war and the crew reportedly had to resort to salvaging 20mm guns from a stricken ship in order to bolster its AA battery. The lack of urgency in upgrading the antiaircraft capabilities of Pacific DEs was a combination of the heavy demand for 40mm guns, the possibility of a surface-ship attack, and the anticipation of the end of the war. Had Allied forces gone ahead with the planned invasion of Japan in the autumn of 1945, the AA capabilities of the large DE force would certainly have to have been increased in order to counter the expected mass suicide attacks by the remaining Japanese air forces. Despite its percieved lack of firepower, *Gendreau* was credited with shooting down four aircraft and assisting in destroying a fifth while serving off Okinawa during the month of April 1945. *Gendreau*'s number one fire room was holed by 150mm gunfire from a Japanese shore battery on Okinawa on June 9, killing two crew members. The damage was repaired at Kerama Retto with parts taken from *Oberrender* (DE 344, *John C. Butler* class). *Oberrender* had been removed from service following a direct kamikaze hit. (19-N-62804)

Fieberling DE 640
The Big F

Named for: USS *Hornet* pilot Lt. Langdon Kellogg Fieberling, killed June 4, 1942, near Midway

Port quarter view of *Fieberling* on April 25, 1944, in San Francisco Bay. An SA antenna is at the masthead with an SL radome immediately below. Two 20mm guns are in a gallery on the stern. The ship is wearing Measure 32/10D. *Fieberling* was built in fewer than twenty-four days, the fastest any escort vessel was put together during World War II. It is a testament to the soundness of the *Buckleys*' design and building process that *Fieberling* did not experience any major structural or mechanical problems during its career. A plane crashed into *Fieberling* on April 6, 1945, toppling the radar at the masthead and leaving a wing on board aft of the bridge. (80-G-236417)

William C. Cole DE 641

Named for: Vice Adm. William C. Cole (1868–1935)

William C. Cole preparing to refuel from the escort carrier *Copahee* (CVE 12) on September 18, 1944, during a voyage from Hawaii to Manus in the Admiralty Islands. The DE is wearing Measure 32/14D. The quad 1.1-inch machine cannon is in a vertical position, showing the barrels of the four guns. (80-G-264238)

Paul G. Baker DE 642

Named for: USS *Lexington* pilot Lt. (jg) Paul G. Baker, killed May 7, 1942, over the Coral Sea

Paul G. Baker on June 25, 1945, photographed from *California* (BB 44) while acting as a screen for a battleship and cruiser force patrolling southeast of Okinawa. A .50-caliber air-cooled machine gun has been fitted to the leading edge of the sky lookout position, just forward of the 12-inch signal light. Many DEs added automatic weapons to various locations along the bridge and superstructure during the Pacific campaign to augment their antiaircraft batteries; photographs of these arrangements are, however, rare. The island was declared secure four days before, on June 21. Although DEs were not originally conceived as escorts for fast combatants like battleships and aircraft carriers, the use of older battleships for shore bombardment and the construction of dozens of escort carriers with merchant ship machinery enabled the usually slower DEs to perform these duties. *Paul G. Baker* is painted Measure 21. The cruiser in the background is *Wichita* (CA 45). (80-G-374261)

Damon M. Cummings DE 643

Named for: Lt. Cdr. Damon M. Cummings, killed November 13, 1942, aboard the USS *San Francisco*

Damon M. Cummings in an undated photograph, probably taken in 1947 when the ship was placed out of commission in reserve. The ship is painted a very light gray overall with its hull number in black. This scheme was used briefly following World War II for ships that were operating as reserve training vessels, but it was soon abandoned in favor of measures uniform with the regular navy. The DE retains its wartime arrangement—including the torpedo tube bank amidships—except that the two 20mm single mounts forward of the pilothouse have been removed. *Damon M. Cummings* screened an LST group during the initial assault on Okinawa, April 1, 1945, and remained on station until May 1. Between February and September 1946, *Damon M. Cummings* operated with American forces along the coasts of China and Vietnam before returning to the United States. (428-G-1043358)

Vammen DE 644

Named for: USS *Enterprise* pilot Ens. Clarence Earl Vammen, Jr., killed June 6, 1942, near Midway

Vammen off San Diego in July 1952, following its conversion into a specialized ASW ship. The ship would remain essentially the same during its tour of Vietnamese waters almost ten years later, in early 1962. *Vammen* was one of four DEs (and the only *Buckley*-class vessel) that underwent SCB 63 and 63A refits in 1951–52 to enhance their antisubmarine capabilities. *Vammen*'s bridge was cut down and enclosed except for a Mk52 director tower that remained at the original flying bridge height. An open conning deck was added at the 02 level, and an elongated platform was built at the 01 level to support two trainable Mk15 Hedgehog projectors, replacing the number two 3-inch/50. The SCB 63 plans called for a battery of four Hedgehogs and a more radically rebuilt bridge, but *Vammen* underwent the less-powerful SCB 63A conversion. All of *Vammen*'s automatic guns have been removed, but the ship now has six paired and two single depth charge projectors, as well as two depth charge tracks at the stern. *Vammen* also received a new sonar during the upgrade. *Vammen*'s foremast supports a World War II–type SA radar antenna at the top with an SU radome below. A mainmast has replaced the X position weaponry and holds radio and communication equipment. The ship retains two 3-inch/50 guns. Note the mesh lifelines around the forecastle. *Marsh* (DE 699) is in the background. After its final decommissioning, *Vammen* served as a reserve training ship out of Long Beach, California. (Courtesy, The Mariners' Museum, Newport News, Virginia, Ted Stone Collection)

Jenks DE 665 (APD 67, canceled)

Named for: Lt. (jg) Henry Pease Jenks, killed October 13, 1942, aboard the USS *Atlanta*

Jenks cruising in calm Atlantic seas on a brilliant October 4, 1944. Four single 40mm guns have replaced the ship's torpedo tubes and two 20mm guns have been added on the stern. The ship is painted Measure 32/3D. *Jenks* shared in the Presidential Unit Citation awarded to the *Guadalcanal* (CVE 60) antisubmarine hunter-killer group (TG 22.3) for the capture of U-505 (Type IXC) on June 4, 1944, off the coast of Mauritania. As the fastest ship in the task group, *Jenks* left on June 9 to carry the captured Enigma machine and documents from U-505 to Bermuda. *Jenks*'s planned conversion into APD 67 was canceled due to the end of the war, and the ship was never officially reclassified. (80-G-281810)

Durik DE 666 (APD 68, canceled)
The Dirty D

Named for: Apprentice Seaman Joseph Edward Durik, killed March 15, 1942, aboard the USS *Meredith*

Durik in 1945, at the end of the war in Europe. *Durik* exhibits the preferred AA upgrade for destroyer escorts, consisting of two 40mm twin mounts on the upper deck aft of the stack and one 40mm quadruple mount in the X position. Due to the paucity of 40mm multiple mounts, few DEs received this refit during wartime, but those ships that remained in commission following the general downsizing of the fleet in 1946 and 1947 received a similar battery. *Durik* underwent an earlier AA refit in 1944, when the ship had its torpedo tubes replaced by four 40mm single mounts. A covered Mk52 director has been added to the top of the bridge. The ship is painted Measure 22. (Courtesy, Mr. F. Niepp)

Wiseman DE 667

Named for: USS *Yorktown* pilot Lt. (jg) Osborne Beeman Wiseman, killed June 4, 1942, near Midway

Wiseman as a power supply ship during the Korean War era. The transformer and covered cable reels are amidships between the stack and the 40mm twin mount in the X position. Except for the torpedo tubes, *Wiseman* has retained all of the armament it had as a World War II escort, although the 20mm single guns have been replaced with Mk24 twin mounts, increasing the number of these guns from ten to twenty, and a Mk52 director has been added to the top of the bridge. Note the awning above the flying bridge, the lack of a canvas covering tied to the railing along the searchlight position at the 02 level, and the tarpaulins on the K-guns. *Wiseman* was converted into a power supply ship at Charleston Navy Yard from December 1944 to January 1945 and then provided electricity and fresh water from its evaporators for Manila, the Philippines, from April to September 1945. *Wiseman* was the only TEG to deploy during World War II. (Courtesy, Mr. H. Clemens)

Yokes APD 69 (ex–DE 668)

Named for: Seaman 2/C William John Yokes, killed October 19, 1942, aboard the S.S. *Steel Navigator*

Yokes as commissioned on December 18, 1944. *Yokes* was the first *Buckley*-class DE reclassified and completed as an APD while still at the shipbuilder's yard. *Yokes* and the five other ships similarly converted were identical to the rest of the *Charles Lawrence* class. *Yokes* is painted Measure 31/20L. (19-N-APD-62-2)

Pavlic APD 70 (ex–DE 669)

Named for: Lt. Cdr. Milton Frank Pavlic, killed November 15, 1942, aboard the USS *South Dakota*

Pavlic at Okinawa, just off Buckner Bay on May 10, 1945. This may be the only wartime photograph of the ship. *Pavlic* was permitted to drop anchor while waiting for its next picket station assignment. The high-speed transport had just returned from escorting the hospital ship *Relief* (AH 1) from Okinawa on its way to Guam. The escort of hospital ships was a violation of the Geneva Convention, but it became necessary after *Comfort* (AH 6) was struck by a suicide aircraft on April 29, 1945, killing twenty-eight people, including six nurses. *Pavlic* operated as a special rescue vessel in the Okinawa area between May 18 and June 27, 1945, and aided numerous ships throughout the campaign. (Courtesy, Mr. J. Boland)

Odum APD 71 (ex–DE 670)

Named for: Fireman 1/C Joseph Roy Odum, killed October 15, 1942, aboard the USS *Meredith*

Odum at anchor off San Francisco in December 1945, following a tour of duty to occupied Japan between September and November. *Odum* is painted Measure 21, overall navy blue. Note the weathering along the hull and lower superstructure compared to the 5-inch blast shield and pilothouse. The crew is assembled on the quarterdeck in dress blue uniforms. (NH 77399)

Jack C. Robinson APD 72 (ex–DE 671)

Named for: Marine Pfc. Jack C. Robinson, killed October 25, 1942, on Guadalcanal

An excellent, detailed photograph of a World War II destroyer escort APD conversion. *Jack C. Robinson* as commissioned on February 2, 1945, wearing the mottled camouflage Measure 31/20L. The ship, like many APDs, carries a heavy complement of rafts for the use of small demolition squads and as life preservers. *Jack C. Robinson* served as a patrol vessel off Okinawa in June 1945 and supported the occupation of Japan following the war. (19-N-78932)

Bassett APD 73 (ex–DE 672)

Named for: USS *Yorktown* pilot Ens. Edgar R. Bassett, killed June 4, 1942, near Midway

Bassett off Norfolk, Virginia, in October 1954. The 20mm gun sponsons at the 01 level on either side of the bridge were removed as part of a general APD refit following World War II, although by the late 1950s most U.S. Navy warships would land their remaining 20mm guns. Only the port depth charge track remains, but two K-guns have now been added on either side of the stern. The mast supports an SU X-band surface-search radar radome and an SA air-search set. *Bassett* is painted overall haze gray, except for the top half of the cargo derrick, which is a darker color. (Courtesy, The Mariners' Museum, Newport News, Virginia, Ted Stone Collection)

John P. Gray APD 74 (ex–DE 673)

Named for: USS *Hornet* pilot Lt. (jg) John Porter Gray, killed June 4, 1942, near Midway

Launching of *John P. Gray* on March 18, 1944, at the Dravo Steel Plant, Neville Island, Pittsburgh, Pennsylvania. No photograph of the ship during its service has been located. Ships built on inland waterways were launched into the water sideways. *John P. Gray* was one of three DEs launched by Dravo that were floated down the Mississippi River and completed as APDs at Consolidated Shipyard, Orange, Texas. *John P. Gray* arrived too late for wartime service, although it participated in the occupation of Korea and Operation Magic Carpet, the transport of service personnel back to the United States following World War II. Note the two LSTs in the background. (BS 62430)

CHASING ECHOES
on a Destroyer Escort

Weber DE 675 APD 75

Named for: USS *Enterprise* pilot Lt. (jg) Frederick Thomas Weber, killed June 4, 1942, near Midway

The lead article of the April 1944 edition of *Popular Science*, featuring *Weber*. Once the destroyer escort program hit full stride, the U.S. Navy used many high-profile publicity campaigns to raise public awareness of the new ship type, as well as to increase production and morale at the shipyards. The Navy trod a thin public relations line in late 1943 and early 1944, since cancellations of DE contracts were announced at the same time DEs were leaving the shipyards in large numbers. (Courtesy, *Popular Science*)

Schmitt DE 676 APD 76

Named for: Chaplain Lt. (jg) Aloysius H. Schmitt, killed December 7, 1941, aboard the USS *Oklahoma*

Schmitt at Great Harbor, Culebra, Puerto Rico, on February 22, 1949, four months before it decommissioned and entered the inactive reserve. The 40mm twin mount that was in the number two position has been removed. (80-G-445313)

Frament DE 677 APD 77

Named for: Pharmacist's Mate 3/C Paul Stanley Frament, killed November 19, 1942, on Guadalcanal

Frament at speed, off San Diego, California, following its return to the United States in January 1946. *Frament* is unique because the ship has a tripod cargo derrick like the *Crosley* class instead of the lattice derrick found on all other *Charles Lawrence*–class APDs. Note the pay-off pennant streaming from the top of the mast to the fantail, the traditional announcement of the end of a naval vessel's current tour and discharging of the crew. (NH 79797)

Harmon DE 678

Named for: Mess Attendant 3/C Leonard Roy Harmon, killed November 13, 1942, aboard the USS *San Francisco*

Harmon at the Mare Island Navy Yard on November 13, 1945, following the replacement of its 3-inch main battery with two 5-inch/38 guns. The eleven *Buckley*-class DEs that underwent this conversion initially retained their high bridge structures, which allowed these ships to be readily differentiated from other DE classes with 5-inch guns. (19-N-91490)

Greenwood DE 679

Named for: Lt. (jg) Frank Greenwood, killed November 12, 1942, aboard the USS *Erie* in the Mediterranean

Greenwood on October 10, 1947, at speed off the Boston lightship. *Greenwood* received its 5-inch battery in the autumn of 1945, but has now undergone further modifications. The single 40mm guns on either side of the Hedgehog have been removed, as well as two of the 20mm tubs around the stack. The 40mm twin mount amidships on the starboard side has also been landed. A mainmast has been added forward of the X position director station to support two DBM radar direction-finder radomes. Note the Mk52 director on top of the aft portion of the bridge and the number one 5-inch gun trained to starboard. *Greenwood* served as a training ship at the Fleet Sonar School, Key West, Florida, from 1949 to 1954. (80-G-452419)

Loeser DE 680

Named for: Lt. Cdr. Arthur Edward Loeser, killed November 13, 1942, aboard the USS *Atlanta*

A bow-on photograph of *Loeser* at the San Francisco Navy Yard on November 26, 1945, following overhaul and replacement of its 3-inch battery with 5-inch guns. The Hedgehog is immediately aft of the 5-inch enclosed mount, but it is not loaded with bombs, thus revealing the firing spigots. The arrangement of the 40mm single guns on either side of the forward superstructure is also clearly shown. Bins for floater nets are along the side of the bridge, above the 40mm sponsons. The sound room has been enlarged forward and a Mk52 director has been installed on the top of the bridge. An SA air-search radar antenna is at the masthead, with an SL surface-search radome below. IFF and TBS are on the yardarm. The aft end of the unidentified inboard ship is identical to that of *Loeser*. Two 20mm guns under light-colored hoods are outboard between the 40mm twin mounts amidships and the 40mm quad in the X position. The K-guns have been moved forward from their previous location to avoid the muzzle blast and size of the 5-inch enclosed mount. A 20mm gallery is forward of the depth charge tracks on the stern. Following World War II, *Loeser* trained regular and reserve navy personnel throughout the 1950s and into the early 1960s. (19-N-93275)

Gillette DE 681

Named for: Lt. (jg) Douglas Wiley Gillette, killed October 26, 1942, aboard the USS *Hornet*

Gillette at the Boston Navy Yard on June 21, 1944, following the replacement of its torpedo tubes with four 40mm single guns and the addition of a stub mainmast to carry an HF/DF antenna. *Gillette* is wearing camouflage Measure 32/3D. (80-G-383848)

Underhill DE 682

Named for: USS *Yorktown* pilot Ens. Samuel Jackson Underhill, killed May 8, 1942, over the Coral Sea

Underhill at the Boston Navy Yard on September 12, 1944. The ship is painted in Measure 32/3D. (Compare *Underhill*'s portside pattern of this camouflage measure with the starboard pattern as shown on *Gillette*, above.) Like many Atlantic Fleet DEs, *Underhill* had its torpedo mount replaced with four single 40mm guns. (80-G-382857)

Henry R. Kenyon DE 683

Named for: USS *Hornet* pilot Ens. Henry Russell Kenyon, Jr., killed June 2, 1942, near Midway

Henry R. Kenyon off San Diego upon the ship's return to the United States on December 17, 1945. *Henry R. Kenyon* and the rest of CortDiv 56 steamed over 120,000 miles across the Atlantic and Pacific Oceans. These ships added a little Atlantic flavor to the Pacific with their 40mm single guns amidships and HF/DF antennas atop stub mainmasts. A Mk52 director is on the open bridge aft of the range finder and was added as the ship

transferred to the Pacific theater. Most DEs, including *Henry R. Kenyon*, conducted vital convoy escort month after month during the last two years of the war. The pride DE crews had in their arduous and unsung duty is reflected in the lean and efficient presentation of their ships. (NH 79815)

Bull DE 693 APD 78

Named for: Lt. (jg) Richard Bull, pilot, lost February 5, 1942, over the Netherlands East Indies

Bull during the landings at Lingayen Gulf, the Philippines, in January 1945. A demolition squad from UDT 14 has disembarked in rubber rafts, just aft of the APD. The battleship *Mississippi* (BB 41) is in the background, bombarding the island of Luzon. *Bull* was sold to Taiwan in January 1966 and ended up being one of the last *Charles Lawrence*–class APDs in existence when it was taken out of service and scrapped in May 1995. (80-G-301857)

Bunch DE 694 APD 79

Named for: USS *Hornet* Aviation Radioman Kenneth Cecil Bunch, killed June 6, 1942, near Midway

Bunch at San Francisco Bay in March 1946, following its return to the United States and two months before its final decommissioning. The ship is painted Measure 21, overall navy blue. (NH 79798)

Rich DE 695

Named for: Lt. (jg) Ralph McMaster Rich, killed June 18, 1942, in an airplane crash

Rich (*left*) moving into position to aid the destroyer *Glennon* (DD 620), which has struck a mine off Utah Beach on June 8, 1944. Minutes after approaching *Glennon*, *Rich* was shaken by a mine that exploded near its starboard side; seconds later a second mine blew off its stern from about frame 130 aft. The doomed destroyer escort then set off a third mine and slipped under the Channel waters. Ninety-one men were killed outright or died of their wounds following rescue. *Rich* was the only American DE lost or severely damaged during the invasion of Normandy, while British DEs suffered two casualties: *Lawford* (K 514) was bombed and sunk on June 8 while acting as a headquarters ship off Juno Beach, and on June 11, *Halsted* (K 556) had its bow destroyed by an S-boat torpedo and was declared a CTL (constructive total loss). (NH 44311)

Spangler DE 696

Named for: Lt. (jg) Donald Hays Spangler, killed November 13, 1942, aboard the USS *Atlanta*

Spangler off San Diego in 1954. *Spangler* was rearmed following World War II to carry a 5-inch main battery; in the ensuing years, as this photograph shows, the ship underwent further changes. The 40mm guns have been removed from the 01 level abreast the bridge, and the fixed Hedgehog has been replaced with a Mk15 trainable version. The foremast carries an SA antenna on top and an SU surface-search radome below. A Mk57 director is on a tower at the aft end of the bridge. Two 20mm tubs are on either side of the aft exhaust uptake. Amidships, the starboard-side 40mm twin mount and director have been removed, as well as two of the K-guns, one from each side. The 40mm quadruple mount has a Mk34 fire-control radar antenna on the starboard set, indicative of a Mk63 director. The tripod mainmast supports an HF/DF antenna. *Spangler* is painted in US 27, overall haze gray. (Courtesy, The Mariners' Museum, Newport News, Virginia, Ted Stone Collection)

George DE 697

Named for: Seaman Eugene Frank George, killed November 12, 1942, aboard the USS *San Francisco*

George under way off San Diego on May 9, 1955. All of the ship's 20mm guns have been removed, since they could no longer counter contemporary aircraft. After receiving a 5-inch battery at the end of World War II, *George* and three other *Buckley*-class DEs (217, 218, and 700) were further modified in 1947 to increase their ASW capabilities. These changes included a cut-down and enclosed main bridge, an open observation deck with canvas canopy added around the pilothouse, the removal of the forward 40mm single guns and the starboard 40mm twin mount amidships, and the addition of a Mk14 (subsequently upgraded to a Mk15) trainable Hedgehog in place of the original fixed version. The rebuilt bridge is reminiscent of the low-bridge DE classes. *Buckley*-class ships selected for similar ASW upgrades in the 1950s, such as *Spangler* (DE 696), underwent the same modifications except that the bridge structure was not as extensively changed. (80-G-664903)

Raby DE 698 DEC 698

Named for: Rear Adm. James Joseph Raby (1874–1934)

Raby in the early 1950s. *Raby* underwent an overhaul at the end of 1945, when its original 3-inch guns and torpedo tubes were replaced with a 5-inch battery and heavier AA guns. In November 1949, *Raby* was modified into an amphibious control ship and received additional communications equipment. The ship was reclassified DEC 696 on November 2, 1949, and returned to DE 698 on December 27, 1957. As a DEC, *Raby* was responsible for coordinating landing craft in a local area. The APD flagship proved to be better suited for this work, and by December 1953, the DEC project was abandoned. (428-G-1043370)

Marsh DE 699

Named for: Ens. Benjamin Raymond Marsh, killed December 7, 1941, aboard the USS *Arizona*

Marsh in harbor at Chichi-shima, Bonin Islands, on June 15, 1952, prior to its second deployment during the Korean War. The ship is quite similar in appearance to the configuration it had at the end of World War II, when power supply equipment was added amidships. The main differences are that 20mm Mk24 twin mounts have replaced the single 20mm mounts it carried during World War II on a one-for-one basis, a Mk52 director has been added at the top of the bridge, and the sonar room has been enlarged and extended forward at the face of the bridge. *Marsh* had been converted into a power supply ship at Pearl Harbor from September to October 1945. (80-G-637375)

Currier DE 700

Named for: Lt. Roger Noon Currier, killed November 13, 1942, aboard the USS *Atlanta*

Currier in harbor at Chichi-shima, Bonin Islands, on July 16, 1952, two weeks after defending three mine sweepers from coastal batteries along the eastern shore of North Korea. *Currier* was the only 5-inch-armed *Buckley*-class DE to see combat. *Currier* has a Mk15 trainable Hedgehog in the number two position, which replaced the Mk14 Hedgehog it received during an ASW upgrade in 1947. The mast supports an elongated SU surface set radome and an SA air-search radar antenna at the top. *Currier* is painted Measure 13, haze gray overall. (80-G-637371)

Osmus DE 701

Named for: USS *Yorktown* pilot Ens. Wesley Frank Osmus, killed June 4, 1942, near Midway

Osmus on April 19, 1944, off the Boston Navy Yard. *Osmus* is painted camouflage Measure 32/6D. Following duty in the Pacific during World War II, *Osmus* was rearmed with 5-inch guns at the San Pedro Navy Yard between October 1945 and January 1946. The DE then returned to the Far East and briefly operated as a customs patrol vessel off Korea until 1947. (19-N-65382)

Earl V. Johnson DE 702

Named for: USS *Yorktown* pilot Lt. (jg) Earl Vincent Johnson, killed May 8, 1942, over the Coral Sea

Earl V. Johnson in early 1944. The ship has an HF/DF antenna atop the mast and is painted Measure 22. *Earl V. Johnson* would have its torpedo mount replaced with four 40mm single guns prior to its redeployment from the Atlantic to the Pacific in January 1945. (NH 53626)

Holton DE 703

Named for: Ens. Ralph Lee Holton, killed June 6, 1942, aboard the USS *Hammann*

Holton at anchor in the Philippine Islands in mid-1945. This is one of the few photographs of *Holton*. The DE is identical to its appearance while serving in the Atlantic Fleet. A stub mainmast supports the HF/DF antenna. The SA mattress array is atop the foremast, with the SL radome immediately below. The yard has two BK ski pole IFF antennas on either side and a T-shaped TBS antenna to port. The torpedo tube mount was replaced by four single 40mm guns while *Holton* was in the Atlantic. (Courtesy, Mr. F. Cameron)

Cronin DE 704 DEC 704

Named for: Chief Gunner Cornelius Cronin (1838–1912)

Cronin in September 1944, following the replacement of its torpedo mount with four 40mm single guns. *Cronin* is painted in Measure 32/3D. *Cronin* took aboard additional communications equipment and was reclassified DEC 704 on September 13, 1950; the ship was returned to DE 704 on December 27, 1957. (NH 90592)

Frybarger DE 705 DEC 705

Named for: Marine Pfc. Raymond Frybarger, Jr., killed September 14, 1942, on Guadalcanal

Frybarger at the San Francisco Naval Shipyard on July 7, 1957. *Frybarger* has two 40mm twin mounts amidships in place of the torpedo tubes and a 40mm quadruple mount in the X position, the standard late-war and postwar AA upgrade for DEs. A Mk34 fire-control radar dish is attached to the quadruple 40mm mount; this radar fed range and bearing information to the Mk63 director's computer belowdecks. An SU radome is beneath the SA air-search radar antenna at the top of the mast. *Frybarger* was modified into a control destroyer escort, like *Raby* and *Cronin*, and reclassified DEC 705 on September 13, 1950. *Frybarger* was returned to DE 705 on December 27, 1957. (NH 73472)

Tatum DE 789 APD 81

Named for: Lt. Cdr. Lawrence Aldridge Tatum, killed September 15, 1942, aboard the USS *Wasp*

An excellent photograph of *Tatum* under way off the eastern United States on February 25, 1944. The ship is painted Measure 32/11D. (80-G-419678)

Borum DE 790 (APD 82, canceled)
The Mighty B

Named for: Navy armed guard Lt. (jg) John Randolph Borum, killed July 20, 1943, aboard a Standard Oil tanker

Borum in 1945, probably at the end of the war in Europe. *Borum* was one of the first *Buckley*-class DEs to have its torpedo tubes replaced with heavy automatic AA guns, in this case two 40mm twin mounts with directors. *Borum*'s original 1.1-inch guns have also been replaced with a director-controlled 40mm twin mount and two 20mm single mounts have been added forward of the depth charge tracks. *Borum* underwent these modifications in mid-1944, in response to its special assignment as a control ship for American PT boats in the English Channel from the June 1944 invasion period until the end of the war in Europe. For much of its career in this theater, *Borum* was in range of enemy air attack. Heavy automatic guns also provided the firepower necessary for battling German coastal forces. The Mk52 director is under a protective hood aft of the range finder. (NH 79820)

Maloy DE 791 (APD 83, canceled) EDE 791
The Fighter

Named for: Chief Watertender Thomas Joel Maloy, killed November 13, 1942, aboard the USS *Atlanta*

Maloy in Boston Harbor on May 22, 1963, more than nineteen years after first commissioning. *Maloy* spent most of its postwar career as a platform for sonar research. The bridge has been cut down and enclosed, with a director tower on top. All automatic weapons have been removed except for a 40mm twin mount in the X position. Two 3-inch/50s and the Hedgehog remain forward of the bridge, but the number three gun on the quarterdeck has been replaced with machinery, including a generator to power the winch connected to the stern crane. The crane was used to lower an experimental variable depth sonar (VDS) into the water. Note that the ship's boat has been relocated from the starboard to the port side. (428-G-1073577)

Haines DE 792 APD 84

Named for: Lt. Richard Alexander Haines, killed November 30, 1942, aboard the USS *New Orleans*

Haines during its first transatlantic crossing on June 2, 1944, fueling from *Mission Bay* (CVE 59). Fuel lines and hawsers are strung between the ships. DEs were refueled at sea every couple of days to keep them topped up in case of an extended action. Fueling at sea was one of the most important skills developed by the U.S. Navy in the interwar period. The ability to fuel at sea was critical to the success of the American Atlantic and Pacific campaigns during World War II. *Haines*'s mast supports an SA air-search antenna on top, followed by the SL surface-search radome. The T-shaped TBS antenna is on the port side of the yard, which it shares with two BK ski pole IFF transponders. (80-G-364376)

Runels DE 793 APD 85

Named for: Ens. Donald Steven Runels, killed November 30, 1942, aboard the USS *Northampton*

Runels in calm seas off New York on June 26, 1944. Four single 40mm guns and tubs have replaced the torpedo mount, and two 20mm guns have been added forward of the depth charge tracks. DEs provided the equivalent assurance to merchant ship crews in convoy as long-range fighter aircraft did accompanying heavy bomber formations over Europe and Japan. (80-G-235525)

Hollis DE 794 APD 86 LPR 86

Named for: Ens. Ralph Hollis, killed December 7, 1941, aboard the USS *Arizona*

Hollis steaming near Newport, Rhode Island, on April 6, 1944. At this time, *Hollis* was engaged in testing countermeasures for the German acoustic torpedo. *Hollis* is painted in Measure 32/14D. Following its conversion into an APD, *Hollis* was refitted as flagship for ComUDT PhibsPac in July 1945. *Hollis* was reclassified LPR 86 on January 1, 1969. (80-G-229730)

Gunason DE 795

Named for: Lt. Robert W. Gunason, killed August 9, 1942, aboard the USS *Astoria*

Gunason at speed in Boston Harbor on April 6, 1944, during its initial deployment as an escort for a Caribbean-bound convoy. *Gunason* was the last World War II destroyer escort on the U.S. Navy register still classified as a DE and was struck on September 1, 1973, while berthed at Stockton, California. (80-G-229733)

Major DE 796

Named for: Ens. Charles Nance Major, killed February 28, 1942, aboard the S.S. *R. P. Resor*

Major in an undated photograph, wearing the short-lived postwar paint scheme of very light gray with black hull numbers, used to distinguish reserve training vessels. The DE retains its final wartime layout, including a Mk52 director atop the aft end of the bridge, a stub mainmast supporting the HF/DF antenna, and four 40mm single guns amidships that replaced the torpedo tubes while *Major* was serving in the Atlantic theater. The 20mm guns forward of the pilothouse, however, have been removed. This photograph was probably taken off the coast of California in the spring of 1948, when *Major* was placed out of commission. (428-G-1043440)

Weeden DE 797

Named for: Ens. Carl Alfred Weeden, killed December 7, 1941, aboard the USS *Arizona*

Weeden at Boston on January 19, 1945, preparing to join the Pacific Fleet after having served as a convoy escort in the Atlantic for the previous six months. The ship is painted Measure 32/30D. *Weeden* was one of the first DEs assigned to train naval reservists following the war and began operating as a training ship for the 11th Naval District (San Diego) in November 1946. (80-G-382805)

Varian DE 798

Named for: USS *Enterprise* pilot Ens. Bertram Stetson Varian, Jr., killed June 5, 1942, near Midway

Varian, photographed when the ship operated out of Miami, Florida, in the summer of 1945. Very few photographs of this ship exist. *Varian*'s torpedo battery was landed in favor of four 40mm single guns and a tripod mainmast was added to support the HF/DF antenna. The ship is painted in an unidentified pattern of Measure 32. A crew from *Varian* boarded U-805 on May 12, 1945, off Cape Race, Newfoundland, and escorted the submarine to the Portsmouth Navy Yard, Kittery, Maine. U-805 was one of the few U-boats to surrender to American forces in the western Atlantic following the capitulation of Germany, since most U-boats were operating in European waters at the time. (Courtesy, Mr. K. R. Jameson)

Scroggins DE 799

Named for: Aviation Radioman 2/C Theodore H. Scroggins, killed June 15, 1942, over the Aleutians

Scroggins at Philadelphia in December 1945. *Scroggins*'s sound room has been expanded forward and a Mk52 director has been added to the top of the bridge. Two 40mm twin mounts have replaced the torpedo battery amidships and a 40mm quadruple mount is in the X position. A *Charles Lawrence*–class ship (possibly *Joseph E. Campbell*, APD 49) in Measure 21 is inboard. A column of four Japanese flags topped with an aircraft silhouette is on the side of the APD's sound room. (Courtesy, The Mariners' Museum, Newport News, Virginia, Ted Stone Collection)

Jack W. Wilke
DE 800 EDE 800

Named for: USS *Hornet* pilot Ens. Jack Winton Wilke, killed June 4, 1942, near Midway

Jack W. Wilke off Key West, Florida, on July 17, 1952, operating as an experimental ASW ship. *Jack W. Wilke* still has 20mm guns around the stack, but all automatic guns around the bridge have been removed. The number one 3-inch/50 has been replaced with a Mk15 trainable Hedgehog. An awning has been stretched across the quarterdeck and stern, shadowing the battery of K-guns and depth charge tracks. *Jack W. Wilke* still retains the number three 3-inch/50 and has a 40mm twin mount and a 20mm gun amidships; a 40mm quadruple mount is in the X position. The mast supports an SA antenna at top and an SU radome below. *Jack W. Wilke* tested various antisubmarine equipment, electronics, and tactics from January 1946 until it decommissioned in 1960. (80-G-444103)

Appendix A
Number of Completed and Proposed DEs by Class and Disposition

Class (Abbr.)	A	B	C	D	E	F	G	H	I	J	K
Evarts (GMT)	65	32[a]	0	0	0	97	3	5	0	8	105
Buckley (TE)	65	46[a]	37	6	0	154	0	0	0	0	154
Cannon (DET)	58	14[b]	0	0	0	72	5	3	36	44	16
Edsall (FMR)	85	0	0	0	0	85	0	0	0	0	85
Rudderow (TEV)	21	0	1	46	4	72	0	0	180	180	252
John C. Butler (WGT)	80	0	0	0	3	83	4	0	206	210	293
Total	374	92	38	52	7	563	12	8	422	442	1,005

Key to Columns:
A Destroyer escorts that remained classified as DEs and served only in the U.S. Navy during World War II
B Destroyer escorts that served in foreign navies during World War II
   [a] Royal Navy, lend-lease
   [b] French navy, lend-lease (6); Brazilian navy, transferred from U.S. Navy (8)
C Destroyer escorts that served as DEs but were later converted into APDs (Note: *Buckley*-class DEs redesignated *Charles Lawrence*–class APDs; *Rudderow*-class DEs redesignated *Crosley*-class APDs)
D Ships launched as DEs but completed and commissioned as APDs during World War II (see note above)
E Ships launched during World War II but not completed and commissioned until after the cessation of hostilities (all four *Rudderow*-class ships were converted into *Crosley* APDs while under construction; two of the *John C. Butler*–class ships were completed as DERs in the 1950s)
F Total numbers of DEs and APDs completed
G Ships launched but canceled before commissioning (all named)
H Ships laid down but canceled before launching (all named)
I Ships canceled before being laid down (28 named)
J Total number of canceled ships
K Total number of destroyer escorts ordered

Appendix B
Statistical Data of *Buckley*-Class Ships

DE	APD	USN Name	RN Name	PNa	Yardb	Laid	Launch	Comm
51		*Buckley*			Hingham	07/21/42	01/09/43	04/30/43
52		*Bull* (1)	*Bentinck*	K 314	Hingham	06/29/42	02/03/43	05/19/43
53	37	*Charles Lawrence*			Hingham	08/01/42	02/16/43	05/31/43
54	38	*Daniel T. Griffin*			Hingham	09/07/42	02/25/43	06/09/43
55		*Donaldson*	*Byard*	K 315	Hingham	10/15/42	03/06/43	06/18/43
56		*Donnell*			Hingham	11/27/42	03/13/43	06/26/43
57		*Fogg*			Hingham	12/04/42	03/20/43	07/07/43
58		*Formoe*	*Calder*	K 349	Hingham	12/11/42	03/27/43	07/15/43
59		*Foss*			Hingham	12/31/42	04/10/43	07/23/43
60	42	*Gantner*			Hingham	12/31/42	04/17/43	07/23/43
61		*Gary*	*Duckworth*	K 351	Hingham	01/16/43	05/01/43	08/04/43
62	43	*George W. Ingram*			Hingham	02/06/43	05/08/43	08/11/43
63	44	*Ira Jeffery*			Hingham	02/13/43	05/15/43	08/15/43
64		*Lamons*	*Duff*	K 352	Hingham	02/22/43	05/22/43	08/23/43
65	45	*Lee Fox*			Hingham	03/01/43	05/29/43	08/30/43
66	46	*Amesbury*			Hingham	03/08/43	06/06/43	08/31/43
67		none	*Essington*	K 353	Hingham	03/15/43	06/19/43	09/07/43
68	47	*Bates*			Hingham	03/29/43	06/06/43	09/12/43
69	48	*Blessman*			Hingham	03/22/43	06/19/43	09/19/43
70	49	*Joseph E. Campbell*			Hingham	03/29/43	06/26/43	09/23/43
71		*Oswald*	*Affleck*	K 462	Hingham	04/05/43	06/30/43	09/29/43
72		*Harmon* (1)	*Aylmer*	K 463	Hingham	04/12/43	07/10/43	09/30/43
73		*McAnn*	*Balfour*	K 464	Hingham	04/12/43	07/10/43	10/07/43
74		*Ebert*	*Bentley*	K 465	Hingham	04/26/43	07/17/43	10/13/43
75		*Eisele*	*Bickerton*	K 466	Hingham	05/03/43	07/24/43	10/17/43
76		*Liddle* (1)	*Bligh*	K 467	Hingham	05/10/43	07/31/43	10/22/43
77		*Straub*	*Braithwaite*	K 468	Hingham	05/10/43	07/31/43	11/13/43
78		none	*Bullen*	K 460	Hingham	05/17/43	08/07/43	10/25/43
79		none	*Byron*	K 508	Hingham	05/24/43	08/14/43	10/30/43
80		none	*Conn*	K 509	Hingham	06/02/43	08/21/43	10/31/43
81		none	*Cotton*	K 510	Hingham	06/02/43	08/21/43	11/08/43
82		none	*Cranstoun*	K 511	Hingham	06/09/43	08/28/43	11/13/43

To APD[c]	Thtr[d]	Decomm	Struck	Remarks[e]
	A	07/03/46	06/01/68	40mm; DER 51 (04/26/49–09/29/54); S 06/03/69
	A	01/05/46	02/07/46	40mm; R 01/05/46; CS EIF (Cnc); S 05/26/46
10/23/44	A/P	06/21/46	09/01/64	S 01/31/66
10/23/44	A/P	05/30/46	12/01/66	Tran 11/15/66 to Chile; Ren *Virgilio Uribe*; Dis 1993
	A	12/12/45	02/07/46	40mm; R 12/12/45; CS EIF (Cnc); S 08/12/46
07/15/44	A	10/23/45	11/16/45	D 05/03/44 (T); IX 182 (07/15/44); S 04/29/46
	A	10/27/47	04/01/65	D 12/20/44 (T); DER 57 (03/18/49–10/28/54); S 01/04/66
	A	10/19/45	12/05/45	40mm; R 10/19/45; CS EIF (Jul 45); S 01/15/48
	A	10/30/57	11/01/65	TEG (1949); KW (Sep 50–Aug 51); S 06/10/66
02/23/45	A/P	08/02/49	01/15/66	S 02/22/66 to Taiwan; Ren *Wen Shan*; Dis 1992
	A	12/17/45	01/21/46	40mm; R 12/17/45; CS EIF (Aug 45); S 05/29/46
02/23/45	A	01/15/47	01/01/67	S 05/19/67 to Taiwan; Ren *Kang Shan*; Dis 1978
02/23/45	A/P	06/18/46	06/01/60	Trgt 07/15/62
	A	11/01/46	09/17/45	40mm; CS; CTL 11/30/44 (M); R 11/01/46 (Cus); S Mar 47
02/23/45	A/P	05/13/46	09/01/64	S 01/31/66
02/23/45	A/P	07/03/46	06/01/60	S 10/24/62
	A	10/19/45	12/05/45	40mm; R 10/19/45; CS EIF (Jul 45); S 12/22/47
07/31/44	A/P		06/25/45	L 05/25/45 (K)
07/31/44	A/P	01/15/47	06/01/67	S 07/03/67 to Taiwan; Ren *Chung Shan*; Dis May 95
11/24/44	A/P	11/15/46	12/01/66	S 11/15/66 to Chile; Ren *Riquelme*; used for spares; Dis 1973
	A	09/01/45	09/17/45	CTL 12/26/44 (T); R 09/01/45 (Cus); S 01/24/47; power hulk at Tenerife; Ren *Nostra Senora de la Luz*; Dis 1970+
	A	11/05/45	12/19/45	R 11/05/45; S 06/09/47
	A	10/25/45	12/05/45	R 10/25/45; S 10/28/46
	A	11/05/45	12/19/45	R 11/05/45; FDS BPF (Aug 45); S 06/20/47
	A			D 08/22/44 (T); scuttled
	A	11/12/45	04/17/46	R 11/12/45; S 06/13/46
	A	12/17/45	01/21/46	40mm; R 12/17/45; FDS BPF (Aug 45); S 06/13/46
	A			L 12/06/44 (T)
	A	11/24/45	01/03/46	R 11/24/45; S 10/25/47
	A	11/26/45	01/03/46	R 11/26/45; S 01/21/48
	A	11/05/45	01/03/46	R 11/05/46; FDS BPF (Cnc); S 1947
	A	12/03/45	02/07/46	R 12/03/45; S 11/20/47

DE	APD	USN Name	RN Name	PNa	Yardb	Laid	Launch	Comm
83		none	*Cubitt*	K 512	Hingham	06/09/43	09/11/43	11/17/43
84		none	*Curzon*	K 513	Hingham	06/23/43	09/18/43	11/20/43
85		none	*Dakins*	K 550	Hingham	06/23/43	09/18/43	11/23/43
86		none	*Deane*	K 551	Hingham	06/30/43	09/25/43	11/26/43
87		none	*Ekins*	K 552	Hingham	07/05/43	10/02/43	11/29/43
88		none	*Fitzroy*	K 553	Hingham	08/24/43	09/01/43	10/16/43
89		none	*Redmill*	K 554	Hingham	07/14/43	10/02/43	11/30/43
90		none	*Retalick*	K 555	Hingham	07/21/43	10/09/43	12/08/43
91		none	*Halsted* (ex-*Reynolds*)	K 556	Hingham	07/28/43	10/14/43	11/03/43
92		none	*Riou*	K 557	Hingham	08/04/43	10/23/43	12/14/43
93		none	*Rutherford*	K 558	Hingham	08/04/43	10/23/43	12/16/43
94		none	*Cosby* (ex-*Reeves*)	K 559	Hingham	08/11/43	10/30/43	12/20/43
95		none	*Rowley*	K 560	Hingham	08/18/43	10/30/43	12/22/43
96		none	*Rupert*	K 561	Hingham	08/25/43	10/31/43	12/24/43
97		none	*Stockham*	K 562	Hingham	08/25/43	10/31/43	12/28/43
98		none	*Seymour*	K 563	Hingham	09/01/43	11/01/43	12/23/43
153			*Reuben James*		NorfNY	09/07/43	02/06/43	04/01/43
154	50		*Sims*		NorfNY	09/07/43	02/06/43	04/24/43
155	51		*Hopping*		NorfNY	12/15/43	03/09/43	05/21/43
156	52		*Reeves*		NorfNY	07/07/43	04/23/43	06/09/43
157			*Fechteler*		NorfNY	07/07/43	04/22/43	07/01/43
158	54		*Chase*		NorfNY	03/16/43	04/24/43	07/18/43
159	55		*Laning*		NorfNY	04/23/43	07/04/43	08/01/43 04/06/51
160	56		*Loy*		NorfNY	04/23/43	07/04/43	09/12/43
161	57		*Barber*		NorfNY	04/27/43	05/20/43	10/10/43
198			*Lovelace*		NorfNY	05/22/43	07/04/43	11/07/43
199			*Manning*		CharNY	02/15/43	06/01/43	10/01/43
200			*Neuendorf*		CharNY	02/15/43	06/01/43	10/18/43
201			*James E. Craig*		CharNY	04/15/43	07/22/43	11/01/43
202			*Eichenberger*		CharNY	04/15/43	07/22/43	11/19/43
203			*Thomason*		CharNY	06/05/43	08/23/43	12/10/43
204			*Jordan*		CharNY	06/05/43	08/23/43	12/19/43
205	59		*Newman*		CharNY	06/08/43	08/09/43	11/26/43
206	60		*Liddle* (2)		CharNY	06/08/43	08/09/43	12/06/43 10/27/50 11/29/61
207	61		*Kephart*		CharNY	05/12/43	09/06/43	01/07/44
208	62		*Cofer*		CharNY	05/12/43	09/06/43	01/19/44
209	63		*Lloyd*		CharNY	07/26/43	10/23/43	02/11/44 01/03/51
210			*Otter*		CharNY	07/26/43	10/23/43	02/21/44
211	53		*Hubbard*		CharNY	08/11/43	11/11/43	03/06/44
212	80		*Hayter*		CharNY	08/11/43	11/11/43	03/16/44
213			*William T. Powell*		CharNY	08/26/43	11/27/43	03/28/44 11/28/50
214	64		*Scott*		PhilNY	01/01/43	04/03/43	07/20/43

To APD[c]	Thtr[d]	Decomm	Struck	Remarks[e]
	A	03/04/46	04/12/46	CS; R 03/04/46; S 03/07/47
	A	03/27/46	05/01/46	40mm; CS; R 03/27/46; S 11/04/46
	A	01/01/46	02/07/47	CS; CTL 12/25/44 (M); R 01/01/46 (Cus); S 01/09/47
	A	03/04/46	04/12/46	R 03/04/46; S 11/07/46
	A	11/01/46	06/22/45	CS; CTL 04/16/45 (M); R 11/01/46 (Cus); S Mar 47
	A	01/05/46	02/07/46	R 01/05/46; FDS BPF (Cnc); S 05/23/46
	A	01/20/47	02/07/47	CTL 04/27/45 (T); R 01/20/47 (Cus); S 01/30/47
	A	10/25/45	12/19/45	CS; R 10/25/45; S 05/07/46
	A	01/01/46	11/13/44	CTL 06/11/44 (T); R 11/01/46 (Cus); S Mar 47; renamed to avoid confusion with DE 42
	A	02/25/46	03/28/46	CS; R 02/25/46; S 04/21/47
	A	10/25/45	12/19/45	R 10/25/46; FDS BPF (Aug 45); S May 46
	A	03/04/46	11/13/46	R 03/04/46; S 11/05/46; renamed to avoid confusion with DE 156
	A	11/12/45	01/08/46	R 11/12/45; TEG (Cnc); S 06/14/46
	A	03/20/46	04/17/46	R 03/20/46; S 06/17/46
	A	02/15/46	03/12/46	TEG (Cnc); R 02/15/46; scrapped 06/15/48
	A	01/05/46	02/25/46	CS; R 01/05/46; S 12/10/46
	A	10/11/47	06/30/68	40mm; DER 153 (03/18/49–10/28/54); Trgt 03/01/71
09/07/44	A/P	04/24/46	06/01/60	S 04/14/61
09/07/44	A/P	05/05/47	09/01/64	S 08/15/66
09/07/44	A/P	06/30/46	06/01/60	S Jul 61 to Ecuador as power hulk
	A			L 05/05/44 (T)
11/24/44	A/P	01/15/46	02/07/46	CTL 05/20/45 (K); S 11/13/46
11/24/44	A	06/28/46		
		09/13/57	03/01/75	LPR 55 (01/01/69); S 12/03/75
10/23/44	A/P	02/21/47	09/01/64	S 08/15/66
10/23/44	A/P	05/22/46	11/27/68	LPR 57 (01/01/69); S 02/17/69 to Mexico; Ren *Vincento Guerrero* (ex-*Coahuila*); Ext 1998
	P	05/22/46	07/01/67	Trgt 04/25/68
	P	01/15/47	07/31/68	S 10/27/69
	P	05/14/46	07/01/67	Trgt 11/30/67
	P	07/02/46	06/30/68	Trgt 2/21/69
	P	05/15/46	12/01/72	S 11/27/73
	P	05/22/46	06/30/68	S 06/15/69
	A	12/19/45	01/08/46	S 07/10/47
09/19/44	P	02/18/46	09/01/64	S 08/15/66
07/01/44	A/P	06/18/46		
		02/02/59		
		03/18/67	04/05/67	S 06/25/67
07/05/44	A/P	06/21/46	05/01/67	Tran 05/16/67 to S. Korea; Ren *Kyong Puk*; Dis 04/30/85
07/05/44	A/P	06/28/46	04/01/66	S 03/05/68
07/01/44	A/P	07/01/46		
		02/18/58	06/01/66	S 03/05/68
	A	01/15/47	11/01/69	Trgt 07/10/70
06/01/45	A	03/15/46	05/01/66	S 07/01/68
06/01/45	A	03/19/46	12/01/66	Tran 07/23/67 to S. Korea; Ren *Jon Nam*; Dis 1989
	A	12/09/49		
		01/17/58	11/01/65	DER 213 (03/18/49–12/01/54); NRF I (Nov 50–Jan 58); S 10/03/66
09/10/45	A	03/03/47	07/01/65	S 01/20/67

DE	APD	USN Name	RN Name	PNa	Yardb	Laid	Launch	Comm
215	65	*Burke*			PhilNY	01/01/43	04/03/43	08/20/43
216	66	*Enright*			PhilNY	02/22/43	05/29/43	09/21/43
217		*Coolbaugh*			PhilNY	02/22/43	05/29/43	10/15/43
218		*Darby*			PhilNY	02/22/43	05/29/43	11/15/43
								10/24/50
219		*J. Douglas Blackwood*			PhilNY	02/22/43	05/29/43	12/15/43
								02/05/51
								10/02/61
220		*Francis M. Robinson*			PhilNY	02/22/43	05/01/43	01/15/44
221		*Solar*			PhilNY	02/22/43	05/29/43	02/15/44
222		*Fowler*			PhilNY	04/05/43	07/03/43	03/15/44
223		*Spangenburg*			PhilNY	04/05/53	07/03/43	04/15/44
563		none	*Spragge*	K 572	Hingham	09/15/43	10/16/43	01/14/44
564		none	*Stayner*	K 573	Hingham	09/22/43	11/06/43	12/30/43
565		none	*Thornborough*	K 574	Hingham	09/22/43	11/13/43	12/31/43
566		none	*Trollope*	K 575	Hingham	09/29/43	11/20/43	01/10/44
567		none	*Tyler*	K 576	Hingham	10/06/43	11/20/43	01/14/44
568		none	*Torrington*	K 577	Hingham	09/22/43	11/27/43	01/18/44
569		none	*Narbrough*	K 578	Hingham	10/06/43	11/27/43	01/21/44
570		none	*Waldegrave*	K 579	Hingham	10/16/43	12/04/43	01/25/44
571		none	*Whitaker*	K 580	Hingham	10/20/43	12/12/43	01/28/44
572		none	*Holmes*	K 581	Hingham	10/27/43	12/18/43	01/31/44
573		none	*Hargood*	K 582	Hingham	10/27/43	12/18/43	02/07/44
574		none	*Hotham*	K 583	Hingham	11/04/43	12/22/43	02/08/44
575		*Ahrens*			Hingham	11/05/43	12/21/43	02/12/44
576	39	*Barr*			Hingham	11/05/43	12/28/43	02/15/44
577		*Alexander J. Luke*			Hingham	11/05/43	12/28/44	02/19/44
578		*Robert I. Paine*			Hingham	11/05/43	12/30/43	02/26/44
633		*Foreman*			SanFran	03/09/43	08/01/43	10/22/43
634		*Whitehurst*			SanFran	03/21/43	09/05/43	11/19/43
								09/01/50
								10/02/61
635		*England*			SanFran	04/04/43	09/26/43	12/10/43
636		*Witter*			SanFran	04/28/43	10/17/43	12/29/43
637	40	*Bowers*			SanFran	05/28/43	10/31/43	01/27/44
								02/06/51
638		*Willmarth*			SanFran	06/25/43	11/21/43	03/13/44
639		*Gendreau*			SanFran	08/01/43	12/12/43	03/17/44
640		*Fieberling*			SanFran	03/19/44	04/02/44	04/11/44
641		*William C. Cole*			SanFran	09/05/43	12/29/43	05/12/44
642		*Paul G. Baker*			SanFran	09/26/43	04/07/43	05/25/44
643		*Damon M. Cummings*			SanFran	10/17/43	04/18/44	06/29/44
644		*Vammen*			SanFran	08/01/43	05/21/44	07/27/44
								02/15/52
								10/02/61

To APD[c]	Thtr[d]	Decomm	Struck	Remarks[e]
01/24/45	A/P	06/22/49	06/01/68	S 12/08/68 to Colombia; Ren *Almirante Brion*; riverine hospital ship (1974); Dis
01/01/45	A/P	06/21/46	03/31/78	Tran 07/14/67 to Ecuador; Ren *Moran Valverde* (ex–*Veintiseis de Julio*); Dis 1989
	P	02/21/60	07/01/72	5-in. (Dec 45); NRF II (Aug 57–May 60); S 08/17/73
	P	04/28/47		
		02/23/59	09/23/68	5-in. (Dec 45); NRF II (Feb 59–Sep 68); Trgt 05/24/70
	P	04/20/46		
		08/01/58		
		08/01/62	01/30/70	5-in. (Dec 45); NRF II (Aug 58–Oct 61; Aug 62–Jan 70); Trgt 07/20/70
	A/P	06/20/60	07/01/72	EDE; S 07/12/73
	A	05/21/46	06/05/46	CTL 04/30/46 (E); scuttled 06/09/46
	A	06/28/46	07/01/65	S 12/29/66
	A	07/18/47	11/01/65	DER 223 (03/18/49–12/01/54); S 10/04/66
	A	02/28/46	12/23/47	TEG (Sep 45); R 02/28/46; S 11/18/47
	A	11/24/45	01/03/46	CS; R 11/24/45; S 11/07/47
	A	01/29/47	02/07/47	CS; R 01/29/47 (Cus); S 04/27/47
	A	10/10/44	11/13/44	CTL 07/06/44 (T); R 10/10/44 (Cus); S 01/09/47
	A	11/12/45	01/08/46	TEG (Cnc); R 11/12/45; S 05/23/46
	A	06/11/46	10/15/46	CS; R 06/11/46; S 09/26/47
	A	02/04/46	04/17/46	R 02/04/46; S 12/14/46
	A	12/03/45	01/21/46	R 12/03/46; S 11/05/46
	A	12/03/45	05/19/45	CTL 11/01/44 (T); R 12/03/45 (Cus); S 01/09/47
	A	12/03/45	02/07/46	R 12/03/45; S Oct 47
	A	03/04/46	04/12/46	R 03/04/46; S 03/07/47
	A	04/25/52	05/14/52	TEG (Sep 45); R 04/25/52 (Cus); Tran UK 05/24/52 (MDAP); R Feb 56 (Cus); S 03/13/56
	A/P	06/24/46	04/01/65	S 06/20/67
07/01/44	A/P	07/12/46	01/01/60	D 05/29/44 (T); Trgt 03/26/63
12/07/45	A	10/18/47	05/01/70	DER 577 (03/18/49–Aug 54); Trgt 10/22/70
	A	11/21/47	06/01/68	DER 578 (03/18/49–12/01/54); S 07/18/69
	P	06/28/46	05/01/65	S 06/01/66
	P	11/27/46		
		12/06/58		
		08/01/62	07/12/69	D 04/12/45 (K); TEG (Jul 45); KW (Sep 50–Sep 51); NRF II (Dec 58–Oct 61; Aug 62–Jul 69); Trgt 04/28/71
	P	10/15/45	11/01/45	D 05/09/45 (K); S 11/26/46
	P	10/22/45	11/16/45	D 04/06/45 (K); S 12/02/46
06/25/45	P	02/10/47		
		12/18/58	05/01/61	D 04/16/45 (K); S 04/21/61 to Philippines; Ren *Rajah Soliman*; lost in typhoon Jun 62; raised and struck 12/03/64; S 01/31/66
	P	04/26/46	12/01/66	S 07/01/68
	P	03/13/48	12/01/72	S 09/11/73
	P	03/13/48	03/01/72	S 11/20/72
	P	03/13/48	03/01/72	S 11/20/72
	P	02/03/47	12/01/69	S 11/10/70
	P	02/03/47	03/01/72	S 05/18/73
	P	02/03/47		
		06/18/60		
		08/01/62	07/12/69	SCB 63A (1951); KW (Aug 52–Sep 52; Oct 52–Nov 52); NRF II (Jun 60–Oct 61; Aug 62–Jul 69); Trgt 02/04/71

DE	APD	USN Name	RN Name	PN[a]	Yard[b]	Laid	Launch	Comm
665		*Jenks*			Pitts	05/12/43	09/11/43	01/19/44
666		*Durik*			Pitts	06/22/43	10/09/43	03/24/44
667		*Wiseman*			Pitts	07/26/43	11/06/43	04/04/44
								09/12/50
								10/02/61
668	69	*Yokes*			Orange	08/22/43	11/27/43	12/18/44
669	70	*Pavlic*			Pitts/Orange	09/21/43	12/18/43	12/29/44
670	71	*Odum*			Orange	10/15/43	01/19/44	01/12/45
671	72	*Jack C. Robinso*n			Pitts/Orange	11/10/43	01/08/44	02/02/45
672	73	*Bassett*			Orange	11/28/43	01/15/44	02/23/45
								12/07/50
673	74	*John P. Gray*			Pitts/Orange	12/18/43	03/18/44	03/15/45
675	75	*Weber*			Quincy	02/22/43	05/01/43	06/30/43
676	76	*Schmitt*			Quincy	02/22/43	05/29/43	07/24/43
677	77	*Frament*			Quincy	05/01/43	06/28/43	08/15/43
678		*Harmon* (2)			Quincy	05/31/43	07/25/43	08/31/43
679		*Greenwood*			Quincy	06/29/43	08/21/43	09/25/43
								10/02/61
680		*Loeser*			Quincy	07/27/43	09/11/43	10/10/43
								03/09/51
								10/02/61
681		*Gillette*			Quincy	08/24/43	09/25/43	10/27/43
682		*Underhill*			Quincy	09/16/43	10/15/43	11/15/43
683		*Henry R. Kenyon*			Quincy	09/29/43	10/30/43	11/30/43
693	78	*Bull* (2)			Defoe	12/14/42	03/25/43	08/12/43
694	79	*Bunch*			Defoe	02/22/43	05/29/43	08/21/43
695		*Rich*			Defoe	03/27/43	06/22/43	10/01/43
696		*Spangler*			Defoe	04/28/43	07/15/43	10/31/43
697		*George*			Defoe	05/22/43	08/14/43	11/20/43
698		*Raby*			Defoe	06/07/43	09/04/43	12/07/43
699		*Marsh*			Defoe	06/23/43	09/25/43	01/12/44
								12/15/61
700		*Currier*			Defoe	07/21/43	10/14/43	02/01/44
701		*Osmus*			Defoe	08/17/43	11/04/43	03/17/44
702		*Earl V. Johnson*			Defoe	09/07/43	11/24/43	03/18/44
703		*Holton*			Defoe	09/28/43	12/15/43	05/01/44
704		*Cronin*			Defoe	10/19/43	01/05/44	05/05/44
								02/09/51
705		*Frybarger*			Defoe	11/08/43	01/25/44	05/18/44
								10/06/50
789	81	*Tatum*			Orange	04/22/43	08/07/43	11/22/43
790		*Borum*			Orange	04/28/43	08/14/43	11/30/43
791		*Maloy*			Orange	05/10/43	08/18/43	12/13/43
792	84	*Haines*			Orange	05/17/43	08/26/43	12/27/43
793	85	*Runels*			Orange	06/07/43	09/04/43	01/03/44
794	86	*Hollis*			Orange	07/05/43	09/11/43	01/24/44
								04/06/51

To APD[c]	Thtr[d]	Decomm	Struck	Remarks[e]
	A	06/26/46	02/01/66	S 03/05/68
	A	06/15/46	06/01/65	S 01/30/67
	P	05/31/46		
		05/16/59		
		08/01/62	04/15/73	TEG (Jan 45); KW (Nov 50–Aug 51; Sep 52–Jul 53); NRF I (May 59–Oct 61); NRF II (Aug 62–1970); S 04/29/74
06/27/44	P	08/19/46	04/01/64	S 03/23/65
06/27/44	P	11/15/46	04/01/67	S 07/01/68
06/27/44	P	11/15/46	12/01/66	S 11/25/66 to Chile; Ren *Serrano*; Dis 1985
06/27/44	P	12/13/46	12/01/66	S 11/25/66 to Chile; Ren *Orella*; Dis 1985
06/27/44	P	04/29/46		
		11/26/57	05/01/67	S 09/06/68 to Colombia; Ren *Almirante Tono*; Dis 1977
06/27/44	P	04/29/46	03/01/67	S 03/05/68
01/01/45	A/P	01/01/47	06/01/60	Trgt 07/15/62
01/01/45	A/P	06/28/49	05/01/67	S 02/18/69 to Taiwan; Ren *Lung Shan*; Dis 1976
01/01/45	A/P	05/30/46	06/01/60	S 07/10/61 to Ecuador as power hulk
	P	03/25/47	08/01/65	5-in. (Nov 45); S 01/30/67
	P	09/02/58		
		08/01/62	02/20/67	5-in. (Dec 45); NRF II (Sep 58–Oct 61; Aug 62–Feb 67); S 09/06/67
	P	03/28/47		
		12/01/58		
		08/01/62	08/23/68	5-in. (Nov 45); NRF II (Dec 58–Oct 61; Aug 62–Aug 68); S Sep 68
	A/P	02/03/47	12/01/72	S 09/11/73
	A/P			L 07/24/45 (HT)
	A/P	02/03/47	12/01/69	S 10/22/70
07/31/44	A/P	06/05/47	06/15/66	S 01/12/66 to Taiwan; Ren *Lu Shan*; Dis May 95
07/31/44	A/P	05/31/46	04/01/64	S 06/11/65
	A			L 06/08/44 (M)
	P	10/08/58	03/01/72	5-in. (Feb 46); NRF I (Jul 57–Oct 58); S 11/20/72
	P	10/08/58	11/01/69	5-in. (Jan 46); NRF I (Sep 57–Oct 58); S 10/12/70
	P	12/22/53	06/01/68	5-in. (Jan 46); DEC 698 (11/02/49–12/27/57); S 07/18/69
	A/P	08/16/58		
		08/01/62	04/15/71	TEG (Oct 45); KW (Sep 50–Feb 51; May 52–Nov 52); NRF II (Aug 58–Dec 61; Aug 62–Apr 71); S 02/20/74
	A/P	04/04/60	12/01/66	5-in. (Dec 45); KW (Apr 52–Aug 52); Trgt 01/11/67
	P	03/15/47	12/01/72	5-in. (Jan 46); S 11/27/73
	A/P	06/18/46	05/01/67	S 09/03/68
	A/P	05/31/46	11/01/72	S 05/30/74
	A/P	05/31/46		
		12/04/53	06/01/70	DEC 704 (09/13/50–12/27/57); Trgt 12/16/71
	A/P	06/30/47		
		12/09/54	12/01/72	DEC 705 (09/13/50–12/27/57); S 11/27/73
12/01/44	A/P	11/15/46	06/01/60	S 05/08/61
	A	06/15/46	08/01/65	S Apr 67
	A	05/28/65	06/01/65	EDE; S 03/11/66
12/01/44	A/P	04/29/46	06/01/60	S 05/19/61
12/01/44	A/P	02/10/47	06/01/60	S 07/10/61
12/01/44	A/P	05/05/47		
		10/16/56	09/15/74	S 07/01/75

DE	APD	USN Name	RN Name	PN[a]	Yard[b]	Laid	Launch	Comm
795		*Gunason*			Orange	08/09/43	10/16/43	02/01/44
796		*Major*			Orange	08/16/43	10/23/43	02/12/44
797		*Weeden*			Orange	08/18/43	10/27/43	02/19/44
								05/26/50
798		*Varian*			Orange	08/27/43	11/06/43	02/29/44
799		*Scroggins*			Orange	09/04/43	11/06/43	03/30/44
800		*Jack W. Wilke*			Orange	10/18/43	12/18/43	03/07/44

Note: All ships equipped with General Electric supplied turbogenerators. Boiler manufacturers: Foster Wheeler Corp., Mountaintop, Pa. (hulls 51–98, 563–578, 665–673); Combustion Engineering Co., Chattanooga, Tenn. (hulls 155, 199–213, 633–644, 675–683, 693–705); Babcock and Wilcox Co., Barberton, Ohio (hulls 153, 154, 156–161, 198, 214–223, 789–800)

[a]PN = Royal Navy pennant number

[b]Shipyards:

CharNY	Charleston Navy Yard, Charleston, S.C.
Defoe	Defoe Shipbuilding, Bay City, Mich.
Hingham	Bethlehem Steel, Hingham shipyard, Mass.
NorfNY	Norfolk Navy Yard, Norfolk, Va.
Orange	Consolidated Shipbuilding, Orange, Texas
PhilNY	Philadelphia Navy Yard, Philadelphia, Pa.
Pitts	Dravo Shipbuilding, Pittsburgh, Pa.
Quincy	Bethlehem Steel, Quincy shipyard, Mass.
SanFran	Bethlehem Steel, San Francisco shipyard, Calif.

Class production by shipyard—number completed (hulls): Bethlehem-Hingham—64 (hulls 51–98, 563–578); Consolidated Steel Corp., Orange, Texas—18 (hulls 668–673,* 789–800); Charleston Navy Yard—15 (hulls 199–213); Defoe Shipbuilding Co., Bay City, Mich.—13 (hulls 693–698, 699–705); Bethlehem Steel, San Francisco, Calif.—12 (hulls 633–644); Norfolk Navy Yard—10 (hulls 153–161, 198); Philadelphia Navy Yard—10 (hulls 214–223); Bethlehem Steel, Quincy, Mass.—9 (hulls 675–683); Dravo Corp., Pittsburgh, Pa.—3 (hulls 665–667). *Hulls 669, 671, and 673 laid down and launched at Dravo, completed at Consolidated.

[c]To APD = Date when DE was reclassified to APD

[d]Thtr = Theater of operations (A = Atlantic; P = Pacific)

To APD[c]	Thtr[d]	Decomm	Struck	Remarks[e]
	A/P	03/13/48	09/01/73	Trgt 12/15/74
	A/P	03/13/48	12/01/72	S 11/27/73
	A/P	05/09/46		
		02/26/58	06/30/68	NRF I (May 50–Feb 58); S 10/27/69
	A	03/15/46	12/01/71	S 01/12/74
	A	06/15/46	07/01/65	S 04/05/67
	A	05/24/60	08/01/71	EDE; S 02/01/74

Abbreviations in Remarks:

(1)	First instance of name reassigned to a later ship
(2)	Second instance of name
40mm	Commissioned with a 40mm Mk1 in the X position; all other vessels equipped with a 1.1-inch quad (USN) or no weapon (RN)
5-in.	Rearmed with 5-inch/38 guns (excluding APD and DER conversions)
BPF	British Pacific Fleet
Cnc	Canceled
CS	Coastal Forces control ship
CTL	Constructive total loss
Cus	Custody only (damaged ships that were officially transferred at a foreign port in preparation for striking but not physically returned to the U.S.)
D	Damaged
DEC	Control escort vessel
DER	Radar picket escort
Dis	Discarded
E	Explosion
EDE	DE used for experiments
EIF	British East Indies Fleet
Ext	Extant
FDS	Fighter director ship
HT	Human-piloted torpedo
K	Suicide aircraft (kamikaze)
KW	Korean War
L	Lost
LPR	Amphibious transport, small (formerly APD)
M	Mine
MDAP	Mutual Defense Assistance Program
NRF I	Naval Reserve Force Group I (USN-commanded)
NRF II	Naval Reserve Force Group II (USNR-commanded)
R	Returned to U.S.
Ren	Renamed
S	Sold (to ship breaker unless otherwise indicated)
T	Torpedo
TEG	Power supply vessel
Tran	Transferred
Trgt	Target

Appendix C
Monthly Totals of *Buckley*-Class Production and Service Deployment, 1942–1945

The numbers of *Buckley*-class vessels laid down (ld), launched (lc), and commissioned (co) by month, June 1942–August 1945, are shown in the following table, along with the numbers of U.S. Navy *Buckley*-class vessels deployed in the Atlantic (A), Royal Navy *Buckley*-type vessels deployed in the Atlantic (BA), U.S. Navy *Buckley*s transferred from the Atlantic to the Pacific (A>P), and those deployed directly to the Pacific (P). The table also lists the number of U.S. Navy and Royal Navy *Buckley*s lost (sunk or CTL) or temporarily removed from service for damage repair in the Atlantic (AL) or Pacific theaters (PL). The running totals of active *Buckley*-class vessels (DEs, APDs, and lend-lease vessels) are indicated in the last columns.

| | | | | | | | | | | Totals | | |
Date	ld	lc	co	A	BA	A>P	P	AL	PL	A	P	A+P
Jun 1942	1									0	0	0
Jul 1942	1									0	0	0
Aug 1942	1									0	0	0
Sep 1942	3									0	0	0
Oct 1942	1									0	0	0
Nov 1942	1									0	0	0
Dec 1942	6									0	0	0
Jan 1943	3	1								0	0	0
Feb 1943	16	5								0	0	0
Mar 1943	10	6								0	0	0
Apr 1943	16	7	3							0	0	0
May 1943	15	15	3							0	0	0
Jun 1943	17	10	5	1						1	0	1
Jul 1943	10	15	8	2						3	0	3
Aug 1943	19	16	12	6	2					11	0	11
Sep 1943	14	16	9	5	1					17	0	17
Oct 1943	10	22	17	7	3					27	0	27
Nov 1943	8	17	21	9	1		2			37	2	39
Dec 1943	1	14	19	2	1		2			40	4	44
Jan 1944	0	5	16	5	8		9			53	13	66
Feb 1944	0	0	15	4	16		4			73	17	90
Mar 1944	1	2	10	8	7		3			88	20	108
Apr 1944		2	4	9	6		1			103	21	124
May 1944		1	4	9	1		2	3		110	23	133

Date	ld	lc	co	A	BA	A>P	P	AL	PL	Totals A	P	A+P
Jun 1944			1	4			1	2		112	24	136
Jul 1944			1	3			1	1		114	25	139
Aug 1944			0				1	1		113	26	139
Sep 1944			0				1			113	27	140
Oct 1944			0			5	1			108	33	141
Nov 1944			0			1		1		106	34	140
Dec 1944			2			5		5	1	96	38	134
Jan 1945			1			9				87	47	134
Feb 1945			2			5	1*		1	82	52	134
Mar 1945			1			5	2			77	59	136
Apr 1945						6	1	2	3	69	63	132
May 1945						5	2		3	64	67	131
Jun 1945				1*		5	1			60	73	133
Jul 1945							1*		1	60	73	133
Aug 1945							1*			60	74	134
Totals	154	154	154	75	46	46	37	15	9			

*Damaged ship repaired and returned to service

Appendix D
German and Japanese Submarines Credited to *Buckley*-Class Ships, 1943–1945

	Sub	Type	Date	Principals (hull/pennant number)	Approximate location	Note
GERMAN:*						
1	U-66	IXC	05/06/44	*Buckley* (DE 51), *Block Island* VC-55	17°17′N, 32°29′W	1
2	U-91	VIIC	02/26/44	*Affleck* (K 462), *Gore* (K 481), *Gould* (K 476)	49°45′N, 26°20′W	1
3	U-212	VIIC	07/21/44	*Curzon* (K 513), *Ekins* (K 552)	50°27′N, 00°13′W	1
4	U-248	VIIC	01/16/45	*Otter* (DE 210), *Varian* (DE 798), *Hubbard* (DE 211), *Hayter* (DE 212)	47°43′N, 26°37′W	1
5	U-269	VIIC	06/25/44	*Bickerton* (K 466)	50°01′N, 02°59′W	1
6	U-286	VIIC	04/29/45	*Loch Shin* (K 421), *Cotton* (K 510), *Anguilla* (K 500)	69°29′N, 33°37′E	1
7	U-358	VIIC	03/01/44	*Affleck* (K 462), *Gore* (K 481), *Gould* (K 476), *Garlies* (K 475)	45°46′N, 23°16′W	1
8	U-371	VIIC	05/04/44	*Joseph E. Campbell* (DE 70), *Pride* (DE 323), *Sénégalais* (T 22), *Blankney* (L 30)	37°49′N, 05°39′E	1
9	U-392	VIIC	03/16/44	*Affleck* (K 462), *Vanoc* (H 33), VP-63	35°55′N, 05°41′W	1
10	U-399	VIIC	03/26/45	*Duckworth* (K 351)	49°56′N, 05°22′W	1
11	U-480	VIIC	02/24/45	*Duckworth* (K 351), *Rowley* (K 560)	49°55′N, 06°08′W	1
12	U-488	XIV	04/26/44	*Frost* (DE 144), *Barber* (DE 161), *Huse* (DE 145), *Snowden* (DE 246)	17°54′N, 38°05′W	1
13	U-505	IXC	06/04/44	*Pillsbury* (DE 133), *Chatelain* (DE 149), *Jenks* (DE 665), *Guadalcanal* VC-8	21°30′N, 19°20′W	2
14	U-546	IXC/40	04/24/45	*Flaherty* (DE 135), *Hubbard* (DE 211), *Varian* (DE 798), *Pillsbury* (DE 133), *Chatelain* (DE 149), *Neunzer* (DE 150), *Janssen* (DE 396), *Keith* (DE 241)	43°53′N, 40°07′W	1
15	U-548	IXC/40	04/19/45	*Buckley* (DE 51), *Reuben James* (DE 153)	42°19′N, 61°45′W	3
16	U-549	IXC/40	05/29/44	*Eugene E. Elmore* (DE 686), *Ahrens* (DE 575)	31°13′N, 23°03′W	1
17	U-618	VIIC	08/14/44	*Duckworth* (K 351), *Essington* (K 353), RAF 53 Sqn	47°22′N, 04°39′W	1
18	U-636	VIIC	04/21/45	*Bazely* (K 311), *Bentinck* (K 314), *Drury* (K 316)	55°50′N, 10°31′W	1
19	U-671	VIIC	08/04/44	*Stayner* (K 573), *Wensleydale* (L 86)	50°23′N, 00°06′W	1
20	U-672	VIIC	07/18/44	*Balfour* (K 464)	50°03′N, 02°30′W	4
21	U-722	VIIC	03/27/45	*Redmill* (K 554), *Fitzroy* (K 553), *Byron* (K 508)	57°09′N, 06°55′W	1
22	U-765	VIIC	05/06/44	*Aylmer* (K 463), *Bickerton* (K 466), *Bligh* (K 467), *Vindex* 825 Sqn	52°30′N, 28°28′W	1
23	U-774	VIIC	04/08/45	*Bentinck* (K 314), *Calder* (K 349)	49°58′N, 11°51′W	1
24	U-841	IXC/40	10/17/43	*Byard* (K 315)	59°57′N, 31°06′W	1
25	U-905	VIIC	03/27/45	*Conn* (K 509)	58°34′N, 05°46′W	5
26	U-965	VIIC	03/30/45	*Rupert* (K 561), *Conn* (K 509), *Deane* (K 551)	58°19′N, 05°31′W	6
27	U-988	VIIC	06/29/44	*Duckworth* (K 351), *Essington* (K 353), *Domett* (K 473), *Cooke* (K 471), RAF 224 Sqn	49°37′N, 03°41′W	1
28	U-989	VIIC	02/14/45	*Braithwaite* (K 468), *Bayntun* (K 310), *Loch Eck* (K 422), *Loch Dunvegan* (K 425)	61°36′N, 01°35′W	1
29	U-1001	VIIC/41	04/08/45	*Fitzroy* (K 553), *Byron* (K 508)	49°19′N, 10°23′W	1
30	U-1051	VIIC	01/26/45	*Aylmer* (K 463), *Calder* (K 349), *Bentinck* (K 314), *Manners* (K 568)	53°39′N, 05°23′W	7
31	U-1063	VIIC/41	04/15/45	*Loch Killin* (K 391), *Cranstoun* (K 511)	50°08′N, 05°42′W	1
32	U-1169	VIIC/41	03/29/45	*Duckworth* (K 351), *Rowley* (K 560)	49°58′N, 05°25′W	8

	Sub	Type	Date	Principals (hull/pennant number)	Approximate location	Note
33	U-1172	VIIC/41	01/27/45	*Bligh* (K 467), *Tyler* (K 576), *Keats* (K 482)	52°24′N, 03°53′W	7
34	U-1191	VIIC	06/25/44	*Affleck* (K 462), *Balfour* (K 464)	50°03′N, 02°59′W	9
35	U-1279	VIIC/41	02/03/45	*Braithwaite* (K 468), *Bayntun* (K 310), *Loch Eck* (K 422)	61°21′N, 02°00′E	1
36	U-?		02/28/45	*Fowler* (DE 222), *L'Indiscret*	34°30′N, 08°13′W	10

JAPANESE:

	Sub	Type	Date	Principals (hull/pennant number)	Approximate location	Note
1	I-16	C1	05/19/44	*England* (DE 635)	05°10′S, 158°17′E	1
2	I-45	B2	10/29/44	*Whitehurst* (DE 634)	10°10′N, 127°28′E	1
3	I-48	C2	01/23/45	*Conklin* (DE 439), *Raby* (DE 698), *Corbesier* (DE 438)	09°45′N, 138°20′E	1
4	RO-55	K6	02/07/45	*Thomason* (DE 203)	15°27′N, 119°25′E	11
5	RO-104	KS	05/23/44	*England* (DE 635)	01°26′N, 149°20′E	1
6	RO-105	KS	05/31/44	*England* (DE 635), *Spangler* (DE 696), *George* (DE 697), *Raby* (DE 698), *McCord* (DD 534)	00°47′N, 149°56′E	1
7	RO-106	KS	05/22/44	*England* (DE 635)	01°40′N, 150°31′E	1
8	RO-108	KS	05/26/44	*England* (DE 635)	00°32′S, 148°35′E	1
9	RO-116	KS	05/24/44	*England* (DE 635)	00°53′N, 149°14′E	1
10	RO-501	IXC	05/13/44	*Francis M. Robinson* (DE 220)	18°08′N, 33°13′W	12
11	YU-?	YU	03/27/45	*Newman* (APD 59)	10°15′N, 123°55′E	13

Notes:

*In addition to the twenty-seven U-boats credited to the actions of *Buckley*-type Captains-class frigates on this list, *Evarts*-type Captains-class vessels single-handedly sank eight German submarines—U-214, 285, 445, 538, 600, 648, 757, 1278—for a total of thirty-five submarines credited to the class.

1. The identity of this submarine has been positively established, or there is general agreement as to its identity.

2. The U-boat was captured. It is currently an exhibit at the Museum of Science and Industry, Chicago, Illinois.

3. This U-boat was formerly identified as U-879. Recent physical evidence has proved that the submarine was actually U-548, a submarine credited to the action of *Coffman* (DE 191), *Natchez* (PF 2), and *Bostwick* (DE 103) on April 30, 1945. It now appears that the U-boat sunk by *Coffman*'s group was either U-857, formerly credited to the action of *Gustafson* (DE 182) on April 7, 1945, or U-879.

4. The U-boat was severely damaged during the attack and subsequently scuttled by its crew.

5. This U-boat was formerly identified as U-965, but the latter is now credited to *Conn*'s action on March 30; see note 6 below.

6. This U-boat was formerly identified as U-1021.

7. The credits for U-1051 and U-1172 have been switched in light of postwar evidence.

8. This submarine was formerly identified as U-246, but postwar analysis has shown this could not have been the case. Wreckage brought back on April 30, 1945, by the destroyers *Hesperus* (H 57) and *Havelock* (H 88) indicated that they attacked U-246 (initially identified as U-242), although the submarine may have already been sunk due to mechanical failure and lying on the sea floor, since it had been expected at base long before the end of April. Niestlé's research indicates that the submarine was most likely U-1169 (p. 109).

9. Although the DEs are given credit for destroying this submarine, recent reassessment cannot confirm the identity of the submarine nor whether a submarine was actually sunk at the time.

10. This submarine was formerly identified as U-869, but this has turned out to be incorrect. The wreck of U-869 was found by divers on September 2, 1991, off Point Pleasant, N.J. The identity of the submarine attributed to *Fowler* and *L'Indiscret* was based on a postwar reading of German records that indicated that U-869 was ordered to change its course to the western approaches of Gibraltar and was then lost at about the same time *Fowler* engaged a target off Africa. The order to change course was apparently not received by U-869. A further reexamination of the records surrounding *Fowler*'s attack reveals that the original assessment was "insufficient evidence for the presence of a submarine," and the record was changed to "probably sunk" after the war. It is likely that *Fowler* did not sink a submarine at the time.

11. It is now generally assumed that RO-55 was sunk by *Batfish* (SS 310) on February 9, 1945. *Batfish* claimed three submarines between February 9 and 11, 1945. The identity of two of these kills, RO-112 and RO-113, has been established beyond a reasonable doubt. The third submarine, however, was initially identified as I-41 until a postwar examination of Japanese records indicated that I-41 must have been sunk by *Lawrence C. Taylor* (DE 415) on November 17, 1944. Consequently, *Batfish* was credited with the destruction of RO-55 instead of *Thomason*, since *Batfish* definitely sank a submarine (debris was recovered), while *Thomason*'s claim was supported by convincing, but less substantial, evidence (subsurface luminous explosion and oil slick); if RO-55 had indeed evaded *Thomason* and *Neuendorf*'s attacks, it could have been in the general vicinity of *Batfish*'s action. Boyd and Yoshida claim that RO-115 is actually the identity of *Batfish*'s third submarine and return credit for sinking RO-55 to *Thomason* (p. 216). This reassessment removes claim for RO-115 from the action of *Ulvert M. Moore* (DE 442) and other ships on February 1, 1945, indicating that no submarine was sunk at that time. No reason for this reassessment, however, was provided by the authors. The possibility that *Thomason* sank an Army YU type transport submarine has also been proposed; see *Warship International* 35, no. 3 (1998): 221.

12. This was the former German submarine U-1224 that was transferred to Japan on February 15, 1944. It was sunk in the Atlantic en route from Kiel, Germany, to Japan.

13. The CO's official crew commendation states a "YU-3 Type" submarine; it is possible that it was a Type C midget.

Appendix E
Buckley-Class Ships That Sustained Heavy Damage or Were Lost, 1943–1945

Date	Name (hull number)	Means	Agent	Approximate location	Consequence	KIA[a]	CTL
05/03/44	*Donnell* (DE 56)	T5 torpedo	U-765	47°48′N, 19°55′W	stern destroyed	29	yes
05/05/44	*Fechteler* (DE 157)	torpedo	U-967	36°07′N, 02°40′W	broken back amidships; sunk	29	—
05/29/44	*Barr* (DE 576)	T5 torpedo	U-549	32°09′N, 22°15′W	stern destroyed	17	no
06/08/44	*Rich* (DE 695)	influence mines		49°31′N, 01°10′W	stern destroyed, forward section holed; sunk	91	—
06/11/44	*Halsted* (K 556)	torpedo	S-boat	49°51′N, 01°30′W	bow destroyed	30	yes
07/05/44	*Trollope* (K 575)	torpedo	S-boat	49°41′N, 00°04′W	bow destroyed	62	yes
08/22/44	*Bickerton* (K 466)	T5 torpedo	U-354	71°42′N, 19°11′E	stern heavily damaged; scuttled	38	—
11/02/44	*Whitaker* (K 580)	torpedo	U-483	55°30′N, 07°39′W	bow destroyed	92	yes
12/01/44	*Duff* (K 352)	mine		51°22′N, 02°44′E	holed amidships below waterline	3	yes
12/07/44	*Bullen* (K 469)	torpedo	U-775	58°42′N, 04°12′W	broken back amidships; sunk	105	—
12/07/44	*Liddle* (APD 60)	suicide aircraft		10°57′N, 124°35′E	bridge destroyed	40	no
12/20/44	*Fogg* (DE 57)	T5 torpedo	U-870	42°02′N, 19°19′W	stern destroyed	15	no
12/25/44	*Dakins* (K 550)	mine		51°25′N, 02°44′E	forward hull ruptured	0	yes
12/27/44	*Affleck* (K 462)	T5 torpedo	U-486	49°48′N, 01°43′W	stern destroyed	8	yes
02/18/45	*Blessman* (APD 69)	aerial bomb		25°05′N, 141°10′E	deckhouse destroyed amidships	47	no
04/03/45	*Foreman* (DE 633)	aerial bomb		26°10′N, 127°11′E	holed amidships below waterline	0	no
04/06/45	*Witter* (DE 636)	suicide aircraft		26°04′N, 127°52′E	wrecked starboard side amidships	6	yes
04/09/45	*Hopping* (APD 51)	shore battery		26°15′N, 127°55′E	machinery spaces holed amidships	2	no
04/12/45	*Whitehurst* (DE 634)	suicide aircraft		26°04′N, 127°12′E	pilothouse destroyed	42	no
04/17/45	*Ekins* (K 552)	mine		51°21′N, 02°45′E	holed amidships below waterline	0	yes
04/17/45	*Bowers* (DE 637)	suicide aircraft		26°52′N, 127°52′E	bridge destroyed	65	no
04/27/45	*Redmill* (K 554)	T5 torpedo	U-1105	54°23′N, 10°36′W	stern destroyed	29	yes
05/09/45	*England* (DE 635)	suicide aircraft		26°18′N, 127°13′E	pilothouse destroyed	37	yes
05/20/45	*Chase* (APD 54)	suicide aircraft		26°18′N, 127°14′E	wrecked amidships	0	yes

Date	Name (hull number)	Means	Agent	Approximate location	Consequence	KIA[a]	CTL
05/26/45	*Bates* (APD 68)	suicide aircraft		26°41′N, 127°47′E	hull ruptured, bridge destroyed; capsized and sunk	23	—
05/27/45	*Loy* (APD 56)	suicide aircraft[b]		26°30′N, 127°30′E	starboard side amidships showered with debris	3	no
06/09/45	*Gendreau* (DE 639)	shore battery		26°03′N, 127°12′E	forward fire room holed	2	no
07/24/45	*Underhill* (DE 682)	kaiten[c]	I-53	19°20′N, 126°42′E	bow destroyed and sunk, stern section scuttled	113	—
Total	28 ships					928	

[a]Killed in action; includes (when known) injured who later died of wounds
[b]Near-miss—explosions, shrapnel, and burning fuel often accompanied the crash of a suicide aircraft close aboard
[c]Suicide (human-piloted) torpedo

Appendix F
U.S. Navy Escort Divisions and Royal Navy Escort Groups Containing *Buckley*-Class Ships, 1943–1945

U.S. Navy Escort Divisions

The escort division (CortDiv) was the smallest administrative unit of U.S. destroyer escorts during World War II and was charged with protecting convoys from enemy surface, air, and undersea attack. The escort division was developed during World War II as a tactical device, and not specifically for DEs. (The first escort division was composed of flush-decker destroyers.) Most escort divisions deployed during the war, however, contained only DEs. Each escort division, based on the preexisting destroyer division concept, usually consisted of six vessels of the same class—often six sequential hull numbers.

The CortDivs listed below are all of those which contained *Buckley*-class vessels. Although individual ships were often associated with one escort division throughout the war, the composition and status of escort divisions reflected the tactical progress of the war and was not dependent on the specific ships that composed the division. Therefore, a ship could be assigned to several different escort divisions throughout its career. As a general observation, however, most DEs operated with a single escort division and remained a part of that division for the duration of the division's existence (which was sometimes less than a year) or until the ship was reclassified or transferred (as in the case of DEs converted into APDs).

World War II convoys varied considerably in number and composition of ships. A supply convoy might consist of fewer than twenty to more than one hundred cargo ships and tankers, while a convoy assembled for a landing operation could include dozens of different specialty vessels, such as floating dry docks, cranes, barges, repair ships, and tugs, that exhibited a range of seakeeping qualities. Most Atlantic supply convoys, however, were kept to about forty-five ships.

Atlantic convoys initially were rated as either slow (7 knots) or fast (10 to 10.5 knots). During the months preceding the invasion of Europe, these designations were modified to facilitate the buildup of material in Great Britain, with convoys rated as slow (8 knots), normal (9 knots), or fast (10 knots), and the average number of ships in convoy increased to about ninety-eight vessels. Following the landings in Normandy, convoys returned to a two-speed system with a lower average number of ships in convoy.

A standard Atlantic supply convoy was organized into nine to twelve columns of ships spaced 1,000 yards apart; each column extended four to five ships deep with 600 yards between each ship in the column. A convoy could present a front of four and a half to seven miles and a depth of one mile or more.

The escort division was designed so that one division could adequately screen a convoy of forty-five or fewer vessels from an enemy attack. The six escorts would patrol established stations along the perimeter of the convoy, ideally with each vessel's visual, radar, and sonar ranges overlapping or abutting the next escort's patrol area. It was the job of the escort division to manage the movements of a convoy as efficiently as possible (which even might entail having the convoy return to port in the face of heavy weather). For larger convoys (more than forty-five vessels), ships from two or more escort divisions were usually deployed.

Because of their assignments, some escort divisions tended to operate as a whole unit more frequently than others. It was quite common in the Pacific theater for only two or three ships from a division to be assigned to a particular mission, since Pacific convoys tended to vary more in both number of vessels and distance between destinations compared to the established Atlantic convoys between the Americas and Europe.

Once HUK operations became as important a function as convoy duty for destroyer escorts, fewer escort divisions were deployed as whole units. Usually one to four ships of a given division were temporarily assigned to a HUK group, leaving the remaining ships of the division to undergo availability, light convoy escort, coastal patrol, or to combine with other escorts to form an adequate company for a supply convoy.

Losses due to enemy action also affected the integrity of escort divisions, and replacement ships were often not of the same class as the ship that was sunk or damaged.

The decision in May 1944 to convert a number of Atlantic theater *Buckley*-class escorts into APDs had the biggest impact on escort divisions. Following this large program of conversions, the seven escort divisions that supplied the ships were dissolved. Although some APDs still participated in convoy protection and antisubmarine patrols, these ships were reorganized into transport divisions (TransDivs).

Division commanders usually had the rank of commander. Division commanders in the U.S. Navy were not assigned to a specific DE, but routinely transferred their flag among the ships of their division. If the division was operating with a CVE, the division commander would often fly his pennant from the carrier. The U.S. Navy system was not like the Royal Navy, where the ship commanded by the most senior officer of the escort group carried the flag. In both the U.S. Navy and the Royal Navy, the safety of the convoy was the responsibility of the escort commander; therefore, the ultimate control of the convoy was his. The ships that made up the convoy were under the command of a convoy commodore (often a retired naval, naval reserve, or merchant marine officer), but while under escort, the convoy commodore deferred to the escort commander.

Escort divisions that served in both the Atlantic and Pacific theaters always served in the former before being reassigned to the latter.

CORTDIV 6

Theater: Atlantic

Name	DE
Charles Lawrence	53
Daniel T. Griffin	54
Donnell	56
Sims	154
Hopping	155
Reeves	156

All converted into APDs except *Donnell*

CORTDIV 12

Theater: Atlantic

Name	DE
Fogg	57
Foss	59
Gantner	60
George W. Ingram	62
Ira Jeffery	63
Lee Fox	65
Bray	709

Bray was a *Rudderow*-class DE that replaced the damaged *Fogg*. All were converted into APDs except *Fogg* and *Foss*.

CORTDIV 17

Theater: Atlantic

Name	DE
Scott	214
Burke	215
Enright	216
Weber	675
Schmitt	676
Frament	677

All converted into APDs except *Scott*

CORTDIV 19

Theater: Atlantic

Name	DE
Amesbury	66
Bates	68
Blessman	69
Bull	693
Bunch	694
Rich	695

All converted into APDs except *Rich*

CORTDIV 21

Theater: Atlantic

Name	DE
Joseph E. Campbell	70
Fechteler	157
Chase	158
Laning	159
Loy	160
Barber	161

All converted into APDs except *Fechteler*

CORTDIV 36

Theater: Pacific

Name	DE
Coolbaugh	217
Darby	218
J. Douglas Blackwood	219
Harmon	678
Greenwood	679
Loeser	680

CORTDIV 37

Theater: Pacific

Name	DE
Lovelace	198
Manning	199
Neuendorf	200
James E. Craig	201
Eichenberger	202
Thomason	203

CORTDIV 39

Theater: Pacific

Name	DE
Spangler	696
George	697
Raby	698
Marsh	699
Currier	700
Osmus	701

Marsh and *Currier* joined the division in the Pacific after Atlantic service

CORTDIV 40

Theater: Pacific

Name	DE
Foreman	633
Whitehurst	634
England	635
Witter	636
Bowers	637
Willmarth	638

CORTDIV 47

Theater: Atlantic

Name	DE
Tatum[1]	789
Borum[2]	790
Maloy[2]	791
Haines[1,3]	792
Runels[1]	793
Hollis[1,3]	794

[1]Converted into APDs
[2]Detached in March 1944 for special English Channel duty
[3]April–May 1944, assigned to Quonset Point, Rhode Island, training facility

CORTDIV 52

Theater: Atlantic

Name	DE
Jordan	204
Newman	205
Liddle	206
Kephart	207
Cofer	208
Lloyd	209

All converted into APDs except *Jordan*

CORTDIV 54

Theater: Atlantic

Name	DE
Francis M. Robinson	220
Solar	221
Fowler	222
Jenks	665
Durik	666
Wiseman	667

Wiseman detached and converted into a TEG for Pacific service in late 1944

CORTDIV 56

Theater: Atlantic, Pacific

Name	DE
Gillette	681
Underhill	682
Henry R. Kenyon	683
Gunason	795
Major	796
Weeden	797

CORTDIV 60

Theater: Atlantic, Pacific

Name	DE
Ahrens	575
Earl V. Johnson	702
Holton	703
Cronin	704
Frybarger	705
Parle*	708

Barr (DE 576) was intended for this division, but during its initial deployment as part of a HUK group, it was damaged by a torpedo and converted into an APD while undergoing repairs.
*Rudderow class

CORTDIV 62

Theater: Atlantic

Name	DE
Otter	210
Hubbard	211
Hayter	212
Varian	798
Scroggins	799
Jack W. Wilke	800

CORTDIV 66

Theater: Atlantic

Name	DE
Buckley	51
Reuben James	153
William T. Powell*	213
Spangenburg*	223
Alexander J. Luke*	577
Robert I. Paine*	578

All converted into DERs beginning in June 1945
*Assigned to U.S. 12th Fleet and operated out of Londonderry under British control as EG 32 (former USN TG 120.1) between April 5 and May 23, 1945.

CORTDIV 73

Theater: Pacific

Name	DE
Gendreau	639
Fieberling	640
William C. Cole	641
Paul G. Baker	642
Damon M. Cummings	643
Vammen	644

Royal Navy Escort Groups

Only Royal Navy escort groups (EGs) that contained *Buckley*-type Captains-class frigates are listed below. Other kinds of vessels, including *Evarts*-type DEs, corvettes, older destroyers, Loch-class frigates, and sloops, were also assigned to some of these EGs. Only the *Evarts*-type Captains-class ships, however, are indicated (*). The ships in these lists were usually attached to the EGs for most of their escort service. Nominal assignments to EGs and those of less than a month are not indicated, but longer assignments are cross-referenced.

Those *Buckley*-type Captains-class ships that were assigned for most of their careers to regional commands (Devonport, Nore, and Portsmouth) instead of EGs are listed at the end.

Regional commands controlled a pool of ships that could be assigned to a variety of support and escort tasks in combination with the various ships under that command at that time. The majority of Captains-class vessels were assigned to a specific regional command at some point in their careers, most notably during the Normandy invasion when large numbers of ships were required to screen the Channel and its entrances, but these assignments are not cross-listed. Similarly, some of these escort groups were deployed as or with support groups (SGs) to provide an additional barrier for marauding U-boats along the western and channel approaches. The composition of SGs is not listed.

The home base for each EG is listed below, as is the flagship (Senior Officer's ship, Group Leader).

1ST EG

Home Base: Belfast

Name	Pennant
Affleck	462
Balfour	464 (see 18th)
*Bentley**	465
Byron	508 (see 21st)
*Capel**	470
*Garlies**	475
*Gould**	476
*Gore**	481
Stockham	562 (see 17th)
*Hoste**	566 (see 18th)
Whitaker	580

Flag: *Affleck*; *Balfour* became group leader after *Affleck* was removed from service

3RD EG

Home Base: Belfast

Name	Pennant
*Berry**	312 (see 4th)
*Blackwood**	313 (see 4th)
*Burges**	347 (see 4th, 17th)
Duckworth	351
Essington	353
Braithwaite	468 (see 10th)
*Cooke**	471
*Domett**	473
Rowley	560

Flag: *Duckworth*

4TH EG

Home Base: Belfast

Name	Pennant
*Bazely**	311
*Berry**	312 (see 3rd)
*Blackwood**	313 (see 3rd)
Bentinck	314
Byard	315
*Drury**	316
*Burges**	347 (see 3rd, 17th)
Calder	349
Conn	509 (see 21st)
*Pasley**	564

Flag: *Bentinck*

5TH EG

Home Base: Belfast

Name	Pennant
Aylmer	463
Bickerton	466
Bligh	467
*Grindall**	477
*Goodson**	480
*Keats**	482
*Kempthorne**	483
Tyler	576
*Gardiner**	478

Flag: *Bickerton*; *Aylmer* became group leader after *Bickerton* was lost

10TH EG

Home Base: Londonderry

Name	Pennant
*Bayntun**	310
Braithwaite	468 (see 3rd)
*Foley**	474

15TH EG

Home Base: Londonderry

Name	Pennant
*Louis**	515
*Lawson**	516
*Loring**	565
*Moorsom**	567 (see 17th)
*Mounsey**	569
*Inglis**	570
Narbrough	578

Flag: *Louis*

17TH EG

Home Base: Greenock

Name	Pennant
*Burges**	347 (see 3rd)
Cranstoun	511
Stockham	562 (see 1st)
*Moorsom**	567 (see 15th)

18TH EG

Home Base: Greenock

Name	Pennant
Balfour	464 (see 1st)
*Hoste**	566 (see 1st)

Flag: *Balfour*

19TH EG

Home Base: Liverpool

Name	Pennant
Bullen	460
*Goodall**	479
Cotton	510

21ST EG

Home Base: Belfast

Name	Pennant
Byron	508 (see 1st)
Conn	509 (see 4th)
Deane	551
Fitzroy	553
Redmill	554
Rupert	561

Flag: *Conn*

The 21st EG operated as two divisions in March and April 1945 in order to clear the Minches channel of U-boats. The 1st Division (*Conn*, *Deane*, and *Rupert*) operated in the northern Minches area, and the 2nd Division (*Byron*, *Fitzroy*, and *Redmill*) in the southern Minches area.

REGIONAL COMMANDS

Home Bases: Devonport, Nore, Portsmouth

Name	Pennant
Duff†	K 352
Cubitt†	K 512
Curzon†	K 513
Dakins†	K 550
Ekins†	K 552
Retalick†	K 555
Halsted	K 556
Riou†	K 557
Rutherford†	K 558
Cosby	K 559
Seymour†	K 563
Spragge	K 572
Stayner†	K 573
Thornborough†	K 574
Trollope†	K 575
Torrington†	K 577
Waldegrave	K 579
Holmes	K 581
Hargood	K 582
Hotham	K 583

†Operated as Coastal Forces control ships

Sources

Between December 1993 and January 1996, the author conducted a twelve-page survey of former U.S. Navy and Royal Navy officers and crew members from 102 different *Buckley*-class ships. In most cases, more than one person from each ship was interviewed. The survey elicited responses about their training, duties aboard ship, other ships with which they operated, any modifications to the ship that they could recall, and significant events that occurred during their service. Many of those who responded also provided documentation, including official histories, privately published histories, log books, photographs, diaries, and action reports.

Photographs were obtained from the U.S. National Archives Still Picture Branch, College Park, Maryland; The Naval Historical Center, Washington Navy Yard, Washington, D.C.; The Mariners' Museum, Norfolk, Virginia; The Imperial War Museum, London; and the National Maritime Museum, Greenwich, England. The author also had the pleasure of corresponding with photographers and photo collectors, including Mr. K. R. Macpherson, Mr. Peter Phelps, and Mr. Ted Stone.

Additional individual ships' histories and action reports were obtained from the Ships History Branch, Naval Historical Center, and the Ministry of Defence, London. This material included: C.A.F.O. (Confidential Admiralty Fleet Orders) 2683, *Alterations and Additions "Captains" Class Frigates (Type "A")*,
12/09/43; C.A.F.O. 2684, *Alterations and Additions "Captains" Class Frigates (Type "B")*, 12/09/43; C.B. 01815D, *Particulars of War Vessels (British Commonwealth of Nations): Half-Yearly Return*, April 1944, October 1944, April 1945.

Ship plans and specifications sheets for the *Buckley* class were obtained from the National Archives, Cartographic and Architectural Branch, holding number RG19/5929/reel 1.

Bibliography

No major work on destroyer escorts or on an individual class of DE, other than this volume, has been published. Three short paperbacks are dedicated to DEs, but all are general overviews of the entire DE program and one is no longer in print. The following books and articles contain information on destroyer escorts:

Adcock, Al. *Destroyer Escorts in Action*. Carrollton, Texas: Squadron/Signal Publications, 1997. (Although some of the photographs are interesting, the text contains numerous factual errors and no analysis.)

Bauer, K. Jack, and Stephen S. Roberts. *Register of Ships of the U. S. Navy, 1775–1990: Major Combatants*. Westport, Conn.: Greenwood Press, 1991.

Boyd, Carl, and Akihiko Yoshida. *The Japanese Submarine Force and World War II*. Annapolis, Md.: Naval Institute Press, 1995.

Brown, David K. "Atlantic Escorts, 1939–1945." In

The Battle of the Atlantic, 1939–1945, edited by Stephen Howarth and Derek Law, 452–475. Annapolis, Md.: Naval Institute Press, 1994.

Cagle, Malcolm, and Frank A. Manson. *The Sea War in Korea*. Annapolis, Md.: Naval Institute Press, 1957.

Carpenter, Dorr, and Norman Polmar. *Submarines of the Imperial Japanese Navy*. Annapolis, Md.: Naval Institute Press, 1986.

Chaikin, William. "Shipbuilding Policies of the War Production Board, January 1942 to November 1945." War Production Board Special Study No. 26. Washington: GPO, 1946.

Chester, Alvin P. *A Sailor's Odyssey*. Miami: Odysseus Books, 1991. (The author was commanding officer of *Cofer* [DE 208/APD 62] during World War II.)

———. "Captains Class Turbo-Electric Frigates." *Warships Supplement, Nos. 80–81* (1984–85): 22–32; 6–15.

Colledge, J.J. "Captains Class Diesel-Electric Frigates." *Warships Supplement, Nos. 78–79* (1983–84): 20–26; 1–8.

Davis, H. F. D. "Building Major Combatant Ships in World War II." *Proceedings* 73, no. 5 (May 1947): 565–79.

Department of the Navy. *Summary of War Damage to U.S. Battleships, Carriers, Cruisers, Destroyers and Destroyer Escorts*. Reprint. Kresgeville, Pa.: Floating Drydock, 1995.

———. *United States Naval Chronology: World War II*. Washington: GPO, 1955.

———. *Naval Ordnance and Gunnery*. Navpers 16116. Washington: GPO, 1944.

———. *Naval Ordnance and Gunnery*. Navpers 16116B. Washington: GPO, 1952.

Elliot, Peter. *Allied Escort Ships of World War II*. Annapolis, Md.: Naval Institute Press, 1977. (This is a major compilation of most of the escort types used by the British Commonwealth navies and the U.S. Navy. It is a fine resource, but contains enough errors to warrant double-checking.)

———. *American Destroyer Escorts of World War II*. London: Almark Publishing Co., 1974. (This brief paperback contains several well-chosen photographs of the Captains-class vessels, line plans of DE weapons, and an overview of the RN modifications.)

Fahey, J. C. *Ships and Aircraft of the U.S. Fleet*. 6th, 7th, and 8th eds., 1950–65. Reprint. Annapolis, Md.: Naval Institute Press, 1980.

———. *Ships and Aircraft of the U.S. Fleet*. Victory Edition. New York: Ships and Aircraft, 1945.

Field, James A. *History of United States Naval Operations: Korea*. Washington: GPO, 1962.

Friedman, Norman. *U.S. Destroyers: An Illustrated Design History*. Annapolis, Md.: Naval Institute Press, 1982. (A well-written, cogent history that contains a chapter on the development of the DE.)

———. *U.S. Naval Weapons*. Annapolis, Md.: Naval Institute Press, 1982.

Hackmann, Willem. *Seek and Strike*. London: HMSO, 1984.

Halsey, Jr., Ashley. "Those Not-So-Little Ships—The DE's." *Proceedings* 69, no. 9 (September 1943): 1201–4.

Hodges, Peter. *Royal Navy Warship Camouflage, 1939–1945*. Surrey: Almark Publishing Co., 1973.

Hooper, Edwin B. *The United States Navy and the Vietnam Conflict*. Washington: GPO, 1976.

Karig, Walter. *Battle Report*. 6 vols. New York: Rinehart & Co., 1946–52.

King, Ernest J. *U.S. Navy at War, 1941–1945*. Washington: GPO, 1946.

Kinney, Sheldon H. "The Case for the Open Bridge." *Proceedings* 70, no. 1 (January 1944): 25–28.

Lenton, H. T. *World War 2 Fact Files: British Escort Ships*. New York: Arco Publishing Co., 1974.

Lenton, H. T., and J. J. Colledge. *British and Dominion Warships of World War II*. New York: Doubleday & Co., 1968.

Lundeberg, Philip K. *American Anti-Submarine Operations in the Atlantic, May 1943–May 1945*. Ph.D. diss., Harvard University, 1953. Ann Arbor: University Microfilms, 1997.

———. "Operation *Teardrop* Revisited." In *To Die Gallantly: The Battle of the Atlantic*, edited by Timothy J. Runyan and Jan M. Copes, 210–230. Boulder, Colo.: Westview Press, 1994.

Macintyre, Donald. *U-Boat Killer*. New York: W. W. Norton and Co., 1956.

Miller, John A. *Men and Volts at War: The Story of General Electric in World War II*. New York: McGraw-Hill, 1947.

Mooney, James L., ed. *Dictionary of American Naval Fighting Ships*. 8 vols. Washington: GPO, 1959–91.

Morison, Samuel Eliot. *History of United States Naval Operations in World War II*. 15 vols. Boston: Little, Brown & Co., 1947–62.

Mowry, G. E. "Landing Craft and the War Production Board." War Production Board Special Study No. 11. Washington: GPO, 1946.

Niestlé, Axel. *German U-Boat Losses during World War II: Details of Destruction*. Annapolis, Md.: Naval Institute Press, 1998.

Powell, Hickman, and Harold Kulick. "Chasing Echoes on a DE Boat." *Popular Science* 144, no. 4 (April 1944): 56A–56G, 212, 216.

Rohwer, Jürgen. *Axis Submarine Successes, 1939–1945*. Annapolis, Md.: Naval Institute Press, 1983.

Roscoe, Theodore. *United States Destroyer Operations in World War II*. Annapolis, Md.: Naval Institute Press, 1953.

Roskill, Stephen W. *The War at Sea, 1939–1945*. 3 vols. London: HMSO, 1954–61.

Ross, Al. *Anatomy of the Ship: The Destroyer Escort England*. London: Conway Maritime Press, 1985.

Rowland, Buford, and William B. Boyd. *U.S. Navy Bureau of Ordnance in World War II*. Washington: GPO, 1953.

Scott, Peter. *The Battle of the Narrow Seas*. New York: Charles Scribner's Sons, 1946.

Silverstone, Paul H. *U.S. Warships of World War II*. Garden City, N.Y.: Doubleday & Co., 1965.

Sternhell, Charles M., and Alan M. Thorndike. *Antisubmarine Warfare in World War II*. Washington: Office of the Chief of Naval Operations, 1946.

Tactical and Staff Duties Division. "Naval Operations in the Assault and Capture of Okinawa, March–June 1945." Naval Staff History, Battle Summary No. 47. London: Historical Section, Admiralty, 1950.

Walkowiak, Thomas F. *Destroyer Escorts of World War Two*. Missoula, Mont.: Pictorial Histories Publishing Co., 1987. (A useful overview of all DE classes, which lists the names and key construction dates of the U.S. DEs. It does not contain information on the lend-lease DEs.)

Walkowiak, Thomas F., and Larry Sowinski. *United States Navy Camouflage of the World War II Era*. Part 1. Kresgeville, Pa.: Floating Drydock, 1988.

Williamson, John A., and William D. Lanier. "The Twelve Days of the *England*." *Proceedings* 106, no. 2 (February 1980): 76–83.

Y'Blood, William T. *Hunter-Killer*. Annapolis, Md.: Naval Institute Press, 1983.

Acknowledgments

I am grateful to the following persons for their contributions to this book: David K. Brown, Alan Hope, Sheldon Kinney, Philip K. Lundeberg, Paul Quinn, Dana Wegner, and John Whithouse read drafts and provided comments and corrections.

R. M. Coppock of the Ministry of Defence, Ed Finney and Cherie Watson of the Naval Historical Center, R. G. Todd of the National Maritime Museum, Ian Carter of the Imperial War Museum, the staff of the National Archives Still Pictures and Cartographic Branches, Thomas F. Walkowiak of the Floating Drydock, Michael McDonald of the National Archives of Canada, and Claudia Jew of the Mariner's Museum provided assistance with obtaining documents, plans, and photographs. Michelle Pointon of NASC managed the reproduction of National Archives material.

Additional photographs, personal accounts, and technical information were provided by H. C. Anderson, S. J. Ballard, Gerard Benkert, Jack Boland, Frank Cameron, Harold Clemens, John P. Cosgrove, Roger Cozens, Alexander E. D'Auriol, C. Dick, Armand DiRienzo, Al Dzurinda, Christopher Eason, D. W. Evans, George Farral, Frank Foltz, George S. Forde, Richard Fowler, F. G. Froud, Don Glaser, Leslie Gomersall, Lou Grasek, A. Hammond, Stanley Horne, Norman Howgego, K. R. Jameson, William Johnson, K. R. Macpherson, L. A. Myhre, Ronald Newbury, Fred Niepp, Sid Pell, Peter Phelps, J. Rettke, E. J. Sikora, Howard W. Smith, Gordon Stewart, Ted Stone, Donald Tillotson, Curtis Toombs, Oscar E. West, Jr., Kimber White, Christopher Wickenden, and Al Wudarski.

Mark Gatlin, senior acquisitions editor, and his colleagues at the Naval Institute Press, including Sandra Adams, Susan Artigiani, J. Randall Baldini, Susan Todd Brook, Tom Harnish, and Brian Walker, guided this book through publication. Jack Brostrom deftly copyedited the manuscript and helped shape the final book. Michael A. Brehm designed and typeset the entire text and jacket, drew the maps, and prepared all of the photographs for production.

My brother Mark was instrumental in obtaining out-of-print British publications and reports. My father Richard L. Franklin, former QM 1/C of the *Neuendorf* (DE 200), edited various drafts, provided photographs, and answered numerous questions over the past five years; without him, this book would not have been possible. Lastly, to my dear Laura Catherine: Thank you for your delightful company.

While writing this book, some of those to whom I am indebted have passed away.

Index

Note: *Buckley*-class vessels are printed in boldface type.

About the Author

BRUCE HAMPTON FRANKLIN received a B.A. in historical linguistics from the University of Pittsburgh in 1985. He was awarded a Century Fellowship in linguistics from the University of Chicago and began a career in publishing, first with the University of Chicago Press and then the University of Pennsylvania Press, where he is currently the publicist. His interest in military history was inspired by conversations with his father, a destroyer escort sailor, and his uncle, a B-17 navigator in the 364th squadron of the 305th Bomber Group based in Chelveston, England, in 1944. Franklin also has a military link on his mother's side as a descendant of Wade Hampton, the Civil War cavalry general and statesman from South Carolina.

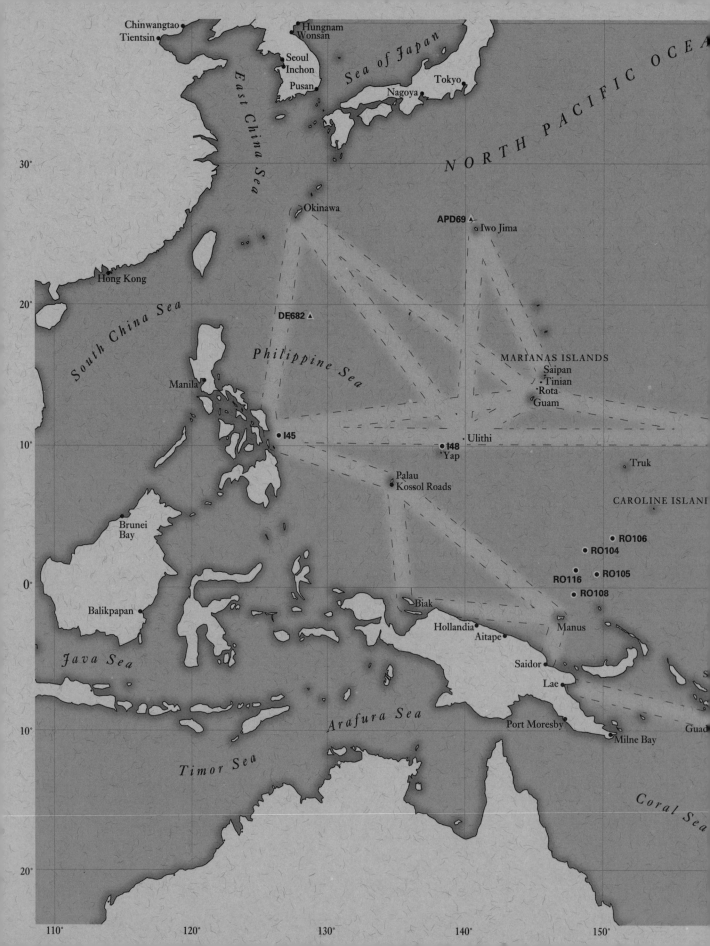